The Wealth and Poverty of Regions

The Wealth and Poverty of Regions

Why Cities Matter

MARIO POLÈSE

The University of Chicago Press
Chicago and London

MARIO POLÈSE is professor of urban economics at INRS Urbanisation, Culture et Société in Montreal and holds the Senior Canada Research Chair in Urban and Regional Studies.

The University of Chicago Press, Chicago 60637
The University of Chicago Press, Ltd., London
© 2009 by The University of Chicago
All rights reserved. Published 2009
Printed in the United States of America

18 17 16 15 14 13 12 11 10 09   1 2 3 4 5

ISBN-13: 978-0-226-67315-8 (cloth)
ISBN-10: 0-226-67315-4 (cloth)

Library of Congress Cataloging-in-Publication Data

Polèse, Mario, 1943–
    The wealth and poverty of regions : why cities matter / Mario Polèse.
        p. cm.
    Includes bibliographical references and index.
    ISBN-13: 978-0-226-67315-8 (cloth : alk. paper)
    ISBN-10: 0-226-67315-4 (cloth : alk. paper)
        1. Urban economics. 2. Regional economics. 3. Regional economic disparities.
    4. Wealth. 5. Economic development. 6. Human geography. I. Title.
    HT321.P65 2009
    330.9173'2—dc22

                                                            2009019773

Contents

Illustrations

Tables

Figures

Maps

Preface

In all nations, some places are better off than others. In every nation, some places are left behind while others surge ahead. Why this is so is the subject of this book.

Much has been written about *national* economic growth, that is, why some nations are richer than others. The recent opus by Harvard economic historian David Landes, *The Wealth and Poverty of Nations: Why Some Are So Rich and Some So Poor* (1998)—part of whose title I have unashamedly borrowed—follows in a rich tradition of scholarship going back to Adam Smith's 1776 classic, *The Wealth of Nations*. The focus of this book is not nations but places, communities, and regions, terms I use interchangeably. My focus is on differences in economic growth *within* nations, between the different places, communities, and regions that make up a nation. Why do such differences exist? That is the question I have set out to answer.

Ever since I can remember, the inhabitants of the Gaspé Peninsula in eastern Canada, the country in which I live, have felt betrayed by the workings of modern economics, not without cause. Somehow, prosperity never reached the Gaspé, at least not if compared to Canada's rich metropolitan centers of Toronto, Montreal, and Vancouver. Unemployment on the Gaspé Peninsula has been above the national average ever since such data was first collected; per capita income there has remained systematically below the national average. Its sons and daughters continue to flock to the bright lights of Canada's big cities. The Gaspé is not an isolated case in Canada. The sons and daughters of the poor outports of Newfoundland continue to flock to Toronto. Prairie farmers in Saskatchewan and Manitoba continue to abandon the land for the growing urban centers of Alberta and British Columbia, as they have done for decades.

As a young university student in the 1960s, majoring in economics, I wanted to understand why such things happened and, with the usual youthful sense of outrage, how to right these "wrongs." This is what drove me into the study of economic geography, regional science, and urban and regional planning.[1] This then also is where the origins of this book lie. Since those early student days, I have continued as a university professor to teach and work in the same field in Canada and elsewhere—with occasional stints in government and in international organizations. I have had the good fortune of visiting and working in a number of nations.[2] My travels have added to my conviction that the subject of regional growth is worthy of a book.

Regional divides exist in almost every nation. Again, ever since I can remember, the inhabitants of France outside Paris have complained that wealth was inordinately concentrated in the Paris region.[3] Little has changed; average incomes in the Greater Paris region today are some 50 percent higher than in the rest of France. In the United States, the South has for decades been poorer than the rest of the nation, although the gap has closed. In Britain, the divide between the south of England—with London today one of the world's most expensive cities—and the old industrial cities of the north seems almost irreparable. Regional differences are even greater in developing nations. At the time of writing, China was easily the extreme case, with differences in average income as high as ten to one between the richest and the poorest regions.[4]

I will return to each of these examples in this book. Faced with facts of this nature, one naturally wonders whether such regional differences are the natural outcome of national economic growth and the workings of modern market economies. Are regional welfare inequalities unavoidable—a necessary condition of prosperity? This "big" question provides the subtext, so to speak, of the book, to which I shall keep returning.

The Industrial Revolution—and what followed—marked a turning point in human history, one of whose consequences was to transform the economic geography of nations. All throughout, I have attempted to adopt a historical perspective, insofar as data and my own (limited) knowledge allow it. Consistent time series data over long periods are notably lacking for sub-national units: regions, communities, places. One of the reasons for this is that the geographic definition of places—of expanding cities, notably—keeps changing over time, precisely because they are growing more rapidly than other parts of the nation. Such data limitations make international comparisons over time difficult. I have nonetheless attempted, when possible, to introduce international comparisons. Indeed, this is one of my main motivations for writing the book. Too much discourse is based on the experience of only a few nations. The chief limitation here is my own knowledge of different nations and places. I have not been to India or to China, although both nations feature in this book. In such cases, I have had to rely on secondary sources and on the advice of colleagues. All errors of fact or interpretation are, of course, my own.

This book is not primarily directed at my academic colleagues, although I hope some will read it. My objective is to make the subject intelligible—and, hopefully, interesting—for as wide an audience as possible. This has caused me to take some liberties—mixing university economics and geography with stories and anecdotes. This is not an easy subject to make interesting, and I am by no means sure that I have succeeded in making it so.

The subject matter of this book does not fall within an established academic discipline. It is neither pure economics nor human geography, but rather a mix of the two, with a bit of urban planning thrown in. I've never been quite sure whether I was an economist or a geographer. The label "regional science" has no meaning outside of a small coterie of insiders, which is a pity.[5] Several designations can be used to describe the field of study covered by this book: regional economics, spatial economics, regional development, local economic development, economic geography, urban and regional economics, to mention the most common.[6] To keep things simple, I shall use "economic geography" as a catchall. But any of the other labels apply just as well to the area of interest of this book.

I lay no claim to a new theory of economic geography. I have my own way of looking at things, of course. Many of the ideas presented were first developed by others in numerous learned journals and volumes, cited in this book.[7] My objective, ultimately, is to distill this rich research tradition—going back more than a century—and present its insights in ways not done before.

Acknowledgments

On the cover of this book, I may well appear as the sole author, but the ideas and insights expressed are by no means solely of my own making. I have been fortunate over the years to have met, worked, and corresponded with numerous colleagues around the world—geographers, economists, urban planners, and others—who have greatly contributed to my understanding of the subject matter of this book. All the good ideas are probably theirs. It is impossible to name them all.

Several colleagues were kind enough to read and annotate previous drafts of the manuscript. My heartfelt gratitude to Prof. William J. Coffey at the Department of Geography, University of Montreal, and to Jeanne Wolfe, retired chair of the School of Urban Planning, McGill University, for not only reading the manuscript but also providing numerous suggestions on how to improve it. At my home institution in Montreal, INRS,[1] I thank my fellow faculty members Andre Lemelin, Christophe Ribichesi, Richard Shearmur, and Nong Zhu (especially for the Chinese content) for taking the time to review and comment on the manuscript. I am truly fortunate in having such associates who were willing to give freely of their time. The book is much better because of them.

The contribution of others is more indirect, via ideas or information shared, sometimes going back many years. I cannot fail to mention (in alphabetical order): Antoine Bailly, retired chair of the Department of Geography, University of Geneva; Jean-Marie Huriot, retired professor of spatial economics, University of Bourgogne (Burgundy); Jean Paelinck, emeritus professor of spatial econometrics, Erasmus University, Rotterdam (now distinguished visiting professor, George Mason University, Fairfax, Virginia); John Parr, emeritus professor of urban studies, University of Glasgow; Jacques Thisse,

Department of Economics, University of Louvain-la-Neuve (Belgium). All
have helped and influenced me in more ways than they realize. Nor can I fail
to thank my many friends and (sometime) fellow faculty, too numerous to
name individually, at the Department of Economics of the Autonomous University of Puebla, without whom the sections dealing with Mexico and Latin
America would have been much poorer.

It is difficult to thank an entire institution. But I would be remiss if I did
not mention the unfailing institutional support of INRS Urbanisation, Culture et Société in Montreal. Since I cannot name everyone in every service
and department who helped me at various moments, I shall limit my thanks
to the current director, Johanne Charbonneau, with the understanding that
this should be understood as thanks to all. Among the graduate students and
interns at INRS who were involved in various stages of the book—drawing
figures and maps, proofreading, data gathering, statistical analysis, etc.—
my thanks to Josefina Ades, Cédric Brunelle, Philippe Rivet, and Geneviève
Polèse. Special thanks also to the secretarial, technical, and professional staff,
especially Viviane Brouillard, Gaëtan Dussault, Elena Pou, and Cindy Rojas.

This book would have been impossible without the financial support of
the Canada Research Chair Program, the Social Sciences and Humanities
Research Council of Canada, and the Fonds Québécois de recherche sur la
société et la culture (Quebec funding council for the social sciences).

If there is a hidden coauthor of this book, his name is David Pervin, senior
editor at the University of Chicago Press. This book is very different from the
manuscript I first sent him, and far better because of him. David Pervin saw
things in the manuscript I did not see. In all honesty, he convinced me to
basically rewrite the book. I wasn't overjoyed at the time. But he was right.
This is truly also his book. David, my enduring thanks.

I also owe thanks to my old friend George Leibson, former owner of
Coliseum Books, one of New York's last great independent bookstores (now
gone), who introduced me to the publishing community and was thus indirectly responsible for me finding a home at the University of Chicago Press,
which turned out to be an excellent choice.

Last but certainly not least, this book could not have been written without
the infinite patience and understanding of my wonderful wife, Céline, and of
my two terrific daughters, Caroline and Geneviève, who never complained
(well, almost never) while I hid in my office rather than being with them. Un
grand merci.

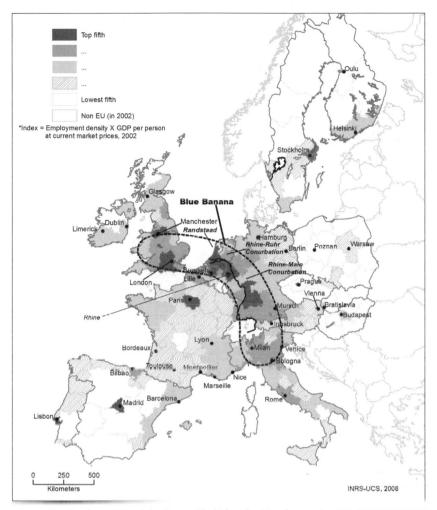

MAP 1. Density of economic activity. Europe. The highest densities of economic activity in western Europe are found in a Banana-shaped arc that largely follows the path of the Rhine, also extending across the Channel into England and across the Alps into Italy. This central feature of Europe's economic geography has remained surprisingly stable in modern times. Elsewhere, activity is densest in and around capital cities: Paris, Madrid, Rome, Stockholm, etc. Note also the high densities in the English Midlands—around Manchester—the birthplace of the Industrial Revolution.

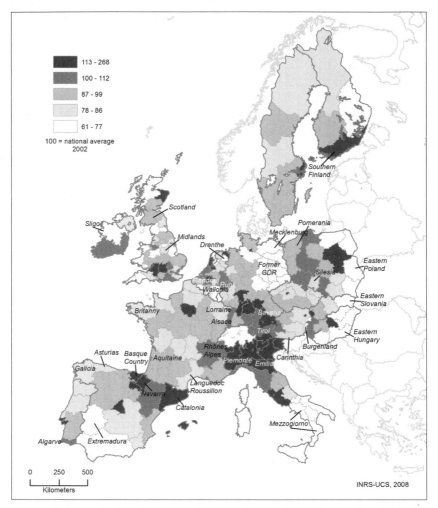

MAP 2. GDP per capita by region, compared to national average: Europe. The map shows GDP (gross domestic product) per person compared to *national* averages for seventeen EU nations. In nations lying outside the Blue Banana, the poorest regions are most often those most distant from it: southwestern Spain, Italy's Mezzogiorno, eastern Poland, northern Scotland, etc. Note the poor performance of the former GDR *Länder* of Germany and of Wallonia in Belgium.

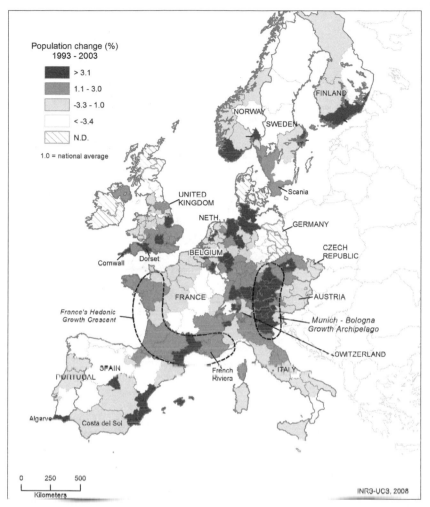

Population change (%)
1993 - 2003

- > 3.1
- 1.1 - 3.0
- -3.3 - 1.0
- < -3.4
- N.D.

1.0 = national average

FINLAND
NORWAY
SWEDEN
Scania
UNITED KINGDOM
NETH.
GERMANY
BELGIUM
CZECH REPUBLIC
Cornwall
Dorset
FRANCE
AUSTRIA
France's Hedonic Growth Crescent
Munich - Bologna Growth Archipelago
SWITZERLAND
SPAIN
PORTUGAL
French Riviera
ITALY
Algarve
Costa del Sol

0   250   500
Kilometers

INR3-UC3, 2008

MAP 3. Population growth, compared to national average: western Europe. The attraction of the south is unmistakable in Britain and Scandinavia. Coastal, Rhine, and southern regions exert the greatest attraction in Germany. The Austrian and Czech populations are being pulled westward. Gray and green migrants, moving to France's hedonic growth crescent, are revitalizing that nation's traditional periphery.

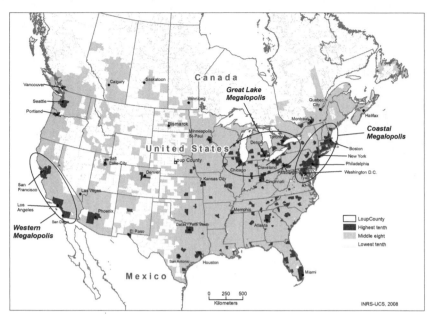

MAP 4. Employment density: US and Canada. The coastal megalopolis—stretching from Boston to Washington, D.C.—is the area of densest activity in North America. A westward extension—jumping over the Appalachians—is centered on the Great Lakes. A second megalopolis has emerged on the Pacific Coast, along an arc stretching from San Francisco to San Diego. Outside the Pacific Coast, note the very low densities in much the West.

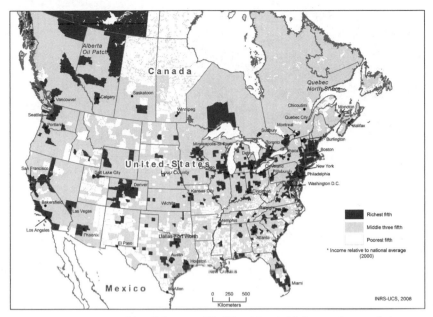

MAP 5. Income per person; richest fifth, poorest fifth: US and Canada. The largest urban conurbations generate the highest incomes. The coastal megalopolis stands out as the greatest concentration of wealth. Note also the high incomes in West Coast and in Texan cities, around Minneapolis–St. Paul and Denver, as well as in south Florida and southern Ontario. High incomes in parts of northern Canada reflect high wage resource industries (lumber, oil, mining, and smelting).

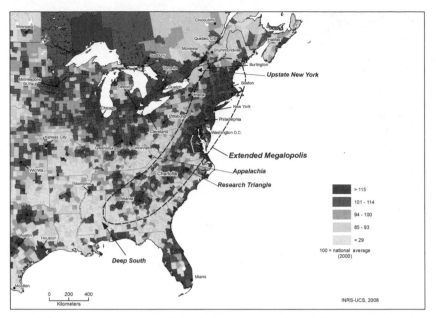

MAP 6. Income per person: eastern North America. High incomes are increasingly generated in city-regions and conurbations of well-connected urban areas. The coastal megalopolis is expanding south, embracing North Carolina's Research Triangle, Charlotte, and Atlanta. The relative poverty of Upstate New York, central Pennsylvania, Appalachia, and the rural Deep South stands out in sharp contrast.

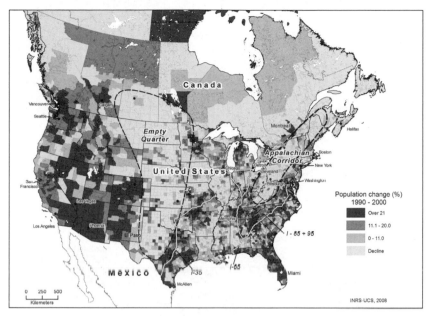

MAP 7. Population growth by place: US and Canada. North America's population continues to move west, to coastal areas, to the Sun Belt, and to large urban centers. In the eastern half of the continent, growth is coalescing along trade corridors of connected cities. Large swaths of North America are losing population: the dry interior (the "empty quarter"), the Appalachian corridor, and Canadian regions east of Montreal.

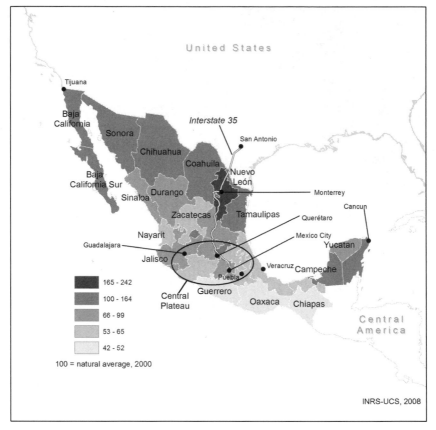

United States

Tijuana

Baja California

Sonora

Chihuahua

Coahuila

Interstate 35

San Antonio

Baja California Sur

Durango

Sinaloa

Nuevo León

Monterrey

Zacatecas

Tamaulipas

Querétaro

Cancun

Nayarit

Mexico City

Guadalajara

Jalisco

Yucatan

Veracruz

Campeche

Puebla

Central Plateau

Guerrero

Oaxaca

Chiapas

Central America

	165 - 242
	100 - 164
	66 - 99
	53 - 65
	42 - 52

100 = natural average, 2000

INRS-UCS, 2008

M A P 8 . GDP per person by state: Mexico. The proximity of the United States, Mexico's chief trading partner, is a key element shaping its economic geography. Northern states have higher incomes, attracting migrants from elsewhere. Mexico City, with the highest incomes, remains the economic center of the nation, but with growth being steadily pulled northwards. The poor southern states of Guerrero, Oaxaca, and Chiapas are both far from the U.S. border and lack a major urban center.

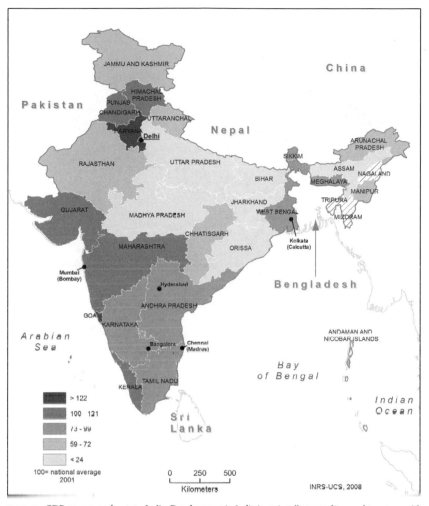

MAP 9. GDP per person by state: India. Development in India is regionally more dispersed; compare with Mexico and China. The high income states of Maharashtra (with Mumbai), West Bengal (with Calcutta), Kerala, and Haryana (plus Delhi) are respectively located in the west, east, south, and north of India. The poorest areas are not in the geographic peripheries, but rather near the center of the nation. Bihar and Uttar Pradesh, among the poorest states, lie along the densely populated Ganges valley in the heart of India.

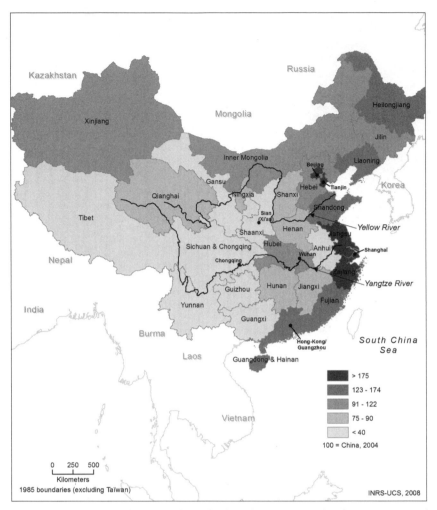

MAP 10. GDP per person by region: China. China's rapid economic growth and uneven institutional reforms—the coastal areas were the first to liberalize—have produced sharp regional disparities. Incomes in greater Shanghai, the richest region, are some ten times higher than in Guizhou, the poorest. Growth has concentrated in the coastal provinces, which also account for the lion's share of foreign trade and of foreign direct investment.

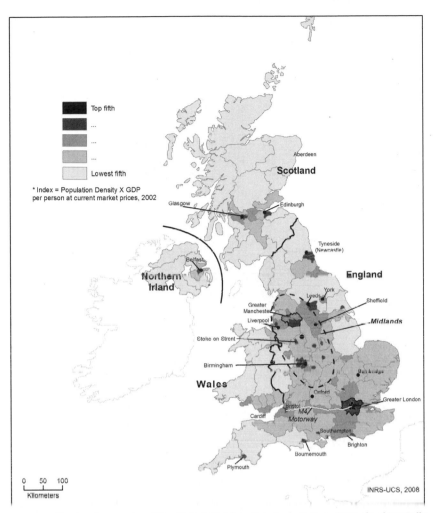

MAP 11. Density of economic activity: United Kingdom. Economy activity in Britain has historically coalesced along a north-south line connecting the Manchester-Liverpool conurbation, Birmingham, and London. Other concentrations are found in Scotland, Tyneside, and Wales. England's economy has drifted southward in recent times. Many industrial cities of the Midlands—vanguards of the Industrial Revolution— have fallen on hard times, while London has continued to prosper.

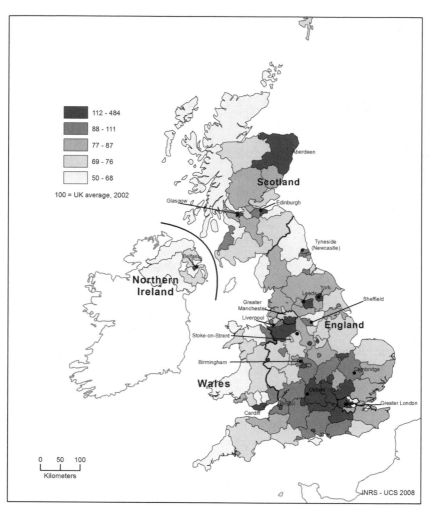

MAP 12. GDP per person: United Kingdom. Regional income disparities, notably between the south and the north, are a persistent feature of Britain's economic geography. London is one of the highest-income and cost places in the world. Knowledge-rich services and industries are concentrated in and around London, often along corridors leading to the university towns of Cambridge and Oxford. Outside the South, Leeds, York, and central Scotland are examples of relatively high-income areas. The high GDP around Aberdeen is an expression of resource rents (oil and natural gas).

Why Do Some Places Generate More Wealth Than Others?

What can people be paying Manhattan or downtown Chicago rents for, if not for being near other people?

ROBERT E. LUCAS

Asking why some places generate more wealth than others is not very different from asking why some people succeed in life while others do not. There are general rules—good health, having loving parents, and growing up in stimulating surroundings—but these alone do not guarantee success and happiness. Individual traits and circumstances count for just as much, if not more. No two individuals are exactly alike. Trying to explain why, within every nation, some places generate more wealth than others is inevitably a balancing act, a constant move back and forth between general laws and particular situations. The quest for grand explanations—and magic recipes—is constantly thwarted by local realities. Simple explanations are the exception, not the rule.

The purpose of this chapter is to bring that message home. I wish to give the reader a sense of the diversity of reasons that explain why some places grow and prosper compared to others. Local success stories abound, as do stories of decline, and chance is all too often the deciding factor. However, I also wish to give the reader a foretaste of the laws of economic geography from which it is impossible to escape. If we pay attention, patterns do emerge underneath the apparent chaos of different destinies, whether they concern big cities, regions, or villages.

Before continuing, a few words are in order on my use of the terms *wealth* and *growth*. All throughout the book, *wealth* is used as shorthand for material welfare or, in more technical terms, as the equivalent of income or product per person, in cases where income data are not available.[1] I shall use these terms interchangeably. *Regional growth*, as used in this book, has a double meaning: growth both in material welfare and in population numbers. In regional economies, the two are generally associated. In open societies, populations will, as a rule, migrate towards places, communities, and regions where incomes are higher.[2]

But why should some places generate higher incomes than others in the age of the Internet, e-mail, and cell phones, in which we are said to have finally vanquished the monster of distance and broken the chains of geography?

Places in a Shrinking World

I turn on my computer and am instantly in touch with almost every corner of the planet. From Montreal—where I am sitting—the price of a telephone call to other parts of Canada is hardly worth mentioning. And the price continues to fall and will soon approach zero. Airplanes carry me to other cities in North America and Europe in a matter of hours. At my local market, day-fresh blueberries from New Jersey and British Columbia are currently for sale, displayed alongside mangoes from Mexico and oranges from South Africa. Yes, the world is shrinking, certainly with respect to the speed at which information travels. Ranchers in Montana have instant access to beef price quotes in Chicago. Bankers in London are able to follow the latest developments on the oil rigs off Scotland as they happen. The IT (information technology) revolution is transforming our world. It no longer matters where one is. All places are equal . . . or are they?

One of the paradoxes of the IT revolution is that *place* now matters more. At the end of this book, the reader will hopefully understand why. I could just as well have called this book *The Wealth and Poverty of Places*; but somehow that doesn't have the same ring as *The Wealth and Poverty of Regions*. The idea conveyed in both cases is that we are dealing with places, communities, localities, towns, cities, urban areas, and regions (the list of labels is almost endless) whose boundaries are not always clearly defined and which are confined *within* a nation. The U.S., Britain, India, China, etc. are patchworks of communities, places, and regions of varying sizes, names, and shapes. Upstate New York is a region, but it is also a place, and some might say that it is a community too. This definitional fuzziness should not bother the reader. Places can have many names and shapes. In more technical jargon, the objects of study are sub-national spatial units, be they villages, towns, cities, or regions. This book attempts to explain differences in economic fortunes *within* nations—between the various places that make up a nation—and not between nations. Explaining why the U.S. or Britain is richer than, say, Nigeria is not at all the same thing as explaining why certain places in the U.S. or Britain are richer—or growing more rapidly—than other places in the U.S. or Britain.

Let us return to the IT revolution. If place no longer mattered, differences in economic fortune *within* nations—between different places—should have disappeared (or at least be in the process of disappearing), certainly within the world's more economically advanced nations. The evidence tells the opposite story. In United States—arguably the world's most mobile society with a long history of free movement and exchange between places—income differences between places are far from insignificant. Average personal incomes in 2006 in the three poorest counties, Loup, Nebraska, and Ziebach and Buffalo in South Dakota, were respectively, $9,140, $11,381, and $12,471 compared to $53,423 in the Greater New York area and $110, 292 in Manhattan.[3] The three poor counties have continued to lose population over the last two decades. Here we have a first indication that *place* does indeed matter or, to be more precise, that *location* matters. Nebraska and South Dakota are neighboring states, located in the center of the North American continent. No two places have exactly the same location. All places in North America do not have the same potential for generating high incomes and job opportunities (maps 5 and 6). Nor do all places in Europe, India, China, and Britain have the same potential (maps 2, 9, 10, and 12). Explaining why this is so is the objective of this book.

The economic value of a particular place is perhaps best reflected in the price people are willing to pay to be there, which can be measured by land and housing prices. In the second quarter of 2008—the subprime crisis notwithstanding—the median price of a single family home in the New York area was twice that in the Chicago area and four times the price in Wichita, Kansas.[4] Similar housing price differences exist between London and smaller British cities and between Paris and the rest of France or, for that matter, between any large metropolis and smaller cities. Only the most fortunate can afford an apartment in central London, Paris, Toronto, Hong Kong, Mumbai, etc. This brings us back to the question of the IT revolution. If, thanks to the Internet and all, it no longer matters where one resides, then why do people continue to pay a small fortune to live in downtown London, Paris, or New York? Why is Chicago "worth more" than Wichita? After all, information is as readily accessible in Wichita as in New York or Chicago, be it via the Internet, cell phone, TV, or Blackberry. Surely, we have missed something.

Why do people continue to flock to big cities? The great cities of China and India will soon reach populations unheard of in the history of mankind. *Place* obviously continues to matter to the millions of Chinese and Indians who, every year, make the move from rural places to urban places. Why do so many put such a high value on some places over others, high enough that they are willing to leave friends and family behind to move there? The

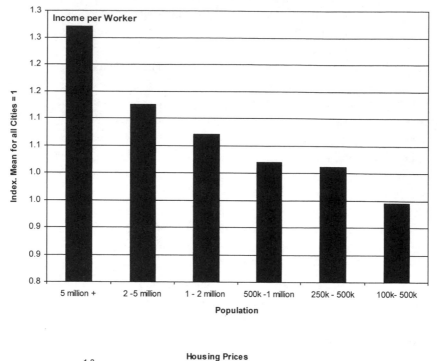

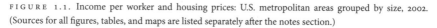

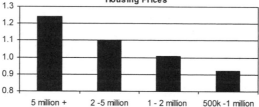

FIGURE 1.1. Income per worker and housing prices: U.S. metropolitan areas grouped by size, 2002. (Sources for all figures, tables, and maps are listed separately after the notes section.)

answer, surely, is that some places generate greater economic opportunities than others. But why?

The previous paragraph provides a second clue. Size matters too. New York is bigger than Chicago and Chicago is bigger than Wichita, and all three cities are bigger than the rural communities of the Dakotas, Nebraska, and Kansas. The positive relationship between city size and higher incomes is one of the best documented in regional economics (figure 1.1). But why should size still matter in the age of the Internet? This question will continue to haunt us throughout this book.

Wealth differences between places exist in every nation[5] (table 1.1). In

TABLE 1.1. Regional Disparities in Selected Nations
Ratio: Richest to Poorest Regions*

Year	1980	2000
Japan	1.50	1.48
UK	1.46	1.59
France	1.60	1.63
Canada	2.41	1.68
Spain	1.97	1.93
US	2.19	2.02
Italy	2.12	2.12
India	3.13	4.81
Mexico	5.08	5.04
Brazil	6.79	5.59
China	7.27	9.07

*Ratio of two regions with highest GDP per person over two regions with lowest GDP per person

the U.S., average product person in the two richest states is about twice that of the two poorest. In developing nations such as India and China, the gap between rich and poor regions is generally much greater. Herein is an additional clue. A link visibly exists between *national* economic development and the scale of wealth differences between places. We shall thus need to examine the relationship between national economic growth and the emergence of regional wealth differences. Why did such differences arise in the first place? Was there ever a time when they did not exist?

Table 1.1 contains another clue. National characteristics also matter.[6] Why should the gap between rich and poor regions be greater in Italy than in Japan or greater in China than in India? Some possible answers are easy to imagine. One should, for example, expect the gap between rich and poor to be less in small nations where people can easily move back and forth between places. But surely the geography, history, and institutions of nations also matter. Here we find ourselves slowly gliding into evermore particular situations, which require knowledge not only of places, but also of the nations in which they find themselves. A small town in the north of England is not necessarily comparable to a small town in the Canadian Prairies, although both may be said to be peripheral in their respective nations.

The reality of place is multidimensional, not easily amenable to one-sentence descriptions. In all nations, the relative wealth (or poverty) of particular places is the outcome of the interplay between general forces—whose impact we are often able to predict—and unique stories. Which of the two carries the day in the end is the kind of question to which social scientists, myself included, are unable to provide simple answers applicable to every place, community, or region.

A PORTRAIT IN CONTRASTS

The two places pictured in figures 1.2 and 1.3 present a striking contrast in economic fortunes. Fist, we see Podung, the new financial district of Shanghai. There is a good chance that Shanghai will one day emerge—perhaps sooner than later—as a the leading global business center, challenging New York and London, and perhaps grow to become the world's largest city. It is already China's largest. It is easily the richest place in China, excluding the special case of Hong Kong. Clearly, Shanghai is favored by both size and location. Its position as a seaport at the head of the vast inland Yangtze waterway system is an obvious advantage, as is its central location on the Chinese seaboard between Hong Kong and Beijing. The size of the Chinese market is an additional factor, as is the direction of trade, a clue that the size and trade relationships of the nation in which a place finds itself will influence its fortunes. Nor can history and politics be excluded. Prior to the communist victory in 1949, Shanghai had developed a proud commercial and cosmopolitan tradition, which set it apart in China. In 1990, the choice by Chinese authorities to establish the first comprehensive free trade zone in Shanghai gave it a head start over other cities. Finally, had the Chinese government chosen not to open the national economy, Shanghai would most certainly have evolved differently. There would probably have been no Podung district of which to take a picture.

Schefferville, Quebec, by contrast, is not a happy story, a sad example of boom and bust. Technology and globalization can be said to be the chief culprits. The 2006 Canadian census puts its population at 202 inhabitants, down from 240 in 2001. In the 1970s, its population exceeded 4,000, a major iron mining center. The mine closed in 1980 because: 1) the demand for iron fell as other lighter materials and alloys (aluminum especially) replaced steel in many products; 2) cheaper iron ore deposits came on stream elsewhere (notably in Brazil) as shipment and transport costs fell. Schefferville ceased to be a competitive location once it became possible to bring in equally high-grade ore from Brazil at lower cost. Within Canada, Schefferville is favored neither by size nor location, situated far from major markets, which in the end precluded a move into other industries after the mine closed. The Schefferville story is an illustration of the double-edged sword that is natural resources: sources of wealth on the one hand, but also potential sources of poverty.

FIGURE 1.2. Growth. Podung, Shanghai's new financial district, a muddy swamp until the 1990s. Photo © iStockphoto.com/Cindy Rojas.

FIGURE 1.3. Decline: Schefferville, Quebec. The sign reads: "Street closed. Drive at your own risk." This was once an upscale neighborhood with big houses, favored by managers and professionals. The town was abandoned when the mine closed. Photo courtesy of Geneviève Polèse.

There is no more fickle resource than a natural resource, a reality that we shall encounter again in this book.

The Schefferville story also tells us that falling transport costs can have both positive and negative consequences, depending on a place's initial location. But wait, if falling transport costs can work both ways, cannot the same reasoning be applied to falling communications costs? Lower transport and communications costs heighten competition between places, bringing them closer. And, as with any competition, there are inevitably winners and losers. Who comes out on top is rarely a foregone conclusion. The relationship between falling communications costs and greater competition provides a first clue as to why the IT revolution might actually increase the importance of place. A shrinking world is not a placeless world. The "place" Schefferville did not cease to exist, but it did decline, a reality which no amount of Internet or IT could alter.

Competition between places, communities, and regions is not exactly the same as competition between nations. The fundamental difference is *openness*. Places, communities, and regions do not have real economic boundaries, although they can have political or administrative boundaries. Only in the European Union, which has almost totally eliminated the barriers to trade and travel between sovereign states, is the distinction blurred. In federal nations such as the U.S., Canada, India, and Australia, constituent states can have considerable economic powers; but they rarely hamper the free movement of people, goods, and money. It is entirely unimaginable that immigration controls should exist between, say, Illinois and Wisconsin or between Alberta and Saskatchewan. Between places, the flow of people, goods, and money is essentially free, held back only by geography, distance, and, in some cases, difference in culture and lifestyles. This is no minor distinction, for it means that a place, unlike a nation, can rapidly gain (or lose) resources, whether human or physical. The wealth of regions is more fragile than the wealth of nations. A region's fortunes can go from good to bad—or the other way around—in the space of a generation, which is exactly what happened in the case of Schefferville, admittedly an extreme case. A place's fortunes can change because technology has changed, because a new transport link was built, because of new consumer fads or because of any number of unpredictable events.

The world of regional economies is a porous one, with places continually exposed to plants opening and closing and people constantly moving in and out . . . and little that communities can do about it, at least not in most cases. Policy levers at the local level are generally limited, although this can vary depending on the size of place and the political structure of the nation.

An American state or Canadian province has more power than a township, county, or city. However, this does not alter the fundamentally open nature of all their economies. Even in a highly regimented society such as China's there is in the end little that local authorities can do to stop migrants from coming into the city.[7] *Places*, by their very nature, are continually exposed to what happens elsewhere.

WHY THE GAP BETWEEN THE NORTH AND THE SOUTH OF ENGLAND?

Britain provides a particularly instructive case, highlighting several reasons why certain parts of a nation might systematically prosper—and draw in populations—compared to others. Urban size alone, which favors London, cannot explain the severity and persistence of regional income and product differences in Britain, specifically between Greater London and the surrounding southeast and the rest of the nation.[8] We need to look at geography and the role of trade. Economic activity is naturally drawn towards places that offer the best access to markets. The EU is Britain's dominant trading partner. When the nation's largest city, London, is located in that part of the nation also best positioned for trade, the result is likely to be an economic divide that consistently favors one region: the south of England in this case.[9]

Historically, economic activity in Britain has largely evolved along a broad northwest-southeast axis stretching roughly from the Manchester-Liverpool duo and nearby Leeds and Sheffield down to Birmingham and, finally, Greater London (map 11). Before the Second World War, it would not have been a total exaggeration to assert that England (I shall concentrate on England, for simplicity's sake) had a bipolar economic geography, with one pole looking west across the Irish Sea and the Atlantic and the other looking east across the North Sea and the Channel. With a little imagination, one could draw an analogy with the United States and declare that Greater Manchester (plus Liverpool) was England's Los Angeles and that Greater London was England's New York, with Birmingham in the middle cast in the role of Chicago. Notwithstanding London's historically dominant role, the other poles were powerful contenders during the nineteenth century and the first decades of the twentieth century.[10] Manchester, as any student of economic history knows, is the birthplace of the Industrial Revolution, rising to become the most important industrial center in the world in the early nineteenth century. Manchester was the site of the first passenger railway between major cities, connecting it with Liverpool in 1830. Manchester in the nineteenth century was one of Europe's leading intellectual and financial centers.

Benjamin Disraeli is reputed to have said at the time that "Manchester is as great a human exploit as Athens."[11] England, in short, had at least two competing centers.

This is no longer so. Manchester, although still a major urban center, can no longer be said to be London's rival as a center of finance and intellectual ferment. London has won. Two symbolic events illustrate the outcome: the Royal Exchange (founded by Manchester cotton traders) closed its doors in 1968; the *Manchester Guardian*, Britain's famed "radical" newspaper, dropped the "Manchester" from its title in 1959 and, adding insult to injury, moved its editorial offices to London in 1970. Britain's economic heartland is today clearly centered in southeastern England, in and around Greater London. The great industrial cities further north remain important, but the center of gravity of the British economy is drifting southward. London is surrounded by a solid block of counties with above-average per capita product (map 12).

There are several reasons for this shift, among them the traditional specialization of northern and Midland cities in declining industries (textiles, steel, coal, etc.). But changing trade routes were also a factor. Just as the shift in trade from the Mediterranean to the Atlantic in fifteenth-century Europe arrested the growth of the great trading cities of Genoa and Venice, so Britain's gradual shift towards Europe and away from the Atlantic has negatively affected Liverpool, Manchester, and other nearby cities. The port of Liverpool was a major lynchpin in the British imperial trading system. With the collapse of that system and Britain's gradual integration into Europe, Liverpool lost its special location advantage, a loss further compounded by the disintegration of the Lancashire textile industry. Both the content and the direction of Britain's trade changed dramatically over the twentieth century. Where trade before was divided between two markets (across the Atlantic/across the Channel), with ups and downs depending on the epoch, the British economy is today solidly tied to Europe, which accounts for the majority of merchandise trade.[12]

Southeastern England is simply closer to Europe. However, geographic determinism must not be pushed too far. We need to introduce a second ingredient: the rise of the service-based knowledge economy. Britain is a prime example of a society that has made the full transition—not without pain, I might add—from a manufacturing-based to a service-based economy. Britain was once the greatest manufacturing power in the world. Today, London is indisputably Europe's primary corporate and business service center with the highest concentration of financial institutions, headquarters, and support services. Indeed, London has even overtaken New York in recent years as the world's dominant center for many financial services. Modern services—financial, corporate, etc.—are the foundation of the London economy, perhaps more so than for any large urban metropolis.

Greater London has three distinct advantages, which made it almost inevitable that modern corporate services should concentrate there: 1) London already had a long tradition as a sophisticated service center, well before the rise of the modern knowledge economy. Even when Britain was primarily a manufacturing nation—much of it concentrated in the Midlands and the north—London was the nation's chief banker and service center. Birmingham's pride was metal, motors, and machines; Manchester's pride was textiles; but London's glory has always been trade and banking. 2) London is Europe's largest city, rivaled only by Paris. No other city can match London in the diversity of available services and firms. 3) The language of London is English. English is today the corporate *lingua franca* of the world. Foreign corporations wishing access to English-language personnel and services will naturally prefer London over other European cities. This does not mean that English-speaking personnel are not available in Amsterdam, Brussels, or Paris, only that they more readily available in London. In the porous world of regional economics, all advantages are relative.

The shift to a modern service economy has favored London over other traditionally more manufacturing-based English cities. In addition, given the almost umbilical connection between high tech industries and modern services (see chapter 2), it is easy to understand why much high-tech manufacturing and R&D has tended as well to locate in the south of England near London. A high-tech cluster, or corridor, has emerged along the M4 motorway linking London to Bristol. Other contributing factors are the proximity of Heathrow Airport and of Oxford University. Birmingham—which lies slightly further north—has started to pick up some of the growth. However, the south of England continues to grow more rapidly and generally generate higher incomes than the north.[13]

PLACES GROW FOR DIFFERENT REASONS. A JOURNEY
TO THE AMERICAN MIDWEST

In few nations are regional economic divides as clear-cut as in Britain. Big-picture explanations, however, run the risk of sliding into geographic or historical determinism. The north of England also contains zones of dynamic growth, although far too few. No two places are exactly alike. It follows that different places will grow (or risk decline) for different reasons.[14] Butte, Montana, is not and never will be anything like Los Angeles. Plymouth (England) is not and never will be anything like London. Why should we expect them to grow (or decline) for the same reasons? By the same token, it seems almost self-evident that such very different communities will face different challenges.

Let me illustrate this with a brief journey to the American Midwest. Chicago has undergone an impressive renaissance in recent years, shedding its traditional, perhaps somewhat overdone, reputation of a tough blue-collar city, built on brawn and muscle, lacking the refinements of New York or Boston. By any measure, Greater Chicago today is a world-class city and has emerged—reemerged would be more correct—as a major center of corporate control, finance, artistic achievement, and higher learning. Chicago was able to achieve this because it was—already a century ago—the *central* place for the entire Midwest, the region's transportation and communications hub, and the natural regional magnet for talent and money. Size was the initial card that Chicago held, so to speak. However, playing this card correctly called for local initiatives that focused on precisely those advantages, which would allow the Chicago area to maintain and even reinforce its position as the "natural" metropolis of the American Midwest. The construction and expansion of O'Hare Airport—the second busiest air transport hub on the continent—is a prime example. The various actions undertaken in the Chicago area in recent decades—downtown beautification and revitalization, public safety and mass transit, major private and public investments in universities, research hospitals, museums, and other institutions—are probably not the outcome of a coordinated strategy (such things seldom are). But they were effective, in large part because of Chicago's initial advantages of size and location.

Chicago could have lost its position at the top of the Midwest urban hierarchy—this was not inconceivable in 1950s when the Detroit economy was in full swing—but it did not. Chicago also won out because Detroit ceased to grow. During the first half of the twentieth century, the rise of Detroit's automobile-based economy was truly spectacular. Detroit has since fallen back.[15] Detroit's troubles can be traced not only to less a propitious location than Chicago but also to a severe case of a negative industrial legacy and ensuing Intrusive Rentier Syndrome (of which more later). Cleveland, another of the Midwest's great cities—with a metropolitan population close to three million—has also seen its growth stunted by the legacy left by its past specialization in heavy industry.

Let me now go to the small Midwestern town of Greensburg, Indiana (population 10,260 in the 2000 census). In July 2006, Honda announced that it would build a large automobile assembly plant there, employing some two thousand workers, ensuring Greensburg's future growth for at least the coming decade.[16] Many other small towns would undoubtedly have liked to attract the plant. However, when we consider the cards that the town held— (small) size, proximity to larger urban centers, and location within the U.S.— the choice of Greensburg is less surprising.

However Greensburg also held another card. Its small size meant that wages and real estate prices were lower there than in larger cities.[17] But proximity was surely what gave the town its edge, strategically located between Indianapolis and Cincinnati, each about fifty miles (seventy kilometers) away. Both are major urban areas with populations over 1 million. Greensburg is located on Interstate Highway 74 with easy access to Interstate 65, one of the major north-south thoroughfares east of the Mississippi. Of the fifteen new car and truck plants that opened in the U.S. between 1980 and 1991, all but two were built along Interstates 65 and 75 (also a north-south highway), which form a narrow corridor running from Indiana and Michigan down through the Ohio valley into Kentucky and Tennessee.[18] Since then, other plants have been built further along I-65, which ends in Mobile, Alabama, in search of ever lower labor and land costs.

Returning to the main point: Greensburg and other small manufacturing towns in the U.S. Midwest and South have not grown for the same reason as Chicago. For Greater Chicago, the crucial variables are not land prices and wages or even labor relations—although they do matter—but rather the capacity to nurture, hold, and attract young entrepreneurs and professionals. Lifestyle issues, urban planning, and local social policies will undoubtedly continue to occupy center stage in "big" places such as Chicago and Minneapolis–St. Paul. For small towns such as Greensburg, future growth will primarily depend on other factors.[19] The Greensburgs of this world are essentially competing on raw costs and on logistics: competitive access to highways, rail links, and, possibly, waterways. Although every place dreams of attracting exciting high-tech industries, for many their natural advantage will lie in middle-range manufacturing. The Greensburgs of this world need to ensure that local wages, land, and infrastructure costs remain competitive. On the other hand, a small town in Montana might not find takers no matter how low its land prices are.

IN SEARCH OF THE SPARK THAT PRODUCES GREAT CITIES

Larger cities produce higher incomes—as a rule—than smaller ones. Why this is so is explained in the next chapter. But understanding how cities become great is quite another matter. Greatness is, of course, a highly subjective notion. We all intuitively know that certain cities in each epoch are *the* cities to be in: where things are happening and tomorrow's new ideas are born. Why did the San Francisco Bay Area (which encompasses Silicon Valley) and not, say, Philadelphia emerge as a magnet for poets, artists, inventors, and dreamers from around America and around the world? The two cities are of comparable size. This is perhaps the most elusive question of all. Most answers end up being circular.

This is a good moment to clarify that throughout this book my use of the word *city* and its many synonyms—urban area, urban center, metropolitan areas, etc.—always refers to urban agglomerations, which can include a variety of political and administrative units: counties, townships, municipalities, boroughs, etc.[20] The competition between such local administrative units—*within* the same metropolitan area—is not the subject of this book. Such intra-metropolitan competition is essentially a fight over shares of the same growing (or shrinking) pie. Whether the growth of the Greater Los Angeles area is captured by the City of Los Angeles—a separate municipality—or the City of Santa Monica (another municipality) is not my concern here. My concern is with the factors that contribute to the prosperity of the metropolitan area as a whole. From the perspective of economics and labor markets, metropolitan areas are the salient unit, for they define the horizon of job and income opportunities.

The quest for the answer of what made some cities great is not unlike trying to discover the secret of artistic talent. Like the arts, it is in part a search for an ideal: a place that will deliver both beauty and prosperity. The early and middle twentieth century, the great heroic period of urbanization in the Western world, gave rise to innumerable projects and city plans whose idealism we can only admire today. Many readers will be familiar with the work of visionary—utopian—architects and urban planners such as Frank Lloyd Wright, Le Corbusier, and Oscar Niemeyer, the latter the chief architect for Brasilia, built from scratch in the 1950s. Such utopian projects have largely gone out of style today. Most planned new towns—built generally between the First World War and the 1960s—have not aged well. The post–Second World War tower blocks and housing estates (called housing projects in New York and HLM[21] in France) have often evolved into slums or ethnic ghettos. The suburban French HLM housing projects were the scene of violent race riots in 2005. As for Brasilia, few today would call it an aesthetic success. I find it a terribly depressing place, dehumanized, like something out of a bad science fiction movie.

The quest for the ideal city will go on. Each epoch will spawn its gurus and utopias. Let me return to the more mundane issue of cities as centers of innovation, industry, and economic opportunity. Why precisely some cities—and not others—emerged as centers of intellectual and economic ferment is a question that continues to haunt scholars. An initial accident of history or geography is often the determining factor. Had not the kings of France chosen Paris as their capital and built the nation's transport system around it, the City of Light might today be no more than another European town. Perhaps no modern scholar has devoted more effort to the study of the relationship between cities, creativity, and economic performance then the British urban historian Sir Peter Hall. In his 1,169-page opus *Cities in Civilization* (1998), Hall attempts to understand what in each epoch makes certain cities—beginning with ancient Athens, through Habsburg Vienna, to Los Angeles today—centers of creativity and innovation. Creative cities in each epoch, Hall finds, were generally cosmopolitan, with a diverse mix of peoples and cultures, places of intellectual ferment, experimentation, and non-conformity, drawing in free spirits from far and wide. In an article published two years later, Hall writes that "creative cities, creative urban milieus, are places of great social and intellectual turbulence: not comfortable cities at all."[22] Hall is undoubtedly right; but this is not terribly useful for predicting where the next creative city will emerge. Hall readily admits in closing, "[O]n reflection, I am far from sure that I have a satisfactory answer. . . . There are no absolute rules in this game; chance happens to great cities too."[23]

At least two problems complicate the search for a growth formula for big cities. First, it is impossible to separate a city's success from that of its surrounding region. It is no accident that San Francisco is in California, with all the magic that that name evokes. The fortunes of regions and cities are hopelessly intertwined. Cities in the knowledge economy are primarily service centers, and as such tied to the fortunes of their market areas, with the possible exception of the very largest mega-cities whose economic space may be an entire nation or even the world. Cities located in stagnating or declining parts of a continent (or nation) will have problems growing, no matter how livable, safe, and culturally vibrant they are.[24] My own city, Montreal, is a good example: a very livable city—certainly in my opinion—but located in a generally slow-growing part of North America. A growing big city in a declining region is almost an oxymoron; for if the big city succeeds in bucking the trend of its wider region, then one would expect the city to pull up the rest of the region, which would then again become a growing region. By the same token, a declining big city in a growing region seems highly unlikely, especially if it is the regional metropolis. In Germany, Munich is growing more rapidly than other major cities, but then so is all of southern Bavaria compared to other parts of Germany.[25]

The second problem is more fundamental. Having a highly skilled and educated population—plus the cultural and higher learning institutions that normally go with this attribute—are obvious advantages. This requires no further comment. The problem—all too common in the social sciences—is one of the chicken and egg, in short, the difficulty of distinguishing between causes and consequences. Which comes first: city growth or an educated workforce? Urban lifestyles—cafés, cultural activities, etc.—often associated with high concentrations of educated young professionals, are not terribly useful as predictors of growth. In this I differ with Richard Florida,[26] one of America's foremost urban scholars, who argues that a bohemian lifestyle and rich cultural scene will per se create the conditions for local economic growth. But, are these attributes the *outcome* of a city that has grown over many decades or are they the *sources* of that growth? I do not believe that a clear answer is possible. Phoenix, one the fastest-growing metropolitan areas in the U.S., certainly does not owe its rapid growth to an initial above-average endowment of educated workers, world-class universities, museums, and café scene. The same might be said of Atlanta, Miami, or Calgary, all of which are rapidly growing cities. Growth attracts talent and money. If Phoenix keeps on growing, we may reasonably predict that it will in time house a more highly educated population and also spawn top-notch universities and cultural institutions, and perhaps even a few trendy neighborhoods where the bohemian classes can hang out. Will these acquired attributes, in turn, produce further growth? Perhaps, but then again perhaps not, since they were not necessary in the first place to spark growth. Nor would Phoenix be the only big city in the U.S. to possess such positive attributes. In the end, it seems unlikely that Phoenix would ever dethrone Boston or San Francisco as a magnet for knowledge workers and the bohemian set.

In all honesty, it is probably not possible to come up with a systematic explanation, that is not circular, of why some cities more than others have prospered and attracted talent and brains (or the other way around). The surest way to attract talent, skills, and money is to be a growing city with plentiful job opportunities and high wages. This is not terribly helpful. All we can do is point out that an educated population and the lifestyles that come with it are indisputably positive assets. But they are also assets that can be acquired and lost. Great cities can lose their young and educated to others. I do not know how many Detroiters have left for Chicago or Los Angeles over the last few decades, but undoubtedly more than a few; a reminder of the porous nature of place economies. Perhaps the closest thing to an answer is that great cities are always the *center* of an urban empire, so to speak, of a wider territory that looks to it as *its* metropolis. A metropolis is always the center of something; call it a hinterland, a market area, or whatever. How certain cities became to be centers is the subject of chapter 3.

History and Industrial Legacies

The past is a force whose continued capacity to shape current events is all too often underestimated, perhaps no more so than in economic geography. The search for general explanations is constantly thwarted by the weight of history. Before proposing general laws, the subject of the next chapter, I invite the reader on a number of journeys, beginning with the stubborn legacy of past industrial glories.

NEGATIVE CLUSTERS: COAL, CUTLERY, AND COTTON

The idea of a negative cluster of industries is not difficult to grasp. All industries must one day decline. High-tech is a fleeting reality. What was a sunrise (high-tech) industry one day is a sunset (declining) industry the next. The metal-bashing industries of Birmingham and the great blast furnaces of the English Midlands were the pinnacle of high technology at the end of the nineteenth century. If an informed observer were asked in 1890 which were the most technologically advanced and innovative places on the planet at the time, he or she would most probably have mentioned Manchester and Birmingham in England and perhaps Pittsburgh in the U.S. and Essen in the German Ruhr—home to great Krupp steel works. Half a century later, if we were to ask the same question, Detroit would perhaps be the first place to come to mind. The automobile industry was the principal driver of the U.S. economy for a good part of the twentieth century. Today, nobody thinks of automobile manufacturing, and even less textiles and steel making, as high-tech industries.

Hence, places that specialized in textiles and clothing or steel and metal production will with time find themselves saddled with negative clusters, *unless* they have managed to diversify into other more dynamic industries. It is precisely this aspect—the ease with which it is possible to move from one industrial specialization to another—that makes some clusters more negative than others. Every industry or occupation—agriculture, fishing, mining, steel making, automobile manufacturing, computer programming, banking, etc.—creates its own culture: a work ethic, pattern of industrial relations, and outlook particular to that industry. Some will be more conducive to change than others. Industrial cultures will have little effect on economic performance in cities or regions where no industry dominates the landscape. But in regions where one industry—or set of industries—with a common industrial culture dominates the landscape, that culture will become the regional norm, which can have either a positive or a negative effect on the local economy. This is a warning to local economic development strategists that the pursuit of clusters—currently much in vogue—also entails risks. Industrial specialization is a good thing while an industry is growing, but it can just as easily turn into an impediment to future growth if it distorts the local labor market or otherwise negatively affects the choices of local businesspeople, workers, and investors, as the next story demonstrates.

THE INTRUSIVE RENTIER SYNDROME

The Saguenay and North Shore regions of northeastern Quebec, Canada, have a population of about 400,000; Chicoutimi, with 150,000 inhabitants, is the largest urban center. Two industries dominate the local economy: pulp and paper mills and aluminum smelting. Economies of scale are important in both industries; both are characterized by enormous, highly capitalized plants, in which labor costs comprise only a fraction of total production costs. This is especially true of aluminum smelting. The transformation of raw alumina into aluminum ingots involves a costly process called electrolysis, requiring vast quantities of electrical power. The combined costs of plant, machinery, and especially electric power far outweigh wage costs. Electrical power is the chief consideration. The reason the aluminum smelting industry is so highly concentrated in this part of Quebec is the availability of vast, relatively inexpensive quantities of electric power, thanks to the immense hydroelectric potential—unparalleled in North America—of northern Quebec. Aluminum smelting plants are located there, rather than on the southern shore of the St. Lawrence River, because of the high transport cost of electricity, whose transmission requires the construction of expensive-to-maintain high-voltage transmission lines and pylons.[27] The Saguenay and North Shore have the added advantage of deep water ports, which can accommodate the freighters bringing in alumina and bauxite from overseas.

The Saguenay and North Shore thus have a clear natural advantage with regard to aluminum production, an advantage that has been exploited with vigor over the last few decades.[28] The parallel with the "natural" advantage a century earlier of the English Midlands for steel making—thanks to nearby coal deposits and ports—is not difficult to make. Aluminum smelting and pulp and paper remain the backbones of the Saguenay and North Shore economies. Precisely because these industries are highly capitalized, with labor only a minor cost, they are able to pay high wages, contributing to the prosperity of the area. Average wages in some communities are above those in Montreal. But the local economy has not diversified into other industries. Hardly any businesses start-ups have taken off in other industries. The area remains solidly wedded to these two big industries controlled as often as not by corporations headquartered in Montreal, Toronto, or elsewhere. The most lucrative jobs by far are those in the large plants that dot the local landscape. The local entrepreneurial class—once dynamic—has all but died out. The Saguenay and North Shore are high-wage economies, but also truncated economies or, perhaps more accurately, stalled economies. Despite high wages, these are places of out-migration and declining populations.

What happened? My colleague Richard Shearmur and I have named the predicament that afflicts regions of this type the Intrusive Rentier Syndrome.[29] In the language of economists, a *rentier* is an individual who lives off an income—a rent—he or she has not truly earned, but rather is the result of particular circumstances or good fortune. As economists cynically put it, we are all rent seekers. Rents can be generated by several circumstances, location among them, which is why economists speak of land rent when referring to income generated by a particular location. But the most common, most visible sources of rents are natural resources. Saudi Arabians, to take an obvious example, are rich not because their economy is technologically advanced or their workforce particularly industrious, but because they enjoy the good fortune of sitting on the world's largest oil reserves.

Back to the Saguenay and North Shore. The combined advantages of geography (deep sea ports) and cheap electric power have generated a potential *rent* for aluminum producers. Firms in the aluminum smelting business are able to generate higher profits here than in other places, not necessarily because of any added efforts on their part, but because of the region's particular attributes. Who captures this rent? Owners and shareholders, of course. Otherwise why invest? Governments will get their share via royalties and taxes. But—and this is my main point—so will workers, by way of higher wages and other benefits. Companies are able, we have seen, to pay high wages thanks to the technological characteristics of aluminum smelting, with large, heavily capitalized plants. Size also produces a second result: large plants facilitate unionization. The Saguenay and North Shore are among the most heavily unionized regions in North America with a reputation of militancy.[30] The labor unions obviously understand the economics of the situation very well and have successfully negotiated advantageous wage packages for their members. Who can blame them?

The outcome is a local work environment in which expectations are in large part set by the practices of large firms and unions. A local resident I met called it the "lunch box" mindset,[31] in which father and then son, and then his son after him, expect in the normal course of things to go to work in the factory with a guaranteed job and a good wage. Here again, a parallel with the English Midlands is not difficult to draw. I remember being in England in the early 1970s during the miners' strike and watching Arthur Scargill (leader of the National Union of Miners) on television, addressing a group of striking miners.[32] His message was simple: my father worked in the mines and my grandfather before him, and my sons and grandsons should be able to do so also. At the time, I found this a shockingly "European" stance—anti-progress and anti-change. But, as my experience in eastern Canada some thirty years later was to demonstrate, such a mindset is not simply an inherited cultural trait, but rather the result of specific local conditions. I found a similar attitude—although high wages and unionization were not at issue in this case—among the fisherman of Newfoundland and the Maritime Provinces of Canada, for whom fishing is more than just work, it is also a way of life: a way of life they do not want to lose. Again, who can blame them?

Let me return to an economic environment characterized by large plants, high wages, and unions. We know who the *rentiers* are—the aluminum companies and their workers. But, why are they *intrusive*? We already have part of the answer: they discourage young workers from looking elsewhere, from starting up a business, for example. The story does not end there. My colleague Richard Shearmur and I met with several budding entrepreneurs in the region. Near Chicoutimi we met with the owner of a small firm producing made-to-measure softwood beams for the U.S. market, a process that required surprisingly sophisticated machinery and technical know-how. His predicament was typical: impossible to hold skilled workers. "Every time I train a young lad," he said, "I lose him a year or so later to a big paper mill or aluminum plant able to pay him twice the salary I can."

The big plants are, in short, doubly intrusive. *First*, they make it difficult, or impossible, to start up a profitable (export) operation in manufacturing in industries that cannot compete with the "artificially" high wages paid by aluminum and paper plants. *Second*, they discourage smaller manufacturing firms from training their workers; for once trained they will leave for a better paying job in a big plant. The combined effect of these "intrusions" is easy to guess: few if any business start-ups in other industries. The few who try, fail more often than not. The entrepreneur we met has since closed shop. Seeing others fail is certainly not an incentive to start one's own business. Little wonder then that the Saguenay and North Shore economies have stalled, seemingly incapable of renewing their industrial structures.

The difficulties of the Saguenay and North Shore are compounded by location. These are peripheral regions, situated some two hundred kilometers from Quebec City and some five hundred kilometers from Montreal. When the costs of distance are added to the disadvantage of a high-wage, unionized environment, the outcome is particularly problematic. The Saguenay and North Shore regions are by no means atypical. Many peripheral resource-rich regions elsewhere find themselves in the same predicament. In Norway, the nation's oil riches have certainly had a positive effect on the national treasury and in turn on the quality of public services, but they have also acted as a break on the development of an export-led high-tech manufacturing sector, unlike Sweden and Finland, which have given birth to high-tech giants such as Ericsson Electronics and Nokia, not dependant on natural resources. Norway is not a region, but a nation; the point, however, remains valid. Resource riches can be both a blessing and a curse. The oil-rich Canadian Province of Alberta is currently going through a resource boom, with extraordinary employment and income growth. Like Norway, the provincial treasury is awash in money—the envy of the rest of Canada. Alberta is the only province to have totally paid off its debt and the only province without a local sales tax. University professors in my field can earn 50 percent more (even double) compared to what they earn elsewhere. Alberta at the time of writing is a high-growth economy, but also a high-cost economy. That, in a nutshell, is the dilemma.

There is nothing natural about natural resources. Technology determines what qualifies as a "resource," not nature. Oil (petrol) was not a resource prior to the invention of the internal combustion engine. Coal ceased being a high-valued resource with the introduction of other—more efficient and cleaner—sources of energy. Changes in the technology of steel making also reduced the value of coal. Indeed, technological progress poses a constant threat to all economic advantages. The introduction of air travel has reduced the importance of ports as centers of finance and corporate control. Steel lost its role as the lead sector in industrialization with the introduction of aluminum, alloys, plastics, and other building materials. The list of industries that have fallen victim to technological change over time is almost endless. No economic advantage is totally guaranteed.

The challenge for resource-rich regions like Alberta is putting its current wealth to good use while it lasts. This is sometimes easier in federations and nations in which regions have a high degree of fiscal autonomy; a share of the resource rents will necessarily be spent in the region on public services and infrastructures. The immense riches of the University of Texas—one of the best endowed in the U.S.—owe a lot to Texan oil. Alberta's oil-based growth has caused its two largest urban centers, Calgary and Edmonton, to reach the

1 million mark. Calgary is in the process of becoming an important corporate and financial center along the lines of Dallas and Houston. However, neither Calgary nor Edmonton has thus far succeeded in creating strong diversified economies. From a North American perspective, both remain comparatively peripheral, not the best places to put a plant or office for serving New York, Chicago, and California markets. Alberta's challenge—like that of many resource-rich regions—resembles a race against time. Can the local economy be primed to sufficient size, in effect, transforming a periphery into a center before the resource runs out or loses its value? The day Calgary's population goes beyond the 2 or 3 million mark, it will have become an economic center. Whether that ever happens, only the future will tell. However, as the history of Detroit, Cleveland, and Manchester demonstrates, size alone is not a sufficient guarantee of future growth.

Wallonia in Belgium provides a particularly harsh example of the debilitating effects of negative clusters, specifically the province of Hainault, historically the heart of Belgium's coal-mining region, centered on the *Borinage* district and the cities of Mons and Charleroi.[33] The landscape of the Borinage is truly dismal; at least, it was when I visited it some years ago. I was not around in the late nineteenth century when the coal mines were in full operation, when iron ore smelters and steel mills were belching out fire, smoke, and soot. I'm sure it was not a pleasant sight. Simply seeing the debris left behind by the coal mines and the tightly packed red-brick row houses beside them, where the miners and their families lived, was depressing enough. I encountered similar landscapes in the English Midlands in the 1970s. Steel and mining—like paper mills and aluminum smelters—are big industries, heavily capitalized, with large workforces, and thus easy targets for unionization. In addition, the horrendous working conditions in the nineteenth and early twentieth centuries made them a fertile ground for social activism—and again, who can blame them? It is not by accident that the traditional European centers of coal and steel—the Ruhr, the Midlands, south Wales, Lorraine, Nord-Pas-de-Calais, the Borinage, Asturias, and Saxony—became strongholds of socialist and sometimes communist parties. The era of violent social conflict and divisive labor disputes is today—hopefully—over. But that era has left a legacy from which some regions have found it more difficult to escape than others. Clearly, the Belgian regions are among those that have found it most difficult.

Many of Europe's old industrialized regions still appear to be under the spell of that legacy. I can find no other explanation of why seemingly well located regions in northern France and in southern Belgium—in the European heartland—should continue to perform so poorly. There is perhaps no better proof of how deeply entrenched those legacies are, and how difficult it is to change perceptions, expectations, and patterns of behavior. This is something about which economic geographers have little to say, another reason why the process of industrial renewal is—in many cases, at least—so slow despite decades of public intervention. The hoped-for transformation is as much sociological as economic. It is revealing that the Ruhr area of Germany—the heart of its old coal and steel industries—seems to have been more successful in renewing its economy than other similar regions in Europe, certainly compared to much of the English Midlands and to southern Belgium. A possible explanation for the difference may be that, when Germany lost the war, it triggered a traumatic self-examination of German society, radically upsetting old social relationships, values, and perceptions. The almost total physical destruction of German industry during the war was undoubtedly an additional factor facilitating change. How valid this explanation is I do not know. But it brings home once gain the importance of history, accidents, and politics, which can annul the advantages that normally come with size and a good location, a useful reminder that no advantage is immutable.

A PARTICULARLY DESTRUCTIVE LEGACY

I do not want to leave the reader with the impression that negative legacies are the unique result of large-scale industries of the industrial era. A step back even further into history reveals other economic specializations—the type of crops cultivated, specifically—that have produced negative legacies, inimical to modern economic growth. The labor requirements of growing cotton or sugar cane are not the same as for dairy farming. The reader will have guessed that I am referring to the sad legacy of slavery, perhaps the most devastating legacy left behind by any industry cluster, so to speak. I do not wish to dwell too long on this (depressing) subject, if only to point out that this is an example—like steel and coal—of geography and technology coming together to create particular social conditions and work environments. It was the technology at the time of picking cotton—to take the most notorious example—that dictated labor requirements and made slavery profitable. Just as the steel and coal industries of Europe gave rise to particular social relationships, so regions founded on plantation economies spawned societies with ways of life and value systems whose impact on regional growth are felt to this day.

The effects of this sad legacy are limited to nations with regions whose climate and soils favored plantation-based crops. Europe thus largely escaped the effects of slavery and plantation economics. The United States, Brazil, and

Mexico were not so fortunate. In each case, sharp regional differences in climate and soils—these are big nations—and the local societies they spawned have shaped the nation's economic geography. Brazil is arguably the most extreme case of the three. Slavery was only abolished in Brazil in 1888. The south-north divide between Brazil's rich south and poor northeast roughly corresponds to the divide between Brazil's temperate south, largely settled by populations of European stock—where slavery was not prominent—and the much hotter sub-tropical and tropical north with a slave-based plantation economy, essentially sugar cane but also cotton. Poor cultivation techniques, plus the inherent propensity of such crops to deplete the soil, has left much of the Brazilian northeast with the dual negative legacy of poor soil—with recurring droughts—and a society on which slavery has left its imprint.

Plantation economies might also be described as intrusive rentiers; but with a major negative difference. In this case, the rentiers—the plantation owners—have driven wages down to zero, the definition of slavery. Various forms of labor exploitation come close to slavery, even if not formally called so. Colonial Mexico had the *encomiendo* system that bound rural Indians and their descendants to particular plantations or haciendas. In many cases, de facto slavery or serfdom—low or zero wages, zero mobility—continued long after the formal abolition of slavery. Plantation economies, founded initially on slavery, have historically found it very difficult to make the transition to a modern industrial society. The American South long remained outside the U.S. economic mainstream—by far the poorest part of the nation—with an almost preindustrial economy until well into the twentieth century. To understand why plantation economies had such a detrimental effect on (future) economic growth, we need to consider both parties in this sad saga: the planters and the slaves and their descendants.

Slavery was a hideous system that broke souls, separated families, and destroyed the normal social fabric of communities. That this left an indelible scar on the populations subjected to slavery and their descendants is obvious. Slavery and the barely less oppressive systems that often followed its formal abolition—Jim Crow in the American South[34]—were necessarily built on violence. One need not be an eminent sociologist to understand that this did not produce terribly happy and productive societies. Trust is a basic ingredient of a smoothly functioning economic environment. Economic growth requires at least a minimum of social cohesion. A society in which a large proportion of the population feels excluded—convinced that it is condemned by history to a life of poverty—is not fertile ground for entrepreneurship and economic growth.

The destructive effect of the legacy of slavery—on economic growth, specifically—is not limited to its impact on the descendants of slaves. Plantation economies, founded on sharp social and racial distinctions, spawned a particular mindset among the ruling, slave-owning classes. Aside from a climate of constant repression and fear (of slave revolts), hard work was not as a rule valued among members of the planter aristocracy. Work, after all, was something associated with the *other* group—the other race—beneath consideration for any socially worthy planter. These were true rentiers, living off the *rents* generated by their fields and captive labor, made possible by slavery.[35] Entrepreneurship and socially progressive thinking were not typically leading characteristics of this rentier class. The mindset and values of that era have in some cases lingered on well after the death of slavery and continue to shape social and economic relationships.[36]

WHOSE EFFECTS LINGER ON IN PLACES ONE WOULD NOT SUSPECT

For many readers this may seem like ancient, best-forgotten history, irrelevant to the understanding of regional growth in modern economies. Let me tell another story. Some years ago, a deputy minister in the Quebec Government, responsible for economic development, asked me to do a study of head office location. Why do large head offices choose to locate in some cities and not in others? This was a subject of some concern at the time—the 1970s and 1980s—because several large corporations were moving or threatening to move their Canadian head offices from Montreal to Toronto. Among the things I examined was the distribution of head offices in the U.S., using the Fortune 500 as my guide. The U.S. city that came out best—for metropolitan areas of analogous size—was Minneapolis–St. Paul. Not only was the Minneapolis–St. Paul metropolitan area home to several large corporations at the time (3M, Honeywell, Control Data, General Foods, Pillsbury, Green Giant, Hormel, etc.), but it was also systematically at the top of the list on many performance indicators: income per person, education levels, unemployment, etc. The location of Minneapolis–St. Paul made its exceptional performance even more intriguing. Like Montreal, it was a northern city with an equally terrible climate. Its location was, arguably, even more peripheral than that of Montreal, lying on the northwestern edge of the North American economic heartland. Truly, this was an interesting case to study.

I thus duly set off for the Twin Cities, as the area is called, with a questionnaire in hand, which methodically listed all the possible reasons why a head office might choose a particular city: size, location, educational institutions, specialized services, etc. The questionnaire also allowed me to weight each factor. After interviewing several executives who were kind enough to receive me, I threw my questionnaire out the window. It was useless. At each occasion, the answer was the same. The company had not chosen to locate there; it was founded there. True, in some cases the initial founders may have come from surrounding towns in rural Minnesota or the neighboring Dakotas, but these were all basically homegrown corporations.

The next question naturally was: why was Minnesota such a fertile ground for rising entrepreneurs. The answer both business executives and academics gave me was the same. This part of the United Sates—where family farms (especially dairy farms) are the dominant form of agriculture—was mainly settled by populations of German and Scandinavian stock with a strong work ethic and, it might be added, a strong stubborn streak. The important Scandinavian presence also left an egalitarian imprint unique among American states, of which Minneapolis–St. Paul's metropolitan form of governance, which provides for income sharing between richer and poorer municipalities, provides an eloquent illustration.[37] The Twin Cities have thus by and large been spared the extremes of racial segregation—and accompanying urban poverty and crime—that characterize so many U.S. cities. Minneapolis–St. Paul, in short, is almost the polar opposite of a society shaped by plantations and slavery. The reader will also have noted that none of the corporations headquartered in the Twin Cities, mentioned earlier, are in big steel or other heavy industry. Many are an outgrowth of agriculture—flour milling, biscuits, frozen vegetables, etc.—while others are in the information technology sector. This is definitely not a Rust Belt city, despite its location in the Midwest. The Minneapolis–St. Paul metropolitan area had the (double) good fortune—in part shaped by geography and by climate—of escaping the negative legacy of both heavy industry and of slavery.

Let us leave Minneapolis–St. Paul, and move to other cities whose recent evolution has been less happy. The problems of many old industrial cities of the Midwest (and the Northeast as well) are not solely due to a history of heavy industry. The legacy of slavery has also left its imprint, whose destructive effects on urban landscapes are still all too visible today. World War I and the decades that followed saw a massive migration of African Americans from the South to the great industrial cities of the North: Philadelphia, Baltimore, Pittsburgh, Cleveland, Detroit, Chicago, Milwaukee, St. Louis, etc. As European migration fell—largely because of more restrictive immigration laws—the descendants of slaves became an important source of labor for the factories of the North. The predictable result was a dramatic shift in the racial makeup of many great American cities. Most of the cities mentioned above—the central municipalities, specifically—today have black mayors. A

less happy result was the creation of racially divided cities, as white populations fled to the suburbs. In many cities, the central business district found
itself, with time, surrounded by inner-city neighborhoods—ghettos (mainly
black)—of extreme poverty, drugs, and hopelessness. Downtown, in some
cases, was all but abandoned, as offices fled elsewhere. Anyone who has visited Detroit will understand what I mean.

The negative consequences of the racial divide permeate many levels of
urban life. The racial divide makes regional collaboration—between the central city and surrounding suburban municipalities—more difficult. To my
knowledge, Minneapolis–St. Paul remains the only American city with anything resembling a metropolitan government. In today's knowledge economy,
where face-to-face contacts are vital, the existence of a well-functioning, safe,
and pleasant central business district is an important asset. This asset has
been squandered in many Rust Belt cities, although some have made Her-
culean efforts since to revitalize their centers.[38] However, turning these cities
into people-friendly, lively, and aesthetically pleasing places is no mean task
in the face of administratively, racially, and fiscally divided metropolitan
areas. This—perhaps more so even than the legacy of heavy industry—constitutes the chief challenge for many old industrial cities of the American
Midwest and Northeast.

Let me return to the South. At about the same time that I was doing
my head office study, I was also working with colleagues at the College of
Urban and Public Affairs at the University of New Orleans, which I visited
on a number of occasions. What struck me in New Orleans was the absence
of large corporate head offices. Indeed, the region had not given rise to any
large nationwide corporations. When I asked my colleagues why, they all fundamentally agreed on the root cause, although sometime stated in different
words. The cause they pointed to was Louisiana's plantation and slave-owning
past. In many ways, the prevailing political and economic ethos of southern Louisiana was more like that of a Caribbean island nation—born out of
slavery—than of North America.[39] The old, mainly French, planter class had
little interest in business and even less, so it would seem, in educating the rest
of the region's unfortunate population. New Orleans was more racially tolerant than the rest of the (Protestant) South—perhaps because of its French
tradition—taking a more relaxed attitude to interracial relations, which was
undoubtedly a factor explaining its cultural vitality, the birthplace of jazz.
That tolerance also reached over into politics; Louisiana acquired an unfortunately justified reputation for corruption, which did nothing to foster good
business relations.

The dominant feature of New Orleans's past, however, was its role as a major center of the plantation economy of the Old South. For a time it was the South's largest city, a focal point for the social elite of the time, together with other slave-trading centers such as Charleston, South Carolina, and Savannah, Georgia. All three cities have a rich architectural heritage that can rival any European city—a reminder of that romanticized past of mint julep and southern belles. But all three have remained economic backwaters, certainly when compared to the economic centers of the New South. It is no coincidence that the South's modern powerhouse, Atlanta, was not a major player in the old plantation economy. Its population—about 10,000 at the time—was barely one-tenth that of New Orleans in the years preceding the Civil War—essentially a frontier town on a railhead. Today, metropolitan Atlanta is more than three times the size of New Orleans,[40] the home of large corporations such as Coca-Cola, CNN, UPS, and Delta Airlines.

The story of the American South does, however, have a (mostly) happy ending. Although states like Louisiana remain poorer than the rest of the nation, regional income disparities have fallen dramatically in the United States. Part of the reason for this positive evolution was the impressive geographic mobility of the American population. It is estimated that some 9 million persons left the Old South between 1910 and 1960, half of whom were African Americans.[41] In the end, many of the descendants of the slaves were able—as we saw—to move to the industrial cities of the North in search of a better life, leaving the plantations (or what was left of them) behind. As we shall see in other chapters, the U.S. is different from most nations—and fortunate in that respect—both in the high degree of cultural integration of its vast territory, facilitating labor mobility, and in the great diversity of geographies that that territory contains.

A first conclusion emerges from this chapter. In order to say anything useful about a place—why it is wealthy or poor, growing or declining—requires at least some knowledge of its past and of the geography of the nation in which it is located. Each story is different. But common threads do run through all stories. We only need to look for them, which provides our point of entry for the next chapter.

Size and Location

The city has always been the centre of civilization. . . . Science, invention, industry, are also urban. They too depend on the division of labor and the wealth which such division makes possible. The larger the city and the more minute the specialization . . . the more easy the production of wealth.

FREDERIC HOWE (1915)

At the most basic level, the wealth-generation potential of a place—compared to others—can be summarized in two rules: 1) location matters; 2) size matters. If a place has both size and a propitious location, its potential will be greater than that of most other places in the nation. If it does not have one it should at least have the other. If a place has neither, the likelihood that it will generate high incomes is reduced, *unless* it has a unique offsetting advantage or is favored by outside events. By the same token, a place's potential for wealth generation can be thwarted, despite size and good location, by negative legacies or unfavorable outside events. Examples of both were presented in the previous chapter.

The Four Golden Rules of Regional Growth

Shorn of all complexity, the geography of wealth can be reduced to what I shall call the Four Golden Rules of Regional Growth. Within nations, where wealth is created and where jobs emerge will in large part depend on four factors: *size, location, cost,* and *unique events*:

Rule 1—Size matters because dynamic industries (the most advanced in each age) are naturally drawn to large cities and places within easy reach. Within nations, rule 1 will produce economic centers—dense multi-city constellations of economic activity. The corollary of *size matters* is that proximity to size—to urban centers—also matters.

Rule 2—Location matters because industries (selling tradable products) are drawn to places best suited for commerce and interaction with markets. Within nations, places located on trade corridors or closest to the nation's major trading partners will be favored.

Rule 3—Costs matter because—failing adequate size or a propitious location—places will grow if they have a clear labor cost advantage or, alternatively, an exceptional resource endowment. However, the latter often precludes the former, as illustrated by the Intrusive Rentier Syndrome.

Rule 4—Exceptions abound because unique events and accidents—history, politics, and technological change—can cause growth (or decline) to occur in places one would not have initially predicted on the basis of the three previous rules.

The purpose of this chapter is to explain the economic foundations of the first three rules. The three are not of equal importance. The choice of *size matters* as the first rule is not accidental. *Size* is at the center in more ways than one. Rules 2 and 3 (location and cost) only make sense if the biggest-sized places—urban centers—already exist. It is in relation to such centers that *location* matters. Being far—peripheral—or close only has meaning with respect to somewhere. In this book, that somewhere is *size*. By the same token, *costs* only have meaning in relation to costs elsewhere. But, in the end, the principal driver is the quest for size—the need to be in or near the biggest places.

The first part of this chapter is thus devoted to the reasons behind rule 1, which I present in the guise of the "seven pillars of agglomeration." The choice of the word *pillar* is not accidental either, for rule 1 is truly the foundation on which much else rests. I follow this with an explanation of how (big) size also produces its opposite number, small size. Smaller cities exist in part because size also implies costs, as we shall see. This chapter is more scholarly than the previous one. I shall be delving into theory, not a subject that lends itself to easy reading, for which I apologize in advance.

The Positive Relationship between Size and Wealth

Let me begin by better defining *size*. I use *size* as shorthand for related concepts such as agglomeration, conurbation, and city-region. Size refers to the economic and demographic weight of a place. Accordingly, the biggest sized places are those with the highest density of economic activity. Size is always relative to other places in the nation. Thus, the biggest sized place in the U.S. is New York. In Iceland, it is Reykjavik, which despite its small size (about one hundred times smaller) occupies a position within its nation similar to that of New York within the U.S. Size is not necessarily limited to cities. The place in question can be a region made up of a dense cobweb of interconnected cities. In the U.S., the Boston–Washington, D.C., corridor is an example; so is the

Randstaad region of the Netherlands, which includes Amsterdam, Rotterdam, and The Hague, forming a dense urban conurbation of cities, the undisputed center of the Dutch economy. Why do such large concentrations of economic activity and people come into being? What is their economic rationale? That is the question I shall attempt to answer in the next few pages.

The recognition that cities facilitate production is by no means new, as the quote, going back almost a century, from Howe attests. An abundant literature has accumulated over the decades attempting to explain why industries are attracted to cities and why *agglomeration* (the term favored by scholars) makes them more productive. The word *agglomeration* has become a catchall for all the attributes that describe a spatial concentration of people and businesses: propinquity, nearness, clustering, density, etc. Economic geographers have coined the term *agglomeration economies* to describe the economic gains—higher output per worker, higher wages, higher profits, higher incomes—that come with the geographic concentration of firms and people.[1]

The reasons why agglomeration raises productivity—and thus incomes— are diverse and not easily amenable to straightforward statistical tests.[2] As a result, much of the literature on the relationship between cities and economic performance remains theoretical or speculative. Yet the positive relationship between cities and higher incomes is indisputable. In all nations for which such data are available, cities, especially larger ones, generate a disproportionate share of wealth; the proportion of national income (or product) cities generate is systematically greater than their population share (table 2.1).[3] Greater New York accounts for some 10 percent of national income but for only 7.5 percent of the American population. Greater Shanghai represents an extreme case with incomes per person some four times above the Chinese average. Urban-rural income differences are generally greater in developing nations, fuelling the rural exodus, a signal that urbanization is still in full swing.[4]

The two cities, Montreal and Manchester, whose income shares are close to (or below) their population shares—a sign of below-average performance for the period studied—are a useful reminder that there are exceptions to even the most solid relationships, which then call for other explanations.[5] Such exceptions notwithstanding, large cities everywhere will, as a rule, generate incomes (or product) greater than their shares of the national population. Why should this be so? Stated differently, why does it make sense for firms to concentrate their operations in cities rather than dispersing them among small villages? Why should they be more productive and profitable in cities, especially big ones?

TABLE 2.1. The Economic Importance of Cities*

Urban area (agglomeration)	Nation	(A) Population Share of national total (%)	(B) GDP or income Share of national total (%)	Ratio B/A
São-Paulo	Brazil	10.5	36.1	3.4
Buenos Aires	Argentina	35.0	53.0	1.51
Lima	Peru	28.1	43.1	1.53
Guayaquil	Ecuador	13.1	30.1	2.30
Mexico	Mexico	14.2	33.6	2.37
All Cities	Mexico	60.1	79.7	1.33
San Salvador	El Salvador	25.8	44.1	1.71
Port au Prince	Haiti	15.1	38.7	2.56
All Cities	Haiti	24.2	57.6	2.38
Casablanca	Morocco	12.1	25.1	2.07
Abidjan	Ivory Coast	18.1	33.1	1.83
Nairobi	Kenya	5.2	20.1	3.87
All Cities	Kenya	11.9	30.3	2.55
Karachi	Pakistan	6.1	16.1	2.64
All Cities	India	19.9	38.9	1.95
Shanghai	China	1.3	5.4	4.20
Beijing	China	1.1	3.1	2.80
Manila	Philippines	12.1	25.1	2.07
Bangkok	Thailand	10.9	37.4	3.43
All Cities	Turkey	47.1	70.1	1.49
Budapest	Hungary	18.0	35.0	1.98
Moscow	Russia	5.8	10.9	1.88
Stockholm	Sweden	20.5	28.5	1.39
London	United Kingdom	12.3	20.0	1.63
Manchester	United Kingdom	4.2	3.9	0.93
Paris	France	18.7	28.3	1.51
New York	United States	7.5	10.1	1.34
Chicago	United States	3.2	3.8	1.17
All Cities (over 100k)	United States	80.0	85.0	1.06
Toronto	Canada	14.2	17.3	1.22
Montreal	Canada	11.4	11.5	1.01

*Results are for years within the range 1985–2005, depending on the source.

The Seven Pillars of Agglomeration

The economic rationale for agglomeration cannot be boiled down to a single factor. I have dubbed them the "seven pillars of agglomeration."

1. SCALE ECONOMIES IN PRODUCTION

Pillar number 1 refers to what economists call economies of scale. Simply put, for many types of goods and services unit production costs will fall as the scale of production increases. This is a basic rule of economics, and applies to any product with fixed costs. Think of a baker. His oven and building are fixed (sunk) costs, which do not change with the number of loaves produced. Flour, yeast, and other ingredients, on the other hand, are variable costs, which do increase with the total number of loaves produced, but whose cost per loaf is probably fairly constant. Because the fixed costs remain precisely that (fixed), the more loaves are baked (up to maximum capacity of his oven), the lower the total cost per loaf since the fixed costs are spread out over an ever larger number of loaves. If the capacity of his oven is superior to that of his competitors, our baker can in principle produce at lower cost and thus

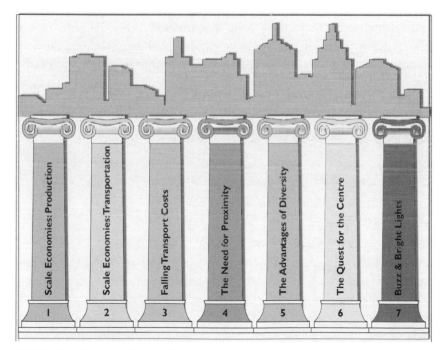

FIGURE 2.1. The seven pillars of agglomeration

capture a greater share of the market. The baker's higher productivity (lower cost per loaf) should also allow him to pay himself and his workers higher wages.

The greater the weight of fixed costs and the greater the impact of scale economies, the greater will be the pull to centralize production in a single location. A more modern example makes this clearer. Economies of scale are obviously important in the production of automobiles. Fixed costs are major: large assembly plants and production equipment that cannot be broken down into smaller pieces. It is apparent to even the non-specialist that producing cars individually in small workshops makes little sense (except perhaps for customized luxury models, which is why they are more expensive to produce). Social scientists have coined the term "Fordist," in honor of Henry Ford, generally thought to be the inventor of the assembly line, to describe methods of mass production based on large plants and standardized output. This is characteristic not only of motor vehicle assembly, but also of industries such as steel, textiles, and (railway) rolling stock, all pivotal sectors in the early days of the Industrial Revolution.

The reality of scale economies inexorably drives firms—notably in manufacturing—to concentrate production in a limited number of locations, thus "creating" cities in the process. Not to do so would be a bad business decision. Little wonder that the largest (in principle, the most efficient) producers end up dominating the market. Scale economies plus the adjacent presence of coal deposit—largely explain the emergence in the nineteenth century of the great industrial cities of the British Midlands, the German Ruhr, and the American Midwest. But the impact of scale does not end here. The natural counterpart of centralized (specialized) production is trade.[6] Large quantities are produced in order be sold to wide markets. But trade requires transport. Transportation and distribution are also subject to scale economies.

2. SCALE ECONOMIES IN TRADE, TRANSPORTATION, AND DISTRIBUTION

The initial economic rationale for cities—well before the Industrial Revolution—was to facilitate trade. Farmers, in order to sell their produce, need a marketplace—a place where sellers and buyers can meet. Here again, size matters. In order for trade to occur in an orderly and efficient manner, distribution and marketing networks and installations need to be maintained, which again involves fixed costs: warehouses and marketplaces (refrigeration, lighting, sanitation, public safety, etc.); transport infrastructures; plus the institutions needed to ensure smoothly functioning markets. A fully stocked warehouse means lower unit costs than one which is half-used. The greater the turnover, the lower the unit costs, something most of us have observed in our daily lives. We know that many items can be purchased more cheaply in large (super) outlets than in small neighborhood stores. This is no less true for cities. Larger cities will, as a rule, provide more efficient distribution and transportation services.

All transport modes (sea, land, and air) are subject to scale economies. A half-empty truck, airplane or ship's hull means that unit transport costs (per ton, say) will be higher. Whether the truck is full or half empty, the driver must be paid, the gas bought, and the truck maintained and paid for. By the same token, no matter how many ships arrive, the docks, cranes, and warehouses must be paid for and maintained. The weight of scale economies in transportation means that all parties gain if goods to be shipped to the same destination are first assembled in a single location before being shipped. By centralizing distribution, shippers can make full use of infrastructures, fill up their vehicles, and ship goods at lower costs.

The effects of scale do not end there. If costs are to be kept competitive, shippers must be able to fill up their vehicle *in both directions*. This inevitably means that the greatest volume of trade will occur between large cities, large ports, railheads, and airports. Those which are centrally located have an added advantage, the subject of pillar 6. This simple truth largely explains the hub and spoke strategy of major airlines today, driven by the need to fill the maximum number of seats. A corollary of the above is that the major transport hubs (air, land, or sea) will offer not only the most cost-effective services, but also the most frequent and diversified services. One is more likely to find a shipping company with regular service to, say, Cape Town in the port of New York than in the port of Charleston, South Carolina.

The upshot of all this is that trade acts as a major force driving the growth of cities. Trade and travel propel the creation of transport hubs, distribution centers, and marketplaces for all manners of exchange. International trade drives the growth of large cities. Returning to the textile mills and steel mills of nineteenth-century Britain—which were not generally located near London—we are now able to better understand why their growth in turn stimulated the growth of London. The rapidly expanding export of British-made goods around the world was founded on efficient transport and distribution networks—but also on a wide array of ancillary services: banking, insurance, advertising, marketing, etc. More exports means more imports, with a parallel growth in distribution, transportation, and ancillary services. It is not entirely by accident that the world's chief financial centers (London, New York, Tokyo, Frankfurt, etc.) have generally arisen around harbors (maritime or fluvial) and transport hubs.

3. FALLING TRANSPORT AND COMMUNICATIONS COSTS

To reap the full benefits of mass production, industries must be able to sell their output to a sufficiently large market. It makes little sense to produce greater quantities if the cost savings—resulting from scale economies—are offset by higher transport costs. All throughout history, transport costs have acted as a powerful barrier to market expansion. Until not so long ago, inter-national—especially transoceanic—trade was a long, costly, and risky affair. I use the term *transport costs* in the broadest sense, including not only mone-tary outlays but also time lost (opportunity costs), plus the effort and frustra-tion that often go with transactions between distant trading partners.[7]

It follows that a fall in transport and transaction costs will stimulate trade and in turn fosters the centralization of production in the lowest-cost loca-tions. This is exactly what has happened in history. As transport and commu-nications costs have fallen, industries have been able to reach ever wider mar-kets, allowing them to realize scale economies. The greater the fall in transport costs and the greater the weight of scale economies, the greater the potential for centralizing production in a limited number of places. Between 1920 and 1990, average unit costs fell by some 75 percent for sea freight, 85 percent for air transport, and over 95 percent for transatlantic telephone calls.[8] Henry Ford could concentrate automobile production in Detroit because innova-tions in transportation, notably paved roads and railways, allowed him to reach the entire U.S. market at a reasonable cost. In the extreme case where scale economies are infinite (unit costs fall continuously as more is produced) and where transport costs are zero, all production would be centralized in a single location, the first (lucky) producer to have arrived at the scene.

Such an extreme case, where all of the world's production is centralized in one location, probably does not exist. However, the film industry comes close. Scale economies are important with large sound studios and often huge budgets. But the crucial element is the very low transport cost of the final product. It costs almost nothing to mail a film clip or DVD and even less if it is done electronically. The centralization of the film industry in Southern California (Hollywood) was only possible because it costs so little to trans-port the final product. The chief barrier to total centralization of the world's filmmaking in Hollywood is culture, language, and differences in tastes. Bol-lywood,[9] the center of India's thriving film industry, continues to flourish because Indian moviegoers want to see Indian actors on the screen, speaking their language, in scenarios that reflect their history, values, and tastes.

That falling communications costs fosters centralization runs counter to much popular perception, especially since the arrival of the Internet. The Internet heralds the death of distance, it is often heard said.[10] Does not modern information technology (IT) free firms from the tyranny of distance, so to speak, from the need to locate in big cities? Witness, for example, the outsourcing of computer programming services to Bangalore (India) and of call centers to smaller-sized cities across North America and elsewhere. To understand what is actually happening, it is useful think of communications or transport costs as if they were tariffs or other barriers to trade. When such barriers fall, say between two nations, competition increases. If one of the two nations is more efficient in the production of good X, it will increase its share of the market, perhaps totally eliminating producers in the other nation. Production of good X is now "centralized" in one nation. The outsourcing of certain services to new places does not mean that distance no longer matters. Rather, it means that the new location can produce the service at lower cost. The fall in communications costs allows production to be increasingly centralized in a new location.

The centralizing impact of IT is consistent with historical experience. The arrivals of the steam engine (railways), of the telegraph and of the telephone, and of the internal combustion engine (automobiles, trucks) have all been accompanied by periods of rapid urban growth. The introduction of the telegraph more than a century ago—as revolutionary then as the Internet today—did not slow down the growth of New York or London. Quite the contrary, it allowed the financial institutions and corporate offices in those cities to expand their reach around the planet. The arrival of radio in the 1920s and the advent of television thirty years later provide vivid examples of the centralizing impact of communications technologies. Before that, much entertainment was produced locally. Almost every town had its own theater. Few remain. Today, for entertainment or news, one turns on the TV, radio, or Internet. For American or British audiences, the person on the other side (actor, singer, newscaster, etc.) will most likely be in New York, Los Angeles, or London.

An obvious implication of the above is that anything that facilitates trade will also foster agglomeration—that is, in places best able to dominate the market. My reference to tariffs and trade barriers was not accidental. World economic integration—globalization—is a powerful force driving agglomeration. Again, going back in history, the rise of London in the nineteenth century as the world's largest city was only possible because it stood at the center

of what was then the largest integrated market—the British Empire—without barriers to trade, the movement of capital, or labor. By the same token,
the rise of New York as London's successor some decades later had its roots in
the expansion (both territorial and otherwise) of the U.S. economy, soon to
become the world's largest wholly integrated market. Large markets produce
large cities, which is why Shanghai is the most likely candidate as the world's
largest city in the year 2050.

In sum, low transport costs and falling barriers to trade allow industries
to centralize operations. But this again raises the question of why they should
want to centralize operations in the first place. We already know part of the
answer: scale economies (pillar 1). However, this is not the whole story. The
majority of city-dwellers do not work in large assembly plants. Much employment is in small and middle-sized firms in almost every imaginable sector
of the economy from legal services to computer software to shirt-making to
financial counseling. Why are such diverse activities drawn to cities?

4. THE NEED FOR PROXIMITY: INDUSTRY CLUSTERS

Pillar 4 refers to the advantages of clustering: the benefits for firms of being
near other firms in the same industry. Economic geographers call such benefits *localization economies*, a sub-class of agglomeration economies. Pillar 4 is
a hybrid, a composite of different elements. Among the myriad advantages of
clustering, I shall focus on four: 1) proximity facilitates business transactions
and the flow of knowledge and information; 2) proximity increases the potential for specialization and facilitates input-outputs relationships; 3) industry
clusters create specialized pools of labor, lowering recruitment and training
costs; and 4) industry clusters lower the unit costs of shared infrastructures.

Observing the concentration of textile mills in the English Midlands in
the late nineteenth century, the British economist, Alfred Marshall, wrote a
paragraph that has been repeatedly quoted since:[11]

> When an industry has chosen a location for itself, it is likely to stay . . . so
> great are the advantages which people following the same skilled trade get
> from near neighborhood to one another. The mysteries of the trade become
> no mysteries; but are as it were in the air. . . . If one man starts a new idea, it
> is taken up by others and combined with suggestions of their own; and thus
> become the source of new ideas.

Marshall's quote, more than a century ago, nicely conveys the often intangible nature of the advances of clustering. Marshall's quote could have been
written today. New York has its garment district, financial district, and Madi-

son Avenue (the advertising "cluster"). Locating near related firms can have definite advantages, not the least of which is being close to where the action is, to where the latest ideas are being hatched and debated.

Economists use the term *externality* or *external economy* to identify this type of advantage. An externality refers to an impact (positive, in this case) whose source lies outside the person or firm profiting from it. A classic example of a positive externality is when Mrs. Jones's neighbors paint their houses, raising the value of all houses in the neighborhood, including Mrs. Jones's house, which was not painted. Mrs. Jones's house is worth more not because she did anything, but because of external factors. Agglomeration economies are a form of externality. In the example illustrated in Marshall's quote, individual firms are more productive and pay higher wages not because of their individual attributes, but because they are located near to each other. The term "cluster," of more recent vintage, conveys the same message.[12]

External economies are notoriously difficult to measure. It is almost impossible to quantify the true impact of being in a place where industry ideas and information float "as it were in the air." The evidence suggests that the benefits of clustering are even greater today than they were a century ago.[13] Why should this be so in the age of the Internet and the cell phone? If information and ideas can be sent over large distances at almost no cost, why is it still so important to be near people? The first part of the answer is simple: advanced economies require more complex information than a century ago. In today's knowledge economy, information, ideas, and know-how have become the primary rare resource. Even firms producing apparently simple products must stay constantly attuned to changing technologies and market conditions.

The second part of the answer is more complex. Not all information can be shared electronically, and most probably never will. Sensitive information continues to require personal face-to-face contact. This is especially so for financial information, a primary reason why banks and brokerage firms are among the most spatially concentrated. Wall Street exists for a reason. Part of the reason lies in the need for trust, and the need to constantly renew trust. A commodity trader, stockbroker, or financial analyst will only share knowledge with a colleague if he or she is convinced that the other will reciprocate. Trust can only be established and renewed through continued personal contact. Body language, facial expressions, eye contact, and tone of voice are all part of the range of signals we use to evaluate another person. We all know and feel that there are some things that simply cannot be explained or said over the telephone. E-mail is even more constraining, for it leaves a data trail.

In cases where creativity, inspiration, and imagination are at play, as is the case of much high-tech manufacturing and modern service industries, personal contact is essential. The ideas exchanged are too unstructured to fit into the constraints of electronic media. Encounters are often informal, even accidental. As anyone who has attended a conference or convention knows, the most useful information and ideas often come out of informal meetings in the hallways, in restaurants, or bars. Think of two scientists sitting together in a local bar scribbling equations on napkins. For firms in rapidly evolving markets, be they in high fashion or computer graphics, the surest way to ensure that their personnel stay on top of the latest ideas, trade gossip, and trends is to be near other similar firms. Technological breakthroughs are more probable if engineers are near other engineers working on related problems. For products that have a physical component, be it a blueprint, a computer animation, or simply a piece of equipment, a common physical presence is required if discussions are to be useful.

Some have gone even further, arguing that IT actually *increases* the demand for face-to-face contacts.[14] Electronic and face-to-face communications are most often complements and not substitutes. Communicating by e-mail or cell phone will often produce a complementary need for meetings. The evidence is persuasive. Business travel, especially air travel, has accelerated since the advent of the Internet and continues to grow. Presumably, all these businesspeople travel because they need to meet. The possibility of communicating by e-mail has not, apparently, reduced the need for trips. For those readers who use e-mail or cell phones, think of your own work experience. How many people do you correspond with or speak to on a regular basis whom you do not also meet from time to time? Probably not many. How many people do you communicate with regularly whom you have never met? Probably even fewer. In most cases, electronic communication is a prelude or a follow-up to face-to-face encounters. The more people communicate, the more they want to meet. Future innovations in IT will most probably further accelerate the demand for face-to-face contact.

The nature of business transactions also pushes firms to locate in close proximity to one another. Proximity is vital where production runs are short, where suppliers and customers are constantly changing, where contracts are transacted on short notice, and where reliability (of delivery) is of the essence. The apparel industry provides a good historical example. In the early 1950s, close to 90 percent of all U.S. employment in cloth-cutting, knitwear, and scarf and hat making was concentrated in New York, much of it in Midtown Manhattan.[15] Rapid changes in fashion, added to the demand for customized items, mean that firms are constantly shifting suppliers (different cloth, buttons, dyes, synthetics, etc.). Transactions will often be concluded with the shake of a hand, with deliveries sometimes expected within the day. This, again, implies a high level of trust and also that suppliers be located nearby. If, say, a customized zipper is needed the same day for an order to be filled tomorrow, then the transaction becomes impossible if no reliable supplier is available at close hand.

Rapid shifts between suppliers and buyers also mean that industry clusters will include a large number of small specialized firms. No one firm will, for example, find it profitable to produce every possible type of zipper and button if this means continually refurbishing machines and constantly hiring and laying off personnel. The clustering of small firms allows each firm to specialize in certain items, yet with the assurance that the cluster contains a sufficient number of (ever-changing) customers to make specialization profitable. The greater the size of the cluster, the greater the potential for special ization. A single producer can focus on making, say, the best no-stick plastic zipper, which he or she can profitably produce in short runs to meet customized requests. The small size of the firms making up the cluster also maximizes flexibility, allowing for constantly changing combinations of suppliers to produce constantly changing collections of clothing products.

The continual negotiation of contracts to buy and sell, sometimes many hundreds a day, is another factor driving the concentration of financial intermediaries, especially if the risks and amounts involved are major. Here, yet again, the need for trust among actors is a major force pulling them together. Decisions to sell or buy (commodities, stocks, etc.) are often made in a split second. Thousands, millions of dollars are committed on the basis of a telephone call, a brief encounter, a handshake. The greater the risks and the amounts involved, the greater the need for relationships that are built on more than e-mail. Investment banking, as one can imagine, is particularly dependant on closely held relationships. No banker worth his salt will invest millions without having met at least once with the principal protagonists. By the same token, no merchant banker will approve a loan worth millions without meeting his potential client.[16] The more customized the good (or service), the more volatile the market, and the higher the stakes, the greater is the need for personal relationships and thus for proximity.

A parallel force driving firms to locate together is the desire to minimize recruitment and training costs. The more knowledge-intensive the industry is, the greater will be the pull of locations where industry-specific labor is most plentiful. Recruitment and training costs are by no means inconsequential. The best proof of their importance is the rapid expansion in recent years of executive-search and other head-hunter services. The chances of finding a knowledgeable, well-connected financial analyst are certainly greater in New

York than in Butte, Montana. By the same token, the chances of finding experienced aerospace engineers or designers are greater in Seattle than in Phoenix. Here we have a true externality. If firm X is able to hire workers with training and workplace experience acquired in neighboring firms, then firm X is profiting from a true positive externality, that is, if the remuneration of the new employee does not totally capture the full value of his past experience and training.[17] The most powerful incentive to cluster for knowledge-intensive industries is, arguably, access to labor. For many firms, the principal constraint to further expansion is the availability of qualified workers.

For other industries, the drive to cluster will be founded on the potential for spreading fixed costs over several firms for infrastructures that cannot easily be divided up: quays, cranes, pipelines, railheads, etc. The petrochemical industry is a prime example. In almost all cities, petrol refineries and related firms will be located together, sharing the same installations. Why, if it has the choice, would a petrol refinery choose to locate alone, thus having to assume the full cost of all installations? By the same token, infrastructures will not be worth installing or maintaining if the number of users is insufficient. Rail lines will be abandoned if volume is not sufficient, a not uncommon occurrence in North America. Once the infrastructure is gone, the area (obviously not a big city), becomes even less attractive for industry, yet another example of how scale economies (in this case, for infrastructures) drive centralization, not only of the infrastructures themselves, but also through their impact on users.

Similar reasoning can be applied to knowledge infrastructures: training facilities, technical colleges, laboratories, etc. Specialized courses in aerospace engineering or design will be easier to run in places where the aerospace industry is present. One expects to find good technical schools in aerospace in Seattle, Wichita, and Montreal. The larger the labor pool (in the industry), the greater the likelihood that specialized learning and training facilities can be maintained, in turn bolstering the area's advantage over others. Specific industry clusters need not necessarily be located in the biggest cities. Examples of industry clusters in mid-sized cities abound: insurance in Hartford (Connecticut) and pharmaceuticals in Lyon (France). Finally, the diverse forces fuelling clustering often reinforce each other. The bigger the cluster of firms and workers in a particular industry, the greater the probability of specialized institutions (laboratories, schools, transport services, etc.) and also the greater the potential for industry transactions, knowledge-sharing, and information exchange. Marshall's statement that know-how is "as it were in the air" remains an apt metaphor for the myriad forces driving industries to cluster.

5. THE ADVANTAGES OF DIVERSITY

The fifth pillar refers to the benefits of locating in cities as such, notably in big cities, called *urbanization economies* by economic geographers. Pillar 4 focused on the advantages of clustering. For many industries, the *size* of the city is crucial. Some will be inexorably drawn to larger cities. Why should this be so?

For the first part of the answer, I return again to scale economies. Not only do scale economies cause firms to concentrate operations in one plant or office, but locating in a big city increases their chances of attaining the desired level of production more rapidly. If a firm's optimal market size is 3 million, then there is a definite advantage to locating in a city of at least 3 million potential customers, where it can reach them all without incurring additional transportation costs. Were the firm to locate in a smaller city (say, of 1 million) then servicing the extra 2 million customers, living beyond the city, would entail additional transport costs. These can be avoided by locating in the larger city.

The combined impact of scale economies and market size is greatest where the crucial consideration is the cost of getting the final product to the customer. If a sufficient number of customers are not present close-by, it will not be profitable to produce the good or service. This is most evident in cases where the "transport costs," so to speak, are borne by the customer. This is typical of services where the customer must personally travel to the location where the service is produced in order to consume it. An example is professional opera. Opera productions are exceedingly expensive to produce, requiring large stage sets, first-class acoustics, a quality symphony orchestra, not to mention the costs of the performers and myriad technicians. Going to the opera is a luxury expenditure and not necessarily everyone's cup of tea. Only a small fraction of the total population can afford or will have the desire to go to the opera. Thus, professional opera houses will normally spring up (and survive) only in the largest cities. Only in the largest cities do they stand a chance of finding a sufficient number of opera buffs willing to regularly buy tickets for a night at the opera.

The opera example illustrates an important point: certain services and products will *only* be available in the largest cities. Typical examples are made-to-measure fashion, specialty caterers, and plastic surgeons. The list is constantly evolving as tastes and technology change. Where this matters most in modern economies is in professional, technical, and artistic services, services purchased primarily by firms rather than individual consumers.[18] Imagine, for example, a firm that needs a Hindi-Japanese-English translator, an expert evaluator of downtown real-estate, a lawyer versed in international trade dispute mediation, or a market analyst specializing in pharmaceuticals. Clearly, the likelihood of finding such persons is much greater in a large city. The more esoteric and the more specialized the service required, the greater the likelihood that it will be available in only the very largest cities. It is this diversity that pulls many industries to large cities.

The benefits of clustering (pillar 4) were in large part founded on the need for ongoing flexible relationships with customers, suppliers, consultants, and others in the *same* industry. The same reasoning can now be applied to firms that need access to a *diverse* labor pool and array of services. This is typical of industries whose products are unstandardized and constantly changing; no two products (contracts) are exactly the same. Advertising agencies and management and accounting consultancies are prime examples. Of the world's top ten advertising firms by income earned, three were located in New York, three in Tokyo, and two each in London and Paris.[19] The world's largest management consultancy, McKinsey & Company, is headquartered in New York. A major reason for this concentration is the need to rapidly assemble varying combinations of expertise and talent. Each advertising campaign (each contract) is unique, requiring a unique mix of abilities and skills. One contract may call for animated cartoons, another for a symphony orchestra and jazz singer, while yet another may require trained chimpanzees. All need to be available on short notice. No management consulting contract is exactly like another. One may call for know-how in copper smelting, another for skills in management-labor relations, while yet another may require a knowledge of the intricacies of glass-blowing.

Major management consultancies and ad agencies are attracted to large cities because that is where the most varied talents are found, but also because that is where human resources from elsewhere can be assembled most rapidly. (Remember pillar 2: scale economies in transportation, especially air travel). Large consultancies and partnerships have associates around the world. It is in cities like London, New York, or Chicago that they can most efficiently bring the needed talents together to work on a particular contract. The need for rapid access to a variety of know-how and talents applies not only to management consultancies and advertising, but to a broad range of professional services: legal advice, accounting, technology consultants, engineering, etc. The same is true of many financial services. Analysts, portfolio managers, and investment bankers often need to draw on a vast (and changing) array of expertise, depending on the nature of the investment or stock under consideration. The knowledge needed to evaluate a possible investment in a copper mine in Zambia is not the same as that needed to evaluate the worth of an IT start-up in San Diego.

The need to constantly bring people back and forth from around the world is also a major factor driving multinational head offices to locate in big cities. Corporate head offices are major consumers of professional, financial, creative, and technological services. Here again, personal contact is essential. For critical decisions concerning a company's image or future, company directors and executives will want not only to be directly involved, but also to personally handle the relationships with outside professionals. The CEO will often wish to directly oversee a major adverting campaign to launch a new product. Before the ad campaign is finalized to the CEO's liking, many meetings will have taken place, viewing and reviewing alternative proposals. For a company planning to launch a major stock offering, the CEO and other executives will first need to spend many hours with potential underwriters and institutional investors to convince them of the company's worth. Other examples are easy to imagine. In short, executives and managers of large corporations spend much of their time in meetings and business lunches. The need for personal relationships explains why at the center of every major metropolis one finds what urban planners call a central business district (CBD) with its office towers and bustling midday crowds. Face-to-face contacts are the glue that holds the CBD together.

CBDs are the heart of the big city. This is where the potential for interaction with others is the greatest, where the advantages of diversity and size come together. The core CBD is, so to speak, the top cluster surrounded by smaller (specialized) clusters, a cluster entirely founded on the need for personal relationships, private meetings, and contacts covering a wide range of subjects. The British weekly, the *Economist*, in a survey of New York,[20] recently wrote, "[T]he jobs which thrive here are those that require or exploit the interaction of people jammed together. . . . Discourse and intercourse— in the broad sense of the word—are the essence and the comparative advantage of New York." I could not have put it better. In other cities, notably in the U.S., alternative CBDs—sometimes called *office parks*—have sprung up in suburban locations, often in reaction to deteriorating social conditions in central neighborhoods.[21] The underlying principle, however, remains the same: offices and office workers cluster in crowded business districts in order to facilitate face-to-face contacts.

The need for a broad range of talents, available at short notice, is also a key characteristic of the entertainment and information industries. It is not difficult to conjure up the diversity of talents and skills needed to keep a daily (or weekly) news or variety program on the air. The film industry relies on a vast array of skills that runs the whole gamut: script writers, composers, actors, sound technicians, musicians, fashion designers, computer programmers, bankers, animal trainers, and so on. The film industry tends not only to cluster (all the major U.S. studios are located in or around the Hollywood area of Los Angeles), but to cluster in what is the second largest U.S. metropolitan area.[22] The need to cluster near other film studios overlaps in this case with the search for diversity. This is true of many modern industries that seek to be close both to similar industries (pillar 4) *and* to a large variety of industries (pillar 5). Large cities can house many different clusters, which, in turn, contribute to their diversity.

6. THE QUEST FOR THE CENTER

It should by now be evident that the various forces driving industries towards cities often work in tandem. As in any edifice, each pillar helps to support others. We know (pillar 5) that firms for which customer access is crucial will seek out cities whose size corresponds to their optimal market range. Industries needing larger markets will be drawn to larger cities. The story does not end there. Not only does size matter, but also location, which brings us to pillar 6.

Firms naturally seek to locate in the geographic center of the markets, notably those for which access to customers is a primary criterion for success, most often service industries. In such cases, the most strategic location for a firm is one that minimizes travel costs for (or to) the maximum number of customers. Economic geographers use the term *centrality*, an attribute of place, to characterize locations in terms of their market potential.[23] Some places are more central than others. The meaning of *central* will be different for different industries, depending on market size. At the lowest level, where scale economies are minimal, say a gas station, a central location will mean a crossroads or a particularly busy street or highway, where the potential number of cars driving by is maximized. This is a basic rule of retailing: locate where the density of potential customers is the highest.

The centrality principle also holds at the national and international level. Consider the airline industry and the performing arts. Broadway, the largest concentration of theaters in America, is located in New York not only because of its population size, but also because of the market potential of theater-goers from outside the city. This market potential is higher in New York for two reasons. First, New York is located in the heart of the most densely populated area of the United States. Greater Philadelphia, with over 5 million people, is a mere ninety minutes' drive away. Second, because of scale economies in transportation, New York is among the best connected cities in the nation, with frequent rail, air, and bus links to other cities. No other city—with perhaps the exception of Chicago—has as many airline connections to other cities. Broadway is Broadway, in sum, because of New York's size, access, and connectivity within the U.S. and the world. Similar reasoning applies to London's West End (the heart of England's theater life) within the United Kingdom.

The search for the center is also a powerful force driving the location of air transport; but in this case geographic centrality matters as much as local market potential. Airlines need to fill up their airplanes if their operations are to be profitable. Each airline seeks to attract the greatest number of paying passengers. This can be done in two ways. The most obvious is by locating in an airport where local market potential is high, necessarily a big city. But an airline can add customers if passengers coming in from other locations choose this airport and airline to make connections to other destinations. The chances of attracting transfer passengers are greater where connections to other destinations are frequent. This again favors the largest cities. However, big cities that are centrally located to service vast market areas hold a particular advantage. The result is a hub and spoke network where a central airport acts as the focal point for feeder lines to other smaller airports. A resident of Indianapolis, wishing to fly to London, will undoubtedly fly via Chicago, just as a resident of Liverpool, wishing to fly to Tokyo, will first fly to London.

Chicago's central location within the United States is one of the sources of its growth. In the second half of the nineteenth century, the transport mode of choice was railways, not airlines. The density of rail connections largely determined a city's centrality. The hub and spoke analogy also applies to rail services. The competition among cities to become the central hub for the American interior was fierce during the nineteenth century, while settlement was still in progress. Chicago eventually won out over Cincinnati and then St. Louis. Today, the Midwest's transport networks are in large part centered on Chicago, the culmination of two centuries of investments in rail lines, roads, and canals. "Centrality" is largely man-made. In Europe and other older, settled regions, transport networks go back further in time. Europe is criss-crossed by canals. The impact over time of such investments is cumulative. Paris is the unchallenged hub of the French transportation network, shaped over many centuries. This cannot be undone. Firms, especially in the service sector, whose market is all of France, will continue to locate in or near Paris, just as firms wishing to serve the entire British market will continue to locate in or near Greater London.

7. BUZZ AND BRIGHT LIGHTS

Recalling the quote by Robert E. Lucas, cited at the outset of chapter 1, what indeed can people be paying Manhattan or central London rents for, if not for being near other people? More succinctly, a participant at a seminar in Toronto on the economy of modern cities summed it up as follows: "It's all about buzz."

Pillar 7 is different from previous pillars. Unlike the others, pillar 7 deals with the motivations and behavior of individuals, rather than businesses. It may well be that people—at least some—also value agglomeration. Not only firms, but also individuals can draw both psychological and material benefits from being in a big city. As with agglomeration economies for firms, such benefits for individuals or families are difficult to measure directly. However, the evidence suggests that such benefits do indeed exist.[24]

With pillar 7, we arrive at arguably the most elusive factor of what makes cities magnets, driving individuals throughout the ages to move to the great cities of their epoch. Why are big cities so appealing, at least to some? The answer is not only a matter of economics. Economics can, we have seen, help to explain why many activities are more profitably pursued in cites. But, manifestly, some people move to cities not simply because they *need* to—to make a living—but also because they *want* to "be near other people," to be in the middle of the buzz. We have swung full circle back to Alfred Marshall's 1890 observation of secrets floating "as it were in the air." However, the buzz in the air affects not only the behavior of firms, but also of individuals. Ultimately, it is the behavior of individuals that drives economies; individuals found firms, invent, invest, innovate, and create.

Ambition, dreams, and the need for recognition are powerful forces driving human behavior. Most of us know instinctively that success depends in no small part in being at the right place at the right time. Many a young man or woman at the start of his or her career will naturally ask: *where* are my chances best of being discovered and of meeting the right people? *Where* in the nation is the potential for career advancement and doing exciting things the greatest? He or she will naturally be drawn to places with the highest concentration of the "right" people, where the lights are brightest and the buzz is loudest. Which is why an aspiring young computer programmer in the Indian countryside will most probably throw his belongings on a train and travel to Bangalore or Mumbai, and why a no-less-ambitious young programmer in rural America will pack his belongings into the back of his second-hand jalopy and drive to Boston or the San Francisco Bay area.

The main impetus behind agglomeration undoubtedly remains economic, but agglomeration also fulfills a social need. Human beings are nothing if not social animals. The life of a hermit may appeal to some, but the vast majority of humanity seeks company. We seek the approval of others, to see others and to be seen. Why indeed are some individuals (at least, those who can afford it) willing to spend a small fortune for an apartment on Fifth Avenue, if it is not to be near the right people, to be seen, to be recognized, and to feel that one is truly at the center of things?[25]

There are also obvious utilitarian reasons why some individuals will be drawn to big cities. The diversity of large cities can, we have seen, constitute an advantage for firms, but this also holds for individuals and families. The chances of finding a job are greater in a diverse labor market and the risks of being unemployed correspondingly less. For a married couple, where each partner has a separate career, the chances of both finding employment is greater in a diverse labor market. And, as we have seen, certain services will only be available in the largest cities. This applies not only to specialty shops, but also to educational and health services. The availability of quality postgraduate teaching institutions is often an important magnet for upwardly mobile couples and youths. Indeed, the value some individuals and couples place on buzz and diversity may mean that they are willing to pay a premium for the privilege of living in a big city. Houses and apartments are more expensive in New York, London, and Paris because some people are willing to pay the price. They obviously feel it's worth it, or there would be no buyers.

Why Smaller Cities Exist

The preceding section was purposely biased towards big cities. The pull of big cities is undeniable, but not everyone lives or wants to live in big cities. Over 85 percent of the American population lives outside metropolitan New York, Los Angeles, and Chicago. Over 80 percent of the British population lives outside metropolitan London. All nations are a patchwork of cities, towns, and villages of varying sizes. To understand how more complex systems of cities and towns come about, we need to identify the countervailing forces that push, so to speak, firms and people out of big cities and into smaller ones.

THE COSTS OF URBAN CONCENTRATION

The impulse to be in the center of things remains the dominant driving force. But concentration also entails costs, called *congestion costs* by economic geographers. These costs essentially affect objects that are geographically immobile, tied to place. Land is a prime example. Land cannot be moved, replaced, or augmented with a piece of land elsewhere. Each piece of land is unique. If a firm wishes to locate in central London, it does the firm little good to know that land costs per square meter are lower in central Leeds. It cannot substitute one for the other. Since the supply of land in central London is essentially fixed,[26] the price of land will necessarily rise as more and more firms and people seek to locate there. In Manhattan and places like Hong Kong, where land supply is constrained by geography (both are islands), the pressure on prices will be even greater.[27] It's a simple matter of fixed supply and rising demand. Rising land prices in central locations are the inevitable result of the growing demand for those locations.

In chapter 1 we saw that urban size and real estate values go hand in hand. Prices are higher because the potential for generating income (per square meter) is greater. How many times have I heard small town mayors say: "One of the great advantages of our community is the low cost of land." I was always tempted to answer (but never did): "Your honor, why do you think your land prices are so low?" The price of land is a signal the market sends out, informing us how the economy values a particular location.[28]

The high price of land in big cities has various repercussions, the most visible of which is the construction of high-rise buildings (office and apartment towers). The higher the cost of land, the greater the incentive to build upwards,[29] to which the skylines of New York and Hong Kong again bear witness. This, again, is a matter of simple economics. The more tenants can be piled into a square kilometer of land, the greater the income generated, justifying the high price of land. High-rise towers have the double effect of both increasing available floor space in central locations and increasing their potential value. That such vertical increases in supply coincide with higher real estate values and higher rents—think again of Manhattan—is yet another manifestation of the economic value of agglomeration. The more users can be jammed into a square kilometer, the greater the potential for buzz and interaction with others.

A second repercussion of high land prices is their impact on local wages. To attract workers of equivalent quality, employers in New York need to pay higher wages than elsewhere. Urban size, we saw, is a good predictor both of wages and land prices. The relationship between housing (and land) prices and the wealth-generation potential of places is in part circular. Wages, and thus also incomes, are higher in big cities, not only because labor is more productive in big cities, but also because higher housing costs push wages up. Disentangling the impacts on wages of higher productivity and of higher housing costs is not simple.[30] The essential point is that both wage and land costs will be higher in big cities, with consequences for the location of industries, as we shall see shortly.

A third cost associated with urban agglomeration is local transport. As with land, substitution is impossible. One has no choice but to use locally available transport infrastructures (shirts can be imported from China, but not roads). Traffic congestion is today the almost inevitable lot of large cities. Besides the general inconvenience, traffic congestion means time lost and higher costs for firms (for fuel, drivers, and equipment). Congestion is not solely due to urban agglomeration. Poor urban management, urban sprawl, and deficient public transit systems also contribute to congestion. Free access to roads also contributes to traffic congestion. Again, this is a matter of elementary economics. If a good is free, it will be consumed freely. This is no less true for roads.[31] In London, the introduction of a road fee for entry into the central part of the city has considerably reduced traffic congestion. By contrast, the aptly named freeways of Greater Los Angeles continue to be plagued by gridlock.

DIFFERENT-SIZED PLACES IN GROWING
NATIONAL ECONOMIES

One reason that different-sized cities exist is that some industries are more sensitive than others to the costs associated with size. The mix of industries that make up an economy changes over time. Imagine a nation at the outset of the Industrial Revolution. The nation is still overwhelmingly rural with the vast majority of its labor force in agriculture. Numerous small towns exist, dispersed throughout the countryside, chiefly market centers for surrounding rural populations. Since transportation is costly and slow, few goods are widely traded. Some larger towns exist, often located on waterways, the least costly means of transport, acting as market centers for the rare goods that can be profitably traded over greater distances. These mid-sized towns are also home to craftsmen producing goods for local consumption. Finally, there is the capital city, the nation's port of entry. Here is where goods arrive from around the world, are processed, and distributed to the rest of the nation. The largest trading houses and financial institutions are located there, as well as an embryonic manufacturing sector.

Let me now push the fast forward button, jumping ahead two centuries to the current era. The population has grown fourfold.[32] The nation is now fully urbanized and industrialized. Agriculture accounts for a mere 3 percent of the labor force (see table 5.1, chapter 5). The urban population has multiplied thirty-six-fold,[33] spread out among the nation's towns and cities, large and small. Why have not all the urban dwellers piled up in the capital? After all, thanks to modern technology and scale economies, most goods can now be efficiently produced in a single large plant; and thanks to modern means of transportation and communication, the whole nation can be easily served from a single central location. In short, the seven pillars of agglomeration should, one would think, be driving most economic activity into the capital.

All economic activity will not end up in one mammoth city because the *relative* weights of the costs and the benefits of locating in a big city are not the same for all firms. All may *wish* to locate in the capital. But this will not be the most profitable choice for all. For some, the higher land and labor costs in the capital will outweigh the potential benefits of size. A firm requiring a great deal of space—an automobile assembly plant, for example—will give *relatively* more weight to land prices than a consultancy, which requires less floor space. The consultancy, in turn, will put a greater weight on face-to-face contacts with clients than would the auto plant. The auto plant would, on the other hand, put a higher *relative* value on the accessibility of road and rail infrastructures and the availability (and cost) of skilled blue-collar workers.

This, however, does not tell us what is continually driving up prices in big cities. Why all the office buildings? The answer lies in the evolution of the employment structure of modern economies (figure 2.2).[34] Manufacturing—as a share of total employment—rises during the early stages of economic growth and then declines. Manufacturing now accounts for about 16 percent of the total workforce in the U.S. and Canada. Why this decline in manufacturing? Essentially, increased labor productivity in manufacturing pushes workers into other activities where it is more difficult to replace human beings with machines, the case for much of the service industry.

I have divided the service sector into two classes: traditional *non-tradable* services and modern *tradable* services. The first group includes services such as retailing (clothing stores, pharmacies, etc.), personal and leisure services (dry cleaners, restaurants, etc.) as well as public and allied services (education, health, etc.). What all these services have in common is that the consumer must physically go to the place where the service is provided in order to consume it. E-commerce, e-learning, e-banking, and analogous innovations have lessened the need for physical presence in some cases. However, the need for some level of physical, tactile contact remains dominant in most cases. The adventure of comparing, touching, and feeling merchandise is one of the pleasures of shopping. And, no matter how sophisticated electronic communication becomes, personal contact at some point between teacher and student and doctor and patient will remain necessary in education and health services.

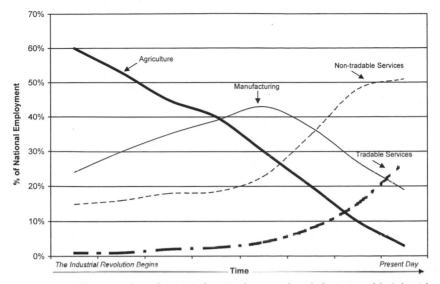

FIGURE 2.2. The structural transformation of a national economy from the beginnings of the Industrial Revolution to the present day

The second, more modern, group is made up of services where all or a major part of the service provided can "travel," either electronically or by the provider going to the customer. Typical examples are consultancies in management, engineering, and computer systems. Part of the service may be sent by e-mail. Other components of the service—advice given, for example—may be transmitted over the telephone. Others, again, dependant on face-to-face meetings, will be delivered by the consultant traveling to the client. Additional examples are broadcasting, advertising, finance, much of the entertainment industry, and functions related to corporate management (head offices), research, and design. Reports, images, sound, and blueprints now travel via the Internet. The essential distinction is between services that can be traded over large distances and those that cannot.

In industrialized economies, tradable services are in the process of replacing manufacturing as the chief source of "productive" employment. Thanks to modern technology, more and more services can be traded, providing an economic base and source of wealth for a growing number of places. Modern services are also increasingly inputs into production, which is why they are sometimes referred to as *producer services*. The decline of manufacturing and the rise of tradable services are not unrelated. Think of a USB device containing hundreds of songs. The service content is greater than the manufacturing content, yet the USB device is nonetheless a manufactured good. The production of many goods is dependent on a wide array of design, research, and marketing occupations, which can take place in or outside the plant. An engineer working in a plant is counted as a manufacturing job. But the same engineer, working as a consultant subcontracted by the firm, will be counted as being in the service sector. The decline of manufacturing is in part deceptive. Tasks that, in the past, were physically part of the production process are now distinct tasks, provided by separate firms. Many producer service occupations did not even exist a few decades ago.

This broad structural change, part of the shift to the knowledge economy, might well be called the industrialization of the service sector. The close link between manufacturing and producer services will shortly help us to explain why much modern manufacturing locates in some small and medium-sized cities and not in others. But I am jumping ahead of myself. We need first to see how the demand for services has historically given rise to networks of different-sized cities. For this, I shall return to an earlier era when tradable services were still the exception.

SMALL AND MID-SIZED CITIES AS SERVICE CENTERS

The primary economic raison-d'être of most towns and cities before the Industrial Revolution was to act as service and market centers—central places—for the surrounding countryside and for smaller settlements. In pre-industrial, rural societies, soil fertility, rainfall, climate, and waterways largely shaped the distribution of service centers. In most nations, the initial pattern of towns and cities, established many centuries ago (more recently in New World nations), has remained largely unchanged. A striking feature of the economic geography of nations is the remarkable stability of urban hierarchies over time.[35] Urban hierarchies, once they have emerged, will only change slowly. A reason for the stability is precisely that most settlements were originally founded on natural attributes that do not change.[36] The construction over time of roads, canals, and other infrastructures consolidates the initial pattern of towns and cities.

For non-tradable services, the crucial variables are local market size and the willingness of consumers to travel. The less distance the consumer is willing to travel, the closer the service provider will need to be to customers. Services for which proximity is vital—food stores, pharmacies, tailors, eating and drinking places, primary education, basic health care, etc.—will give rise to numerous small centers. Services that require larger markets and for which consumers are inclined to travel greater distances will only be found in larger service centers. These are normally services that are less frequently consumed or entail large household expenditures—fashion clothing, book-stores, specialized medical care, postsecondary education, etc. Each service provider will seek out the center of its market, recalling agglomeration pillar 6. A grocery store that needs only a small local market to be profitable, say, one thousand potential customers, will seek out a central location that allows it to capture such a market, which might be a small town or a neighborhood shopping street. Economic geographers use the terms *low order* and *high order* services to distinguish between those that are more geographically dispersed and those that are more concentrated.[37] The result is a hierarchy of services and of service centers—towns and cities—of different sizes, called *central places* by economic geographers.[38]

Small and middle-sized towns and cities will exist as long as the consumption of services requires a physical presence. Travel takes time and money, especially time. Indeed, it can be argued that the true cost of travel has increased, since people place a higher value on time in richer societies.[39] Non-tradable services have continued to grow in modern societies. This is not the result of an explosion of jobs in retailing or barber shops. The principal factor is the growth of the welfare state since World War II, with a corresponding growth of employment in education, health, and public admin istration. More recently, the growth of leisure-related employment—notably in eating places, bars, and amusement facilities—has fueled further increases. People will continue to demand education and, increasingly, health services and continue to need plumbers, electricians, and other professionals to fix and service the latest gadgets, not forgetting the eternal joys of shopping and going out to the occasional movie, restaurant, or football game.

Competition between service centers is much greater today than in the past. Travel is much easier today than in the past. The age of the automobile and paved roadways cannot be compared with the age of dirt roads and the horse and buggy. The main victims of improvements in local travel have been the smallest service centers at the bottom of the urban hierarchy (recall agglomeration pillar 3). People are able to travel greater distances today to shop, see a doctor, or just go out. As road conditions improve and as automobile ownership spreads, small town retailers lose customers to larger nearby towns. The small town general store has all but disappeared in the American Plains and the Canadian Prairies. Yet—improvements on travel notwithstanding—the geographic concentration of many service industries remains severely constrained by the need for the consumer to be physically present at the place of consumption. As long as this remains true, small and mid-sized towns will not disappear.

The preceding paragraphs call for a caveat. Non-tradable services rarely provide an economic base for a community and, as such, are rarely a true source of wealth, precisely because they are not tradable. In the past, when the majority of the population worked on the land, surrounding rural populations provided a guaranteed market for local service centers. Before the Industrial Revolution, few products were traded over large distances.[40] Most communities were largely self-contained. This is no longer the case. Today, employment in non-tradable services depends ultimately on employment in other sectors of the local economy, which *can* be traded and bring money into the community.

SMALL AND MID-SIZED CITIES AS MANUFACTURING CENTERS

Small and mid-sized towns did not disappear with the decline of agriculture and surrounding rural populations. Other activities found it profitable to locate there, most notably in manufacturing and related industries. Modern manufacturing arrived on top, so to speak, of the preexisting hierarchy of cities and towns.

We may again ask, for manufacturing this time, why all activity did not concentrate in the capital. The first answer is the same as for consumer services: transport costs. The transport of goods is not free, and never will be, despite remarkable improvements in transport technologies. The bulkier, the heavier, the more perishable or fragile a product is, the greater will be the countervailing force of transport costs. Firms producing perishable goods— or other goods that need to be gotten to the customer fast—will behave like non-tradable services, locating close to customers. For example, industrial bakeries will be found in the capital city, but also in mid-sized cities to supply regional markets. In this case, the potential advantages of greater scale and agglomeration are outweighed by the need to rapidly deliver the product to consumers.

The trade-off between transport costs and the benefits of agglomeration will not be the same for all manufacturing firms. Those for which agglomeration economies are high and transport costs low will concentrate their production in the capital. The fashion industry and pharmaceuticals are typical examples. For both, the cost of transporting the final product—compared to its value—is low and both are highly responsive to the advantages of clustering. On the hand, firms that require large plants with a lot of floor space will find it more profitable to locate in smaller cities with lower land prices. The production of machinery and other heavy equipment are typical examples.

Not all industries need highly skilled, highly paid labor and will thus find it more profitable to locate in cities where wages are lower.

What I have described here is what economic geographers call crowding out, the process whereby high land, labor, and congestion costs drive manufacturing firms out of larger cities towards smaller ones.[41] In more technical terms, I am again referring to a trade-off between benefits and costs; in this case, between the benefits of agglomeration on the one hand and land, labor, and congestion costs on the other. For firms that are crowded out, the latter outweighs the former. Crowding out, it is important to note, does not run counter to the basic principles of agglomeration. Industries are still agglomerating, only not automatically in the largest cities. They are clustering in particular cities, which need not be the largest ones.

Another reason why some plants will choose to locate outside the largest cities is the high cost of transporting inputs. We are again talking about a trade-off: between the cost of transporting outputs and inputs in this case. If the latter outweigh the former, then the firm will be naturally drawn to locations where the inputs are available, which need not be large cities.[42] Economic geographers refer to such cases as resource-oriented or weight-losing industries in cases where the input is a primary product—of the land or the sea [43] As the term suggests, these are typically industries tied to natural resources, generally in the first processing stages. Their essential attribute is that the final product weighs less, and thus costs less to transport, than the inputs needed to make it. Paper mills are a prime example. The primary input for making paper is timber. Raw logs are more cumbersome and costly to transport than finished rolls of paper, which use only a part of the logs.[44] Thus paper mills will generally locate close to sawmills in areas where timber is plentiful. This allows paper mills to save on the cost of transporting timber, the most costly to transport.

The paper mill example can be restated as a general rule: firms will attempt to avoid or minimize transporting the good, input *or* output, which is the most costly to transport. If it is the output, the firm will seek to locate near its customers. If it is an input, it will locate close to its suppliers. The notion of transport costs can also be applied to other inputs, such as power. Electricity is costly to transport. Transmission lines and power grids are costly to build and maintain. As noted in chapter 1, electricity is a major input into the production of aluminum. Aluminum production in North America is largely concentrated in mid-sized towns in northeastern Quebec, where power is available at low cost.

Aluminum smelting provides another illustration that place advantages are always dependant, at least in part, on prevailing technology. Quebec's location advantage for aluminum production is founded on two technological conditions: the production of aluminum requires large amounts of electricity; electricity is costly to transport. Let us imagine that the second condition has disappeared: a new technological breakthrough makes it possible to send electric power over large distances at almost no cost. Electricity now costs the same price in New York as in Quebec. Were this so, there would no longer be any advantage for aluminum plants to locate in Quebec. We would now expect many plants to locate closer to New York or Chicago, in the heart of the North American market for aluminum products.

The prevailing technologies of each epoch confer advantages on specific places, which can be lost or won, as we saw. The technology of steel production, which dominated the second half of the nineteenth century and part of the twentieth century, favored places close to iron ore and coal deposits. By the same token, the technology of weaving and cloth making (textiles) in the earlier parts of nineteenth century favored locations close to cheap and abundant water power, spurring the growth of mid-sized towns in New England, to which Manchester (New Hampshire) and Lowell (Massachusetts) bear witness. There is no evidence that technological change systematically favors larger over smaller cities. Technological innovations in steel making in the latter part of the twentieth century reduced the weight of scale economies, made smaller plants profitable, and thus facilitated the move to smaller cities.

Summing up, manufacturing, notably mid-tech manufacturing, will often seek out smaller cities for one or a combination of reasons: lower land costs, lower labor costs, and availability of inputs that are costly to transport. The first two reasons only hold if land and labor costs are indeed higher—and continually rising—in big cities, which brings us back to the question of what is driving up prices in large metropolitan areas.

THE RISE OF THE MODERN METROPOLIS

For the majority of modern tradable services, the push to locate in the largest cities is overwhelming. For North American cities, the concentration of employment in scientific, technical, and professional services[45] varies systematically with size[46] (figure 2.3). Large urban areas are systematically more specialized in these modern services than smaller places.[47] Only the largest metropolitan areas (with populations above 1 million) exhibit concentrations above the continental average. The highest concentrations are found in the

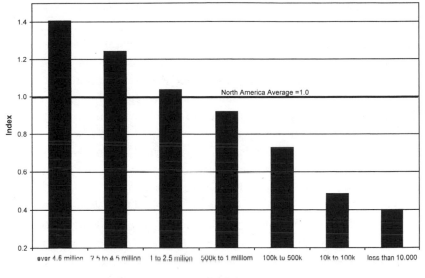

F I G U R E 2.3. Share of employment in professional, scientific, and technical services by city size (compared to the North American average), 2000

very largest class, which includes New York, Los Angeles, Chicago, Boston, San Francisco, and Toronto.

I am not entirely correct in referring to producer services as modern, although most did not exist a century ago. Many producer services are in effect the heirs of the great commercial institutions and merchant houses of the past, which in each epoch identified the leading trading cities, Venice in the fifteenth century, Amsterdam in the seventeenth century, London in the nineteenth century, New York today, and perhaps Mumbai and Shanghai tomorrow. It is in the nature of such activities to seek out the dominant cities. What self-respecting world-class bank or corporation can fail today to have an office in London or New York? The difference with the past is not only that the spectrum of services has expanded greatly, but also that the geographic range over which they are traded has expanded. A report written in New York can now be e-mailed to almost anywhere in the world at no additional cost.

Not all producer service firms will locate in the capital. The principal constraint on the total concentration of tradable services in a single metropolis is the need for face-to-face contacts. All corporate head offices will not automatically concentrate in the largest city. A chief executive can indeed electronically communicate with his subordinates in other locations. But, he or she will also feel the need to visit them from time to time to reassert his or her authority and to learn things which simply cannot be learned via electronic means. A corporation whose operations are chiefly located in the Midwest will have its head office in Chicago, Minneapolis, or another Midwestern city. Service providers (lawyers, accountants, bankers, etc.) will follow. The greater the face-to-face component—compared to electronic communication—the greater will be the limits on geographic concentration. In cases where frequent personal contact is essential, the service firm—a management consultancy for example—will set up shop not only in the capital, but also in other cities, providing local corporate demand warrants it.

But, why do many of the largest service firms absolutely want to locate their head office in the nation's largest city, leaving regional markets to junior offices? The largest international ad agencies and accounting and management consultancies are, we have seen, concentrated in New York, London, and other world cities. For these truly high-order services, all the pillars of agglomeration are simultaneously at work with no countervailing force. The largest city is simply the most profitable place to be. It is the most central location for serving national and international markets (pillar 6) with the best travel connections to the rest of the world (pillar 2) with the greatest concentration of talent in the profession (pillar 4), offering the widest range of contacts and business opportunities (pillar 5). And it is where the young and ambitious in the field want to be (pillar 7), where, in short, it is easiest to attract the best and the brightest from around the nation. Why would a growing merchant bank with international ambitions choose to locate anywhere else but in the nation's financial capital and largest city?[48]

Corporate headquarters and producer service establishments locate in the largest cities because—unlike most manufacturing—they *can*. Producer service firms are able to generate high revenues with little floor space and can thus afford to pay high rents. By concentrating in large cities, they become the principal force driving high office rents. Each new arrival further increases the value of real estate, a process, if it continues, that becomes self-reinforcing. The more banks, brokers, consultancies, corporate headquarters, etc. are jammed into a given area, the more valuable that piece of real estate becomes, and the more "central" it becomes. A self-selection process is set in motion. Only those establishments—the most prestigious bank and the largest headquarters—for whom a location in the largest city is essential and are thus willing to pay the highest rents will locate there, pushing out those less able to do so. Thus the modern metropolis is born, its economy almost entirely dependent on specialized producer services.

In New York, almost no manufacturing or wholesaling activities have survived in Manhattan. The old industrial and blue-collar neighborhoods have been either replaced by office towers or by expensive condos and chic cafés. In New York, as elsewhere, it is the shift of the national economy towards tradable services that is the driving force behind the crowding out of manufacturing.[49] Their continuing rise puts continual pressure on land values, housing prices, and wages, pushing out industries unable to bear such costs. Nonmanufacturing activities that are extensive users of space such as wholesaling, warehousing, and trucking will also move to smaller cities. Some "tradable" services that do not require highly skilled workers may also move to smaller cities where wages are lower. Examples are call centers, data entry, and credit card processing.

In the end, it is entirely possible that the balance between different-sized cities remains largely unchanged over time. That is, the growth of corporate and producer service employment in large cities systematically offsets employment losses to smaller cities. This is exactly what appears to have happened in most industrialized nations, and explains why big cities will continue to grow and be more expensive and why smaller-sized cities will not disappear.[50]

Location

So far I have only considered *size*. But, what of *location*? Should we expect a small town in Montana to attract the same industries as a small town within an hour's drive of Chicago?

NOT TOO CLOSE, BUT NOT TOO FAR EITHER

Figure 2.4 shows the concentration of manufacturing employment in North America by place size. An additional twist has been added. Places with populations under 500,000 have been divided into two groups: 1) those that are within a ninety-minute drive of an urban area with a population over 500,000, and 2) those that lie beyond that distance. Ninety-minute driving time roughly defines the range within which a comfortable two-way journey is possible for business meetings. Within that radius a businessman can attend a morning meeting and still be back in time for lunch.[51]

The evidence confirms what we already suspect. Larger urban areas have proportionately less manufacturing employment than others. Manufacturing activity has, in short, been crowed out of large cities. But it is equally apparent that not *all* smaller cities have benefited from this movement to the same degree. Being close to a large city makes a difference. Places within a

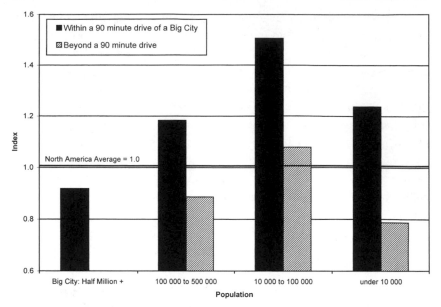

FIGURE 2.4. Share of employment in manufacturing by city size and location (compared to the North American average), 2000

ninety-minute drive show higher concentrations of manufacturing employ-ment than places farther away. Cities with populations between 10,000 and 100,000 within a ninety-minute drive of a metropolitan area are the most successful in attracting manufacturing employment. Places with populations below 10,000—and located beyond the ninety-minute threshold—have been the least successful.

Why is proximity to a large city so important? The answer has, in part, to do with the rise of modern producer services. The concentration of pro-ducer services in big cities and the need for proximity to large cities are not unrelated. We saw that manufacturing and services are increasingly inter-twined. In the daily life of a typical manufacturing plant, executives, consul-tants, programmers, suppliers, and bankers are constantly traveling back and forth between the plant and offices in the city. As the need for services grows, so does the need to be near the city. But the plant will not necessarily locate *in* the big city for reasons we now know. If the firm is looking for a site where land and labor costs are lower than in the big city, the plant will need to locate beyond commuting range of the city. The ideal location for the plant is one that is sufficiently far to not be affected by the high labor and land cost in the big city, but not so far as to make travel to the big city overly onerous.

Plants, in short, are being pulled in two opposing directions. 1) The need for business meetings pulls plants towards the big city, travel time being the essential consideration. 2) The need for adequate floor space, unencumbered merchandise transport, and lower labor costs pulls plants in the opposite direction, towards smaller cities. In modern economies, the growing importance of business meetings and the growing opportunity cost of time are reinforcing the location advantage of small places within easy reach of large ones. The balancing act between the parallel need for proximity—to be *in* the city—and the requirements of less costly labor and land also means that larger firms with several plants will often separate their administrative and production functions, the former going to the big city and the latter to smaller ones. The national or regional head office will be in the big city with plants located elsewhere. In such cases, the need for continuous communication with the head office becomes an additional reason for locating plants within easy reach of the big city. A firm headquartered in Chicago will give preference to small cities closer to Chicago over those further away. The coalescing of manufacturing near, but not necessarily in, large urban centers is today a dominant feature of the economic landscape of most nations.

PROXIMITY TO LARGE CENTERS MATTERS MORE FOR SOME PLACES

The trade-off between size and distance will not be the same for high-tech industries as for more standardized industries.[52] For high-tech manufacturing and associated R&D activities, the forces pulling plants towards large urban centers will be stronger than those pulling in the opposite direction. For industries such as aerospace, scientific equipment, and pharmaceuticals, for example, the need to be in a major urban center will often overwhelm all other considerations, including higher wages and land costs. In short, for many high-tech industries, location trumps direct costs.[53] This is simply a restatement of the often intangible—difficult to measure—advantages of agglomeration for knowledge-rich activities.

Other factors also encourage manufacturing plants to locate within easy reach of a large city. If the big city is a distribution center, as it usually is, for merchandise coming into and going out of the region, then proximity will reduce transport cost both for inputs (coming in) and for outputs (going out). The greater the weight of exports in a plant's output—or imported inputs in production—the greater will be the benefits of locating in or near a big city. By the same token, the proximity of a busy airport is an obvious cost advantage for firms engaged in long-distance trade.

The history of automobile assembly plants—once a symbol of advanced technology—provides an illustration of the changing trade-off over time between distance and city size. Automobile assembly is subject to scale economies: large plants requiring large amounts of space. In neither the U.S. nor Japan or Germany is the industry today concentrated in the nation's largest city. Toyota's principal plant is located near Nagoya; Volkswagen's plant is in the town of Wolfsburg near Hannover; while the American auto industry continues to cluster in and around Detroit, with new plants—including those foreign-owned—gradually moving out along a southward axis into Ohio, Kentucky, and further on, in search of ever lower land and labor costs. Proximity continues to matter. New plants are, as a rule, located in small towns within easy reach of a larger center (recall the Greensburg story).

The move to small and mid-sized towns in the American South, at ever greater distances from the original industry core in Detroit, has further repercussions. *First*: by locating in small towns, automobile plants contribute to the survival of small towns. But, by moving on—ever further—to new small towns, they also help to keep them small; a concentration of plants beyond a certain number would raise land and labor costs, defeating the very purpose of the move to a small town in the first place. *Second*: automobile plants and other mid-tech industries will only move to more distance locations if the place in question—small or mid-sized town—truly offers a compensating cost advantage, in the form generally of lower land and wage costs.

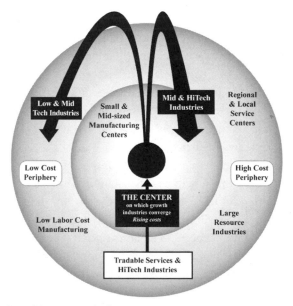

FIGURE 2.5. An evolving economic landscape

A Simple Template

After this admittedly somewhat arduous journey into theory, let me draw a simpler—and necessarily stylized—picture of how economic geographies are formed. Every nation and place is different, of course. Nonetheless, we should generally expect to find:

- One or two (sometimes more) dominant cities or urban conurbations, where incomes are higher than elsewhere, specializing in corporate and business services and other rapidly growing tradable services (broadcasting, entertainment, etc.), pushing up real estate prices and wages. For manufacturing, only high-tech industries will remain together with industries highly reliant on face-to-face contacts (publishing, high fashion, etc.), able to bear the high costs of operating in the largest cities.
- Smaller places within easy reach of large urban centers—but beyond commuting range—with strong manufacturing bases. The largest among these will have specialized in a mix of mid- and high-tech industries, with some having developed clusters around particular industries. Smaller cities will have specialized in low- and mid-tech industries with, again, the emergence of industry clusters in some. A condition of success will be lower wage and real estate costs compared to larger cities.
- Places that have neither the advantages of size nor proximity, the periphery, in short. Some will have specialized in resource-based industries, others in industries dependent on low labor, providing they have a cost advantage that compensates for their small size and distance.

The initial spark is technological change, driving the constant structural transformation of national economies. During every epoch, some industries will grow while others will decline, each with its distinct location needs. Expanding knowledge-rich industries—often in the service sector—will put growing cost pressures on the largest cities, for that is where they need to be. The largest city—the *center*—combining the advantages of size and of location, is the place all actors aspire to, but not all can afford. The greater the numbers that converge on the center—driving up costs there—the greater will be the incentive of others to seek out alternative locations. The picture— if I may be forgiven a bit of poetic license—resembles that of a fountain (figure 2.5). The greater the water pressure, the higher the fountain gushes, and the farther the spray is potentially carried (with a little help from the wind). If wind conditions are favorable, the spray may go very far, hopefully fertilizing distant locations.

There are limits to the distance that the spray will be carried. This is where *real* geographies enter the picture. Larger nations—where more places

are far—are also more likely to produce peripheries where economic opportunities are scarce. In a small nation, such as the Netherlands, where the great
majority of places fall within easy reach of a large city, places with truly poor
locations will be few. Also, in larger nations such as the U.S., India, or China,
several large urban centers have emerged, although one is necessarily on top.
Real geographies include mountains, valleys, rivers, lakes, oceans, and differences in climate, soil fertility, and geology. The larger and more diverse the
nation—the larger the area of profitably inhabitable land—the greater will
be the diversity of locations with a potential for generating wealth. The real
world—as economists are wont to say—is rarely as simple as theory would
like it to be.

Yet, looking at the world through this lens—schematically depicted
here—provides a useful template for thinking about the economic geography of nations.[54] Some things are predictable. Distances from large urban
centers continue to be powerful predictors of wealth in the U.S. and elsewhere.[55] Returning to the story of Greensburg, the fact that wages are lower
there than in Indianapolis should no longer hold any secrets for the reader,
nor should the decision to locate an auto plant there. By the same token,
Chicago's position as the metropolis—the center—of the Midwest is a good
predictor both of its relative wealth compared to other Midwestern cities,
but also of the types of industries that are most likely to flourish there. But
Chicago is also a good illustration of the delicate balance between general
explanations and particular circumstances. Chicago does, as we would predict, exhibit the highest income per person among cities in the Midwest, with
one exception—Minneapolis–St. Paul—thus calling for other explanations
beyond size.[56]

The Regional Origins of Wealth: Where It All Began

Global economies always have a center, one city at the heart of business logistics: from it information, goods, capital, credit, men, commands, and invoices move back and forth. . . . The city at the top changes only very rarely. When such a change does occur, it is always of great significance. [author's translation]

FERNAND BRAUDEL (1979)

A fundamental question remains unanswered: why are size and location so important today? Did not size matter before? Did not location also matter? Why did not industries move into cities or near cities before? The answer, simply, is that most were not free to do so.

When Location and Size Mattered Less

The location of economic activity—the question at the heart of the previous chapter—would for the most part have interested few people in preindustrial times. Scholars in medieval and Renaissance Europe would undoubtedly have been mystified why anybody would find the location of economic activity a subject worthy of consideration; that is, beyond the obvious explanations provided by Mother Nature: soil fertility, resource endowments, climate, and the presence of good harbors and navigable waterways. The great majority of the workforce was tied to land, whose location, so to speak, was preordained. True, the emergence—and later decline—of the great textile centers of Flanders (Bruges and Ghent) and the great trading cities of Italy (Venice and Genoa) would certainly have been deemed worthy of interest, and have been the subject of study by economic historians since.

Differences in place prosperity existed in all great preindustrial civilizations. Some towns were larger and richer than others. Peasants, tradesmen, and aristocrats were richer in some areas than in others. Urban hierarchies existed in premodern times. But on the whole, the question of why some businesses choose to locate in one place and not another would have seemed odd to most people. Indeed, the very notion of a business free to choose between different locations for its facilities would have seemed foreign to most. Outside of agriculture, most activity—primarily trade and crafts—was regulated by royal charters, guilds, and other covenants that, among other things, stipulated where the activity could take place, often in which neighborhood of which town. In any case, such activities concerned only a small fraction of the working population, as the overwhelming majority toiled on the land or were engaged in activities linked directly to the land and its resources.

Concerns with what we today call regional income disparities—between regions of the same nation—would also have seemed bizarre to most observers in preindustrial times. The modern nation state with its (more or less) well-defined borders and shared sense of national destiny is a recent invention. Most inhabitants in preindustrial times—the overwhelming majority of whom were miserably poor by today's standards (and disenfranchised)—would probably have had few concerns beyond that of their immediate community or clan, which, in any case, kept getting shifted back and forth between competing loyalties, fiefdoms, and kingdoms. Not only did statistics not exist until very recently (the twentieth century, in most cases) that drew attention to the gaps between poorer and richer parts of the nation, but the notion that citizens should be concerned with such welfare differences is of recent vintage, part of the long social transformation that led to the modern welfare state.

Historical evidence on development differences *within* nations in preindustrial times is understandably sparse. The little evidence that exists suggests that regional welfare differences were, as a rule, less acute than those found in many nations today.[1] This may seem surprising, but is less so when one reflects that the overwhelming majority of the population lived on very meager incomes that on average varied little from one place to another; if indeed they had "incomes" at all in the modern sense of the word. Income differences between social classes—between local aristocrats and peasants—were huge, of course; but those privileged few were in most places but a fraction of the total population, with the result that *average* incomes per person (as a statistician might have calculated them at the time) did not vary greatly between regions. Such is the tyranny of statistics.

A traveler at the time, say in Renaissance Europe, would have found great differences in customs, dress, and cuisine as he or she moved from place to place, *precisely* because so few goods were traded between places and precisely because communication between places was difficult and costly. Globalization was still far off. Most of what was consumed was produced locally. In an epoch when only a fraction of what was produced could be traded (over any reasonable distance), the relative wealth of most places was indeed largely explained by natural conditions. With some exceptions, prevailing technologies used to produce and move goods did not vary fundamentally over space; animal, water, and wind power were almost everywhere the sole sources of energy, as they had been for centuries. Each region had its market and trading centers. But, such trade as there was beyond the region was limited to non-perishable primary products (grains, spices, etc.) and to a few high value-added and easy to transport fabricated products (jewelry, custom-made swords, leather goods, specialty cloths, etc.). The majority of artisans and town laborers (blacksmiths, leatherworkers, bakers, etc.) continued to be tied to place. The idea that artisans could actually *choose* where to locate their workshops would, indeed, have seemed bizarre. Why even ask the question?

For *location* to matter—for it to become a subject of concern as it is today—three things needed to happen. First, transportation technologies needed to change so that goods could move profitably over longer distances, allowing producers to choose where best to locate their production facilities. Second, a sufficient number of people needed to be lifted out of poverty so that sufficient demand existed for non-agricultural products, whose production was not tied to the land. Third, production technologies needed to change so that the vast majority of workers were no longer tied to the land and to the production of foodstuffs. Only when the production of goods and services was finally freed from the tyranny of the land did the question of "why here and not there?" take on the urgency it has today, which is the appropriate point of entry for looking at the creation of economic centers. How did the center (the fountainhead in our template) come into being in the first place?

Water and Waterways

The time has come to leave imagined geographies behind and to give real names to places. Where *did* the largest cities spring up? This is not a question that lends itself to a simple answer. Chance, geography, and serendipity are generally part of the story, which varies from nation to nation. I will concentrate on western Europe and on North America—the two historical heartlands of the industrialized world.

In all western European nations, the largest city—usually also the capital—is located on or near a river, lakefront, waterway, or harbor. The major exception is Madrid, where the location of the capital was strictly a political decision, motivated at the time by the desire for a geographically central capital city, based in Castile, in what was then—the fifteenth century—a recently unified nation, following years of war, subject to strong centrifugal pressures. Madrid is also an exception in that it is located in a relatively dry region with comparatively low population densities. But Madrid is just that, an exception.

Why were water and waterways so important for the creation of large cities? Much, again, has to do with transport costs. Large cities, we know, are normally important distribution and trading centers. Indeed, this was often their initial economic function. A first reason why cities typically sprung up on river or harbor fronts is that these are natural break-bulk points. Caravans arriving at a river—without a bridge—needed to unload their wares, put them on a boat or raft, and then reload them again. Caravans had no choice but to interrupt their voyage. The suffix "ford" in many English place-names bears witness to the early significance of river crossings as stop-off points. In the case of ocean ports, discharging and recharging cargo is an absolute necessity. Ocean-faring vessels can go no further; the journey stops there. Goods must be unloaded and put on other transport modes if they are to be sent further inland.

Moving from one transport mode to another—unloading, handling, and reloading—all involve costs and time lost, costs that traders and producers will attempt to avoid if they can. Why stop to unload and reload if not required to do so? Since break-bulk points mean that their merchandise will be unloaded and handled in any case, it makes economic sense to make use of such compulsory interruptions to do something else. Thus break-bulk points will often become distribution centers. The merchandise is already on the dock (say, cotton from Egypt) and will in any case need to be transferred to other transport modes (river barges, coaches, etc.). It is easy to see why warehousing, trading, and wholesaling activities will spring up in the same location. Why set up a distribution center elsewhere only to incur unnecessary break-bulk costs? By the same token, it makes sense to establish manufacturing activities there, especially if the final good is less costly to transport than bulky primary inputs. Historically, great port cities have often been centers for milling, reducing wheat into flour, and more recently petrol-refining, and transforming crude oil into gasoline and petrochemical products.

But the story of water does not end there. Transport by water has historically been the least expensive transport mode and still remains so in many cases, especially for bulk transport. Until the advent of the steam engine and railways in the mid-nineteenth century, waterways were by far the most efficient means of transport. It took much less effort to move goods across water than across land. Until the advent of the railway, overland travel was hazardous, generally on unpaved roads, and largely dependent on horsepower. Without waterways, the possibilities for trade were severely limited by the high cost of transporting goods. Indeed, much of the modern history of trade has been the story of the search for water routes to markets and suppliers. The discovery of America was spurred by the search for a water passage to Asia.[2] Trade was equally the incentive behind the Suez Canal and the Panama Canal, the greatest engineering projects of their time. Western Europe north of the Pyrenees is criss-crossed by canals, many dating back several centuries.

Water remains the least costly and most energy-efficient mode of transport for long-distance merchandise trade. This has important consequences for ocean-bound traffic. The combination of high initial fixed costs (harbors, ships, etc.) and low marginal costs per additional distance traveled means that traders have an incentive to send their goods as far as possible by water once they are on a boat. Why unload before, only to switch to a more expensive transport mode (truck, train, etc.), unless absolutely necessary? The shipper will normally aim for the port city closest to the market—bypassing other ports on the way—before changing to another transport mode. If the customers of an American exporter are in Berlin, the shipper will most likely choose to unload his wares in Hamburg before transferring them to a train or truck, whose costs per ton-mile are higher. Were he to unload his wares farther away in Le Havre, France, he would have to bear these higher transport costs over longer distances. This simple truth of transportation economics has had a major impact on the economic geography of nations.

The cost advantage of water transport over other modes—particularly for long-distance bulk shipments—also applies to inland voyages. This, in turn, gives cities with access to inland waterways an advantage over competitors and explains the vital role played by canals during the early days of the Industrial Revolution. Returning to the Berlin-Hamburg example, Hamburg, besides being a seaport, also has an inland water link to Berlin, which further strengthens its cost advantage. Places well-positioned for both ocean and inland trade have an advantage over other places. New York's magnificent natural harbor coupled with the Hudson River—and later the Erie Canal—gave it such an advantage.

Water also has a more basic impact on economic development. Water is necessary for agriculture, as well as providing a source of energy. Population densities—potential markets, in short—are generally greater in regions with abundant water. It is no mere accident that the first civilizations in Mesopotamia, Egypt, India, and China sprung up along rivers. Rivers served the double purpose of transport facilitators and of sources of soil fertility.

However, we must beware of geographic determinism. Civilizations have also sprung up in regions with few rivers, most notably in the Americas. The Aztecs and the Incas were quite sophisticated empires in their time, before they came to an abrupt end with the arrival of Europeans. Mexico and Peru are singularly lacking in navigable rivers. By the same token, in other parts of pre-Columbian America, technologically advanced civilizations did *not* automatically spring up along the banks of the Hudson River and the fertile valleys of Ohio or along the shores of the La Plata River (which fronts Buenos Aires) and the fertile plains of the Argentinean Pampas. The emergence of New York and of Buenos Aires as centers of wealth has as much to do with historical accident as with geography. The first unique event—the initial spark—that determines where the center emerges is often an accident,[3] the subject to which I shall now turn.

A Tale of Two Continents

That the Industrial Revolution initially took off in England in the seventeenth century may properly be called an accident. This is not because explanations are lacking. The purpose of this book is not to explain the origins of the Industrial Revolution. I simply observe that Britain *was* where it took off. My interest lies in what this has meant since for the economic geography of nations. It is an accident because the starting-point could plausibly have been elsewhere in Europe, in the Low Countries or northern Italy, for example, with histories of economic achievement and intellectual ferment no less remarkable than that of Britain prior to the Industrial Revolution. Indeed, it was not preordained that China or Japan were not to be the birthplaces of an earlier Renaissance and Industrial Revolution, their explorers—and not those of Portugal, Spain, Holland, and England—criss-crossing the oceans, followed by conquest and by colonization. But, this is an accident that did not happen.

Thus the Industrial Revolution started in the northwest corner of Europe on the British Isles,[4] its fruits spreading over time to neighboring countries. Here we have a first manifestation of the importance in history of distance and geography. The next European nations to industrialize were located in the same part of the continent: Belgium, the Netherlands, France, and Germany.[5] The percentage of the labor force in agriculture was already well below 50 percent by the end of the nineteenth century in these four neighboring nations. Together with Great Britain, these were the most urbanized parts of Europe at the time. The importance of geographical proximity to the initial starting point—compared to culture or religion—is brought home by the fact that two of these early industrializing nations were overwhelmingly Roman Catholic (Belgium and France). In Germany, the largely Catholic Rhineland was among the first to industrialize in the nineteenth century, while Protestant Prussia, east of the Elbe River, remained largely rural. Which brings me to the essential question: where *within* nations did development eventually concentrate?

Europe's Blue Banana

One of the most striking features of the economic geography of western Europe is the concentration of population and economic activity along a banana-shaped corridor stretching from southern Britain in the northwest of the continent down to northern Switzerland, with an interruption in the Alps, and then picking up again in northern Italy (map 1). This banana-shaped band largely follows the path of medieval trade fairs linking the merchant towns of Flanders, the Rhineland, and northern Italy. North of Italy, this high-density corridor—with England and Switzerland at each end—covers most of the Netherlands and Belgium, much of western Germany, as well as parts of northwestern France. The term *Blue Banana* has become popular among economic geographers as a handy shorthand to describe it, generally attributed to the French geographer Roger Brunet, who, beginning in the 1970s, produced a number of maps in which this banana-shaped region was colored blue.[6]

The geographic center of the European economy is, in short, not difficult to identify. More than three hundred years since the inception of the Industrial Revolution, Europe's economic development is still pretty much centered on the same general area. Admittedly, some of the earliest centers of industrialization, notably the coal- and steel-producing regions of Britain, Belgium, and France, have fallen on bad times. But Europe's economic center of gravity has not catapulted to some other distant part of the continent. Some high-income centers did spring up elsewhere during the twentieth century, most notably in the northern tier of the continent, but nothing to compare with the density and magnitude of the economic activity of the Blue Banana. The consequences for the distribution of wealth are predictable (map 2). By and large, incomes in Europe are higher in regions in or adjacent to the Blue Banana.[7]

Why and where this center arose is not difficult to understand, once we think back to the first two rules of regional growth. Industries will coalesce in and around urban centers and along trade corridors. The contours of the Blue Banana in continental Europe, the reader will have surmised, largely follow the axis of the Rhine River, Europe's preeminent navigable waterway, from Rotterdam on the North Sea to Basel in Switzerland. The Rhine has given birth to some of the most densely urbanized areas in Europe, notably the Dutch Randstad and the Rhine-Ruhr and Rhine-Main conurbations.[8] But here again, we should beware of falling into the trap of geographic determinism. No equivalent economic corridor developed along the Danube and its confluents, one of Europe's other great navigable waterway systems. What was needed for the Blue Banana to develop was the *simultaneous* presence of a waterway system—the North Sea included—and an "accidental" spark close by, which set off the Industrial Revolution. The trading relationships between England and its partners across the Channel and the North Sea were already well-established at the time of the Industrial Revolution.

This is not the end of the story. Human endeavor, aided by geography, helped to reinforce the central position of the Blue Banana over time. The Rhine is blessed by several confluents and adjoining river systems (the Main, Meuse, Moselle, etc.) which are, at least in part, navigable. Over time, these rivers together with others (Weser, Elbe, Seine, etc.), were linked by a complex web of canals, creating what is arguably the densest navigable waterway system in the world. The potential for trade and agglomeration economies is easy to understand. We know that lower transport costs foster economies of scale and agglomeration. The addition over time of other transport infrastructures—paved roads, highways, and rail—enhanced not only the internal potential of the Blue Banana for interaction and trade, but also its central position at the heart of European transport networks. Trade between the two sides of the Alps has been greatly facilitated by man-made tunnels—Gotthard, Simplon, etc. The Chunnel auto-rail link across the Channel is only the latest in a long series of infrastructures tying the European heartland ever closer together, and the rest of Europe to it. Europe's four busiest hub airports are located either directly in the Blue Banana—Heathrow, Schipol, Frankfurt—or are within close range (Paris). A new multibillion rail-freight connection is currently being built between the port of Rotterdam and the Ruhr-Rhine region of Germany.

The center, once established, will tend to reinforce itself, especially during the early stages of economic growth. The chief culprit, so to speak, in this story is transport infrastructure. Once a central point is born, all other places will aspire to be linked to it. What follows is a transport network (man-made) with the principal roads converging on the center, further strengthening the geographical centrality of the center (repetitions intended). Paris within France provides an eloquent example. Paris's preeminent position within France was not geographically preordained. But, centuries ago, when Paris became France's capital of what was to become a highly centralized state (and still is), the understandable priority of any local prince or prefect was to have a road or water) link with Paris. Since many local princes and prefects got their wish, the end result was (and still is) a national transportation system centered on Paris. One of the ironies of transportation planning—a good example of the law of unintended consequences—is that transportation investments ostensibly made to help peripheral places end up strengthening the center. If all communities in the United States—above some population size—succeeded in obtaining a direct air link to New York, that would undoubtedly be a good thing for each community, taken individually, but the collective result would be the strengthening of New York as the central hub from which to serve all communities.

A first conclusion flows from this European journey into the origins of continental and national heartlands. Their location on the map is not pre-ordained. Accidents and unique events will in part determine where they first emerge. However, once a center comes into being, generally early on in the development process, it becomes a geographical fact, which can no longer be undone. The natural forces of agglomeration and accompanying investments in infrastructure will combine to consolidate its initial advantage. Paris cannot be undone, nor can London, nor any other major city. They become irreversible facts on the ground. I have already remarked upon the stability of urban hierarchies, once established. In every European nation, the largest city in 1900 is still the largest city today and, I believe, this is equally true for the second-ranking city within today's borders. Economic geographies, grounded in many centuries of investment and interaction, once established, are devilishly difficult to reverse.

The Paris example suggests an additional conclusion. Besides the founding accident, which established where the Industrial Revolution would ignite on European soil, the sites of national capitals are also accidents—for accidents they generally were—of some significance. The principal high-income or high-density places outside the Blue Banana are national capitals and their surrounding areas: Stockholm, Madrid, Rome, Vienna, Paris, etc. In Europe, the capital, once established, generally became the nation's dominant city, an expression of the importance of the state in European history, quite different from the North American experience, as we shall see.

A CONTINENT OF BORDERS, CULTURAL AND POLITICAL

European history is replete with what I call accidents, not all of them happy ones. I do not need to recall that more than 50 million Europeans perished in the twentieth century in two world wars. Over the last century, Europe has witnessed economic and political upheavals (in the east, from capitalism to communism and back again), civil wars, genocide, massive population transfers, and major boundary changes. Indeed, east of Switzerland, with only minor exceptions, no international boundary existing in 1900 is still intact today.[9] The economic geography of most European nations cannot be understood without reference to such accidents of history. Boundary changes can affect the relative fortunes of cities and regions, even to the extent of transforming a center into a periphery. Before World War I, Berlin could be said to have had a central location within Germany. Today, it finds itself on Germany's eastern periphery, less than 60 kilometers from the Polish border.

Nations with a long history of political unity, stable borders, and a strong central state will normally have more dominant national economic cores, usually centered on the capital city; France, Spain, and Sweden are examples in Europe. In nations whose borders are more recent, development will often be less polarized. Italy illustrates the tug of war between the pull of the continental heartland—the Blue Banana—and the pull of a fairly recent national capital. Italy is one of the few cases[10] where the national capital (Rome) is not clearly the nation's largest city. Milan is about as big and Italy's economic capital. A primary reason for Milan's preeminence within Italy is its location. The prosperous Italian north, centered on the fertile Po Valley, is part of the historical European heartland, the southern progression beyond the Alps of the Blue Banana. Its trade links with regions north of the Alps predate the Industrial Revolution. The other reason for Milan's economic dominance is, precisely, Italy's recent unity. Rome only became part of the Italian state in 1870, following the fall of the Papal States. Had Italy been united for a thousand years, à la française, with Rome as its capital, the latter would undoubtedly have emerged as the nation's undisputed economic center with a population much larger than today.

Vienna presents the opposite case: an old capital whose empire suddenly shrunk as a result of border changes. In 1919, after the fall of the Austria-Hungary, the newly created Austrian Republic, a mere fraction of the old empire, found itself saddled, so to speak, with a capital that was too big for its needs. The expression at the time was *Wasserkopf* (loosely translated as "bloated head"). The young republic did not know what do with the huge ministries and hordes of civil servants it inherited from the defunct empire. Firms based on an internal market of 50 million, which had suddenly shrunk to 6 million, were forced either to close down or to downsize.[11] The predictable outcome was a city whose population ceased to grow. Greater Vienna's population today is still below that of 1910, the last census before World War I. Vienna is an example of cities adjusting to the size of their natural market areas, which are often defined by borders, be they political or cultural.

Returning to the Blue Banana, perhaps the most striking feature of Europe's economic geography, despite the momentous upheavals and disruptions of the twentieth century, is that it continues to occupy such a central position in the continent's economy. Knowledge-rich activities in today's Europe continue by and large to converge on its cities and towns. Two Scandinavian researchers, Tomas Hanell and Jörg Neubauer,[12] looked at several indicators for Europe's knowledge economy: the distribution of highly educated populations; employment in high-tech manufacturing and in knowledge-intensive services; patent applications filed; number of edited scientific journals; and leading university cities. The picture that emerges is of a string of knowledge-rich metropolitan areas (around which hover small and mid-sized university towns and high-tech manufacturing clusters) that almost exactly reproduces the contours of the Europe's Blue Banana.[13] I can think of no better evidence of the underlying force of the rules of regional growth.

HOW BORDERS SHAPE CENTERS AND PERIPHERIES

The crowding out principle explained in chapter 2 (recall the sprays gushing from the fountain), informs us that the Blue Banana should also generate countervailing pressures, pushing out manufacturing and ancillary services to other less congested parts of Europe.[14] Those places closest to the Blue Banana should be the first to gain in accordance with the second golden rule of regional growth (location matters). However, in Europe the presence of a cobweb of international boundaries means that both the pull of the center and the dispersal of employment away from the center will not follow an uninterrupted geographic progression. In Europe, borders continue to act as barriers to the free flow of labor and of direct investments (in plants and other facilities), despite the EU. Differences in language, culture, and professional accreditations, as well as the non-transportability of social benefits such as health care and pension plans, considerably reduce the mobility of labor. Investors in new plants or offices will, given the choice, prefer to begin with locations that fall within their cultural sphere and established network of business relations. A Paris-based owner will as a rule feel more at ease managing a plant in another part of France than in Germany.

The presence of international borders adds a new dimension to the notion of distance: distance from where, the national or the continental center? A place may be far (in the periphery) from a national perspective but not from a continental perspective, or vice versa. The Dutch province of Drenthe, located in the northeast corner of the Netherlands, some 100 kilometers from Amsterdam, is peripheral from a Dutch perspective; but less so from a European perspective, located almost in the Blue Banana. The region of eastern

Slovakia, by contrast, is peripheral both within Slovakia—some 200 kilometers from the Slovak capital of Bratislava—and within Europe, a good 1,000 kilometers east of the Blue Banana.[15]

The advantage of proximity to the continental center is most apparent where international borders intervene. For almost all nations lying entirely outside the Blue Banana, the wealthiest regions are those located closest to the Blue Banana; that is, close to the nearest border: the Basque Country in Spain, southern Sweden; western Hungary (map 2). Where such regions have the added attribute of size—housing the nation's largest or second-largest city—their relative advantage *within* their respective nations is enhanced, as in southern Finland (Helsinki), western Slovakia (Bratislava), and Catalonia (Barcelona). At the other end of the spectrum, the poorest regions are systematically located at the periphery of each nation, the farthest removed from Europe's Blue Banana.[16] The examples should no longer come as a surprise: the most easterly regions, respectively, of Hungary, Slovakia, Poland, and Austria; the southern regions of Spain and Italy; the northern regions of Finland and Sweden; and finally, the peripheral northern and western regions of the United Kingdom and the Republic of Ireland.

Nothing better illustrates the impact of borders than the juxtaposition of poor and rich regions facing each other across an international boundary, which in Europe can almost be formulated as a general rule[17]: wealthy regions in nations outside the Blue Banana will be located across from poor regions of nations closer to the Blue Banana. The wealthiest regions *within* each nation—abstracting from national capitals—are often located near the border with the next nation in line, standing between it and the Blue Banana. The Spanish-French and Hungarian-Austrian borders are examples. In the former case, the wealthiest Spanish regions are bunched up along the French border across from the regions of Roussillon-Languedoc and Aquitaine, relatively poor within the French context. The Austrian-Hungarian example is even more telling. Austria's poorest *land*, Burgenland, at the eastern extreme of the nation, sits across from the three richest provinces of Hungary (barring Budapest) in the western part of the nation. This is as close to a pure border effect as one can get; before the First World War, Austria and Hungary were part of an economically integrated whole with no true international border separating the two nations. The instauration after 1919 of an international boundary between Austria and Hungary—a boundary reinforced by the iron curtain between 1947 and 1990—made Burgenland into a peripheral region within Austria.[18] Burgenland is not a "natural" peripheral region; borders made it so.

Studying map 2, the perceptive reader may well ask why the border effect is not visible—or less so—for Poland and the Czech Republic for their respective borders with Germany. Should not these western border regions be wealthier? This is where accident and history creep back into the picture, never far from the surface in Europe, especially here, that part of Europe which used to be referred to as Central Europe (*Mitteleuropa*), a designation which has largely fallen into disuse. The border areas of Poland and the Czech Republic were the scene of expulsions of ethnic Germans after World War II, subsequently resettled, respectively, by Poles and Czechs. I make no moral judgments on these populations transfers. In terms of regional economics, however, this legacy means that these are atypical regions for Europe, more akin to newly settled territories. This also suggests—although I have no proof of this—that these are still relatively under-exploited regions, which should grow rapidly in the future, eventually attaining higher income levels, consistent with their favorable location *within* their respective nations.

For nations lying wholly or partially within the Blue Banana, patterns are more complex, in part because of the weight of negative clusters inherited from the past, precisely because these were often the first regions to industrialize based on coal and steel: Wallonia, Lorraine, the Ruhr. In old industrialized nations, high relative levels of wealth will most often be the result of a combination of size, location, *and* the absence of a negative industrial legacy. Examples are southern Bavaria with Munich at its center and the Rhône-Alpes region of France with Lyon at its center. Within France, GDP per person in the Rhône-Alpes region is surpassed only by that of Paris and of Alsace, the latter squarely located in the Blue Banana on the banks of the Rhine.

Europe also adds another dimension to location. Being on a peninsula or on a part of a continent jutting out into the sea far from the heartland is also a handicap, by virtue of what we have learned about the economics of water transportation. Brittany, on the western tip of France, and Galicia, on the western tip of Spain, draw little economic advantage from their location on the Atlantic Ocean. Most shipping bypasses them, in search of ports closer to the European heartland. The same reasoning can be applied to southern Italy.

Finally Europe reminds us that a lack of harbors or waterways is a handicap. This is not a constraint for most European regions because of the continent's geography, where seas or rivers are rarely very far. The interior of Spain and parts of the Balkans and eastern Europe are exceptions and exhibit correspondingly low per capita products. However, Europe west of Russia has nothing comparable to the vast landlocked regions of North America, the continent to which I now turn.

North America's Bipolar Destiny

The emergence of North America's economic heartland was no less accidental. The accident may be summed up in two statements: 1) they came from the east, and 2) they came from Europe's economic heartland—England, France, and Holland. Had North America been "discovered" and colonized from the west by, say, the Chinese or the Japanese, then the continent's economic geography would look very different. What is today San Francisco might have become America's financial and corporate center—not New York. The Sacramento and Central Valleys of California—not the Great Lakes—might have developed into the continent's industrial heartland. But that did not happen. The first settlers came from Europe. The first towns were founded on the East Coast.

The fact that the first colonists came from those parts of Europe where the Industrial Revolution was progressing most rapidly is no less critical. If the Portuguese or the Spanish, and not the English, had arrived first along the eastern seaboard, things might also have turned out differently.[19] Had the English conquered and settled Mexico, perhaps Mexico would have developed into the continent's economic powerhouse instead, and gone on to conquer much of the rest of the continent. Nor was it foreordained that those first English-speaking settlers should occupy the entire East Coast with only a few interruptions (New Netherlands and, briefly, New Sweden), which were soon absorbed, leading to the creation of a vast linguistically unified space between the French settlements to the north—future Canada—and the Spanish settlements to the south. What is today the United States might, like Europe, have found itself divided up into numerous cultural and linguistic units, each with its own sovereign state. But that did not happen either.

North America's economic center thus sprang up on the East Coast, gradually spreading west. Some four centuries after the first settlers arrived, the greatest concentrations of economic activity are still found east of the Mississippi River, with the highest concentrations along trade corridors and urban centers. The forces of agglomeration and the "search for the center" were no less powerful in shaping North America's economic geography than Europe's. As in Europe, an economic "center" emerged in North America, although not as geographically neat as Europe's Blue Banana. The similarities and the differences with Europe are instructive. Let me begin with the similarities.

The most obvious similarity is the importance of seafronts and of waterways. The greatest concentration by far of economic activity is found along a corridor extending from Greater Boston down to Washington, D.C., encompassing other great cities such as Baltimore and Philadelphia, and of course

New York. The French geographer Jean Gottmann first coined the term *megalopolis* in 1957 to refer to this dense string of cities.[20] All lie on the coast; all are port cities. This coastal megalopolis is the historical starting point of the American economy and remains its densest point. A second corridor of activity, though not as dense as the first, is also visible on the map of North America, appearing as a westward continuation of the coastal megalopolis. Just as the Alps form a barrier between Europe's Rhine-centered Blue Banana and its southern extension into Italy, so do the Appalachian Mountains (although far less formidable) between North America's coastal megalopolis and its westward extension. Depending on the eastern starting point, this mid-continent concentration of economic activity can be viewed as either a Toronto-Chicago or a Pittsburgh-Chicago corridor. Other cities along this corridor are Buffalo, Cleveland, Detroit, and Milwaukee. All, save Pittsburgh, lie on the Great Lakes, North America's great inland waterway system and natural gateway to the West.

Other cities also owe their existence to water transport. Montreal, Canada's first industrial center and today its second largest city, is the principal port, or break-bulk point, for entry into the Great Lakes system, the farthest point west that most ocean shipping can go before transferring to ships appropriate for inland waterways or to other transport modes.[21] Cincinnati (on the Ohio) and St. Louis and Minneapolis (on the Mississippi) are located on major rivers. In short, as in Europe, waterways were a major factor shaping North America's early economic landscape. And, as in Europe, human investments in infrastructures further compounded initial natural advantages. The best-known example is, of course, the Erie Canal, built in 1825, which established a water transport link between New York and the Great Lakes system. New York already had a considerable natural advantage because of the quality and size of its harbor and its position at the head of the Hudson River, penetrating north into the interior.[22] By connecting the Hudson River with the Great Lakes, the Erie Canal allowed traffic to move directly between the rapidly growing American interior and the port of New York, cutting through the Appalachians. By the same token, Chicago's favorable position on the southwest shore of Lake Michigan was reinforced by a spiderweb network of canals, railways, and highways, as noted earlier.

In short, an economic heartland—continental center—also emerged in North America, and, as in Europe, its location was much influenced by coastlines and waterways.[23] And, as in Europe, we must avoid geographic determinism. The Mississippi and Missouri Rivers, which flow into the Gulf of Mexico at New Orleans, never gave rise to a concentration of economic activity comparable to that which emerged in the coastal megalopolis or along the

Great Lakes. North America's economic center, once established, was not easy to challenge. The principal challenge would come from the Pacific Coast, as we shall see shortly. In this respect, North America is different from Europe.

Another difference, perhaps not obvious at first glance, is in the composition of the two continental centers. Europe's Blue Banana constitutes, by any measure, an impressive concentration of economic power. But the cities it houses are generally smaller than those found in its North American sister. The population of New York is considerably larger than that of London, the Blue Banana's largest urban center.[24] The great urban conurbations of the Rhine notwithstanding, there is really nothing on the continental portion of the Blue Banana to compare with the cities of Philadelphia and Boston, both of which have metropolitan populations of over 6 million. Also, nowhere on the European continent do we find the equivalent of the uninterrupted strip of urban development stretching from Boston to Washington, D.C., with some 50 million people. In short, despite approximately equivalent total populations (about 300 million each), North America has produced urban concentrations of a greater magnitude. I might add that Greater Los Angeles, with some 17 million inhabitants, also has no equivalent in Europe. But I would be jumping ahead.

What does this difference tell us? Urban concentrations will be larger where there are fewer barriers to trade and, more importantly, to the movement of people. Recall my earlier comments on the linguistic unity of the United States. Indeed, abstracting from the French-speaking parts of Canada, the U.S. and Canada constitute a largely homogenous cultural space, with no barriers to movement within the United States—which after all accounts for 90 percent of North America's population north of the Rio Grande—and until not too long ago fairly open borders with Canada.[25] Larger cities emerged because nothing stopped people from moving there. The forces of agglomeration, described in chapter 2, operated freely without hindrance, and still do. Europe has smaller cities because its nations, within which people move freely, are smaller. Only Russia, perhaps, has the potential of matching New York one day, providing its population ceases to decline. Greater New York, with its 20 million people, was only possible because of the eventual large size and cultural unity of the United States of America. Had things evolved differently, as I mused earlier, New York might still exist, but not in its current size.

The relative absence of international borders, plus the federal character of both Canada and the U.S., is mirrored in the limited importance of capitals as fountainheads of economic activity. New York is neither the capital of a state nor of a nation; neither are Chicago or Los Angeles. The capitals of their respective states, Albany (New York), Springfield (Illinois), and Sacramento (California) are urban centers of secondary importance. In Canada, the largest city, Toronto, is a provincial capital (of Ontario), but the next two largest urban centers, Montreal and Vancouver, are again not political capitals. Both in the U.S. and in Canada, the federal capital is not the nation's largest city. In the end, this a reflection of an economic tradition different from that of most European nations, a tradition of less state intervention—especially in the U.S.—in which market forces and migration are more easily accepted. This relative freedom from state guidance played a major role in shaping North America's economic geography. We find no equivalent of Paris on the map, an imperial city whose national economic preeminence (and architecture, I might add) are in large part the result of the political will of its rulers.

THE EMPTY QUARTER AND THE SECOND CORE

The emergence of a vast culturally unified and economically integrated American Republic, occupying the heart of the continent, is a result of human intervention, of what I have called "accidents." However, North America's physical geography is also distinctive on a number of counts, with major consequences for the evolution of human settlement, to which I now turn.

Large parts of the heart of the continent are relatively dry and lack navigable waterways. This vast funnel-shaped north-south region, set roughly between the Mississippi River and the western reaches of the Rockies, is not particularly propitious for human settlement. Joel Garreau, in his 1981 book *The Nine Nations of North America*, used the term *empty quarter*—which is quite fitting—to describe North America's sparsely settled western plains and mountain regions.[26] This western-middle part of North America remains sparsely settled, despite growth in some areas. Indeed, some portions of the Great Plains and prairies, characterized by steppe and desert-like conditions, should perhaps not have been settled, or at least as densely as they were following the first waves of settlement arriving from the East and from Europe in the nineteenth century. Many of those first settlers—and their descendents—were, we can now say with hindsight, clearly overly optimistic regarding the carrying capacity of the land, leading to over-exploitation and an ever-receding water table as increasingly marginal land was devoted to agriculture. The sad result was the dust bowl of the 1930s, with recurring droughts over a decade, which devastated large parts of Kansas, Oklahoma, and neighboring states.[27]

The dry heart of the continent is, in short, not well-suited to produce large concentrations of economic activity, comparable to Europe's Blue Banana or America's East Coast megalopolis. However, if we move further west (as many early settlers did), we fall upon a second distinctive feature of North America's geography: a second seaboard, replete with harbors, fronting this time on the Pacific Ocean. Although short in navigable rivers, the West Coast of North America counts a string of potentially fertile interior valleys, tucked between the Rockies and coastal mountain ranges, propitious for human settlement and economic activity.[28] What eventually emerged does not need to be recounted at length, since the reader undoubtedly knows the end of the story. A string of large urban centers developed on the West Coast, rivaling the great urban centers of the East Coast megalopolis. The Los Angeles–San Diego urban conurbation is not far in size and economic weight from that of the New York metropolitan area. The San Francisco Bay Area is in every respect a rival of Boston, both as a center of higher learning and of high technology. Seattle on the West Coast is the home of Microsoft and Starbucks, two icons of the Internet age. In Canada, Vancouver, on the Pacific Coast, may one day overtake Montreal as the nation's second largest city.

The point is this: a second "Blue Banana" has emerged in North America. Although not as dense as the first, its presence is undeniable and its continued growth highly probable, at least in the foreseeable future; which is why I speak of North America's bipolar destiny. Why large urban centers sprung on the West Coast should by now be obvious, considering what we learned about the importance of seacoasts. Yet this is not a sufficient explanation. The reader may well ask why a second center—along the North American model—did not also develop in Europe on that continent's second coastline along the Mediterranean. The Mediterranean, after all, saw the birth of the great civilizations—Greece, Rome—of antiquity. Important cities such as Barcelona, Marseille, and Genoa have emerged in modern times on Europe's Mediterranean coastline. But these do not compare with the great industrial centers farther north and certainly do not equal Los Angeles or San Francisco in size and economic importance.

Why the difference? The answer lies in the location—across the sea—of each continent's principal trading partners. This is where we jump from a continental to a global perspective. The direction of international—intercontinental—trade influences the emergence of economic centers *within* each continent.

A major reason that Europe's Mediterranean coast did not give birth after the Industrial Revolution to anything rivaling the economic powerhouses of California—notwithstanding similarly pleasant climates and landscapes—is that the trading partner on the other side is not terribly dynamic. North Africa and the Middle East, on the other side of the Mediterranean, have not emerged as important economic centers. Had Algeria or Egypt become major economic powers, along the lines of Japan or South Korea, things might have turned out differently. But they did not. Yet another accident that did not happen. In short, the Mediterranean, compared to other seaboards, did not in modern times open the door to very lucrative markets and still does not. Admittedly, the Suez Canal opened a door to wider markets. But this is not the same as free ocean access. The West Coast of North America, in contrast, found itself facing dynamic trading partners on the other side of the Pacific, beginning with the emergence of Japan in the late nineteenth century, followed since by the rise of the Korean, Taiwanese, and now Chinese economies. If current trends continue, and there is little reason to believe they should not, east Asia will soon house the world's largest economy, surpassing that of the European Union or of North America. The ports of the West Coast are the natural points of entry (and of exit) for trade with the east Asian economies.

The importance of intercontinental, cross-ocean proximity is not limited to trade, but also extends to investment and the flow of ideas and people. Person-to-person links are naturally easier between regions (nations, continents) that are closer. This means that ideas, fashions, and innovations coming from Asia will generally penetrate first on the West Coast of North America. No person who has traveled to the West Coast, whether in the U.S. or Canada, can fail to perceive the impact of Asia, be it simply in the number of Asian faces on the street and the numerous Asian restaurants of every imaginable kind. As was true for Europe, business relationships will also be closer between regions that are closer or share cultural affinities. Asian investors (in plants, resources, etc.) will, given the choice, prefer West Coast to East Coast locations. This does not mean that they will not invest elsewhere in North America, only that, proportionately, their presence will be more strongly felt on the West Coast.[29] The need for face-to-face contacts and personal relationships, to which I have often referred, also affects cross-continent ties. Very simply, for a Japanese corporate manager, the flight to Los Angeles is shorter than to New York, and perhaps the chances of finding good Sushi better.

The introduction of cross-continent trade and ties allows us to approach North America's megalopolis and Europe's Blue Banana from a different perspective. Seen globally, the two continental centers are closely linked. Historically, each has been the other's principal trading partner, source of investments, and ideas. The economic vitality of each *within* its respective continent is, in part, linked to the economic vitality of the other. The *relative* decline the East Coast megalopolis within North America during the twentieth century can in part be traced to the *relative* decline of Europe as an economic power and trading partner. From a global standpoint, New York is less well situated today than a century ago, when the only other real center of economic power and wealth lay in Europe, across the Atlantic. By the same token, the vitality of Europe's Blue Banana has, historically, been linked to cross-Atlantic trade. One of the reasons that the urban centers of northwestern Continental Europe were able to maintain their dominance is that they were ideally suited for trade and interaction with the world's other rising economy, across the Atlantic. The rise of cities on the Atlantic coast and along the Rhine river and canal system was, it is useful to recall, in part the result of a dramatic shift in the direction of intercontinental trade, as the Atlantic replaced the Mediterranean as the main axis of commerce, following the fall of Constantinople in 1453. One of the unforeseen consequences of that shift was the "discovery" of America.

WHY SOUTHERN ONTARIO DID NOT GO THE WAY OF THE MIDWEST

International boundaries have played less of a role in shaping economic geographies in North America than in Europe. However, their impact has been major for America's two neighbors. Let me begin by looking north. Canada's population, as in Britain, is being pulled south. But, unlike Britain, the southern limits of Canada are not set by geography, but by human hands— although the Great Lakes do form a natural barrier along part of the border. Canada, as a separate nation in North America, is a product of the American Revolution, or, more correctly, of two population groups that refused to join that revolution—the original French-speaking settlers and their descendents in the Saint Lawrence Valley (*les Canadiens*, as they called themselves) and the English-speaking Loyalists who fled the new American Republic to settle in what are now the Canadian provinces of Ontario, Quebec, and New Brunswick.[30] Following American independence, an international border was drawn between what was left of British North America—today's Canada— and the young republic to south.

That international boundary established the context that allowed the Province of Ontario—its southern tier to be exact—to acquire a uniquely favorable location *within* Canada, much like the south of England *within* Britain. But, southern Ontario's privileged position was *not* predetermined by geography. Nothing in its location predisposed it to become the economic powerhouse it is today. Indeed, southern Ontario is squeezed between two archetypical slow-growing Rust Belt cities—Buffalo and Detroit. Toronto, southern Ontario's metropolis, lies across from Upstate New York, one of the least dynamic parts of the American Northeast. Had the American Revolution not occurred or, alternatively, had Canada been absorbed into the United States, there is good reason to believe that southern Ontario would have gone the way of most of the Rust Belt, and Toronto would be another big Great Lakes city—let's say, on the model of Cleveland—falling under the influence of New York and Chicago.

But, viewed within a purely Canadian context, "protected" by a man-made border, southern Ontario comes very close to holding a monopoly on size and location and other positive attributes: it is home to the Canada's largest city, Toronto; the region has the densest network of mid-sized cities in Canada; the region is home to more top Canadian universities than any other; the region is the closest to major U.S. markets; it is the center of the Canadian market. Finally, Toronto's rise to prominence to become Canada's number-one city was considerably helped by a fortuitous accident (fortuitous for Toronto, that is), which caused Montreal to yield that honor to its old rival (see chapter 6). Viewed in this light, it not difficult to understand why Ontario—unlike the U.S. Midwest and Northeast between which it lies—has managed to maintain its dominant position within Canada. Its share of Canadian GDP (over 40 percent) has remained fairly stable over the last hundred years

South of the Border—Mexico

The time has come to repair an omission. I have so far limited my definition of North America to the United States and Canada, failing to include Mexico. This is not entirely correct. Nor is it entirely incorrect. Most Mexicans would agree that Mexico's sense of being part of North America remains ambiguous and is quite recent, following the signing of the North American Free Trade Agreement (NAFTA) in 1994 with the United States and Canada. In that sense, it is not entirely inappropriate that I should have waited until now before approaching Mexico. There are also two good reasons for dealing with Mexico separately. First, the Mexican story is substantially different from that of the rest of North America. Second, Mexico provides a particularly telling example of how the interplay between continental centers, national centers, international borders, and trade shape the economic geography of nations.

A first obvious difference between Mexico and its two northern partners is in economic development. Although no longer a truly poor nation, Mexico's average real income per person is about a third that of North America's two other nations.[31] In strictly economics terms, Mexico is still a developing nation. A second important difference lies in Mexico's history of settlement.

Unlike the United States and Canada, Mexico is not a "new" nation, created by waves of immigrants from overseas. The Aztec Empire, to which the Mexican Republic traces its roots, predates the arrival of the Europeans; its capital, Tenochtitlan (today's Mexico City), was already a major urban center at the time of the Spanish conquest.[32] The urban system that evolved during the Spanish colonial period was basically superimposed on the preexisting pattern. This is aptly illustrated by the decision of the Spanish to build their colonial capital on top of the ruins of the old Aztec capital.[33] The settlement pattern of New Spain—as it was then called—was essentially a continuation of what existed before, with the overwhelming majority of the population concentrated, as it still is today, in a broad stretch of central valleys and plateaus extending, roughly, from Guadalajara in the west to Puebla in the east, respectively Mexico's second and fourth largest cities. Mexico City lies in the middle of this vast central area of settlement—Mexico's heartland—which is home to over 60 million people.

Unlike the U.S. and Canada, Mexico's story is not one of settlers moving from east to west as they sought to occupy an ostensibly empty continent. Unlike the U.S. and Canada, the overwhelming majority of Mexico's population is descended—totally or partly—from the land's first inhabitants, whose roots go back to the Aztecs and other pre-Hispanic peoples. The deep historical roots of its settlement pattern put Mexico closer to Europe than to Canada and the United States. Mexico is also closer to continental Europe because of the weight of the state in its history. Both the Aztec Empire and the Spanish State which followed it were highly centralized, authoritarian monarchies buttressed by powerful church hierarchies,[34] a legacy that continued long after independence. Even though Mexico is formally a federation and democratic society—at least since the late 1990s—centuries of centralized and authoritarian rule have left their mark. With a population of more than 18 million, making it North America's second largest city after New York— larger than any European city—Greater Mexico City is as dominant within Mexico as is Paris within France.

Mexico's historical economic heartland, centered on Mexico City, developed independently of the emerging continental—New York–centered— heartland farther north. For many centuries, the vast dry and desert-like regions to the north of Mexico City, which straddle today's Mexico-U.S. border, remained a major barrier to settlement and to trade. Unlike the U.S.-Canada border, no continuous corridor of dense settlement tied the two nations together. The traditional overland trade route linking Mexico's heartland with the U.S. industrial heartland—via Monterrey and San Antonio— remains sparsely settled to this day.

Mexico's geography makes it different from its northern neighbor (and from Europe) on at least three counts: the almost complete absence of navigable waterways as noted earlier, the tropical nature of most of its coastal regions, and the contrasting temperate climate of its Central Plateau and valleys. Mexico's economic heartland did *not* develop along coastlines and waterways. Populations settle and multiply where their chances are best *relative* to other places. I am not equipped to comment on why a pre-Columbian urban civilization sprung up in Mexico and not, say, in New York State or in Michigan. This is an "accident" of the same order as the birth of the Industrial Revolution in England. However, once this initial birth occurred—in ancient Mexico, in this case—it was not an accident that population centers sprung up primarily in the temperate and comparatively well-watered higher altitudes. Before the arrival of modern medicine, tropical regions were to be avoided.[35] By the same token, pre-Colombian settlement in much of tropical Central and South America tended to concentrate in highlands—where available—removed from the sea. Rivers exerted little attraction because they were rarely navigable and, subsequently, waterborne trade failed to develop in most cases.[36]

Let me draw this story to a close. For most its history, Mexico's economic geography evolved independently, by and large, of what happened farther north, and with an economy that was considerably less advanced. Let me now jump forward to modern times. What happens when a less developed economy—Mexico—which evolved outside the continental heartland[37] finds itself progressively tied to the richer heartland via trade, investment, and even migration? The same question applies to European nations lying outside Europe's economic heartland that are now part of the EU. Mexico's location within North America is not unlike that of Poland and Spain within Europe.

The predictable result for Mexico is that northern Mexican states, nearer the U.S., are wealthier on average than those to the south. As the Mexican economy progressively integrates into that of the rest of North America, its center of gravity is slowly but systematically being pulled north. North of the border, the great urban centers of the U.S. and Canada are magnets for poorer Mexicans. But for Mexicans mobility is greatly reduced by the presence of an international border, which is a true barrier to the movement of people, much more so than most borders in Europe, the large flow of undocumented workers notwithstanding. As such, Mexico provides a particularly telling example of the impact of borders on the economic fortunes of regions.

The higher incomes per person of northern Mexican states cannot be understood without reference to the border. The northern states would hold no special advantage *within* Mexico if the border disappeared. Why, in the absence of a border, would a firm choose to put an assembly plant in Monter-rey, Mexico, if it could also locate in, say, Raleigh, North Carolina, which is much closer to the richest urban markets? Migrants from southern Mexico would no longer stop at the border. The cost advantage of a lower-wage (cap-tive) labor force would consequently disappear. The border will, of course, not disappear, certainly not in the foreseeable future. As long as North Amer-ica's wealthiest markets and chief sources of direct investment are situated north of the border, the advantage *within* Mexico of the northern Mexican states is secure. Since this is not about to change, northern states will con-tinue to generate higher incomes than the Mexican average.

But Mexico has its own historical heartland where *internal* demand and market access are highest. Incomes in Mexico City and surrounding areas are also above the national average. This is a classical case of two competing centers—fountainheads—drawing in resources. Firms seeking to maximize market access to *both* continental and internal markets will be pulled in both directions, meaning that places between the two can become attractive loca-tions, specifically those located on transport corridors between Mexico City and wealthy U.S. markets. If we add in size, this favors places located in or near urban centers along the principal trading corridors with the U.S. Among the most rapidly growing Mexican urban areas (populations over 500,000), all are located either directly on the U.S. border, on a major highway lead-ing north, or within easy reach of a larger metropolis.[38] Querétaro is a good example—the fastest growing major city in Mexico not directly on the U.S. border. Querétaro is located within easy reach of Mexico City (about 200 kilometers) on the major highway leading north to the richest U.S. markets. Querétaro, in short, is well-located for both internal and continental markets and close enough to Mexico City to be a potential site for industries "crowded out" of the capital.

The three largest cities close to Mexico City—Toluca, Cuernavaca, and Puebla—have grown rapidly in recent years, a sign that the deconcentration of manufacturing from the *national* center—crowding out—is proceeding. Farther north, the rise of Monterrey (located on the Mexico City–Texas trade corridor) as a major industrial powerhouse is an eloquent example of the importance of good access to the *continental* center. At the end of the nine-teenth century, its population was barely 40,000, the seventh largest city in the republic at the time. Today its population is well over 3 million, and may soon overtake Guadalajara to become Mexico's second largest urban area.

This leaves the Mexican south as the odd man out. It has neither the advantages of size nor location. The three poorest states of Oaxaca, Guerrero, and Chiapas are handicapped on three counts: they house no truly large city, which could act as an industrial magnet; most places are too far from Mexico City to draw any significant benefits from the crowding out of industry from the capital; the three states are poorly located for trade with the continental economic heartland. Why locate a textile or clothing factory in Oaxaca or Chiapas if one has the option of locating farther north, unless there is a compensating cost advantage?

The principal compensating advantage they have to offer is lower wages, which is not the happiest prospect for a region that is already the poorest in the republic. Per capita product in Chiapas is less than a third of that of the state of Nuevo León. The relative absence of manufacturing in the poor states of Guerrero, Chiapas, and Oaxaca tells us that even this difference is not sufficient to compensate for the disadvantages of distance and the absence of a large city. The effect of distance is amplified by the still rudimentary nature of transportation infrastructure in the Mexican southeast. The region's location handicap is compounded by cultural differences and a particularly difficult political heritage. Both states have been the scene of political turmoil in recent years,[39] in part a reflection of their poverty. This truly is Mexico's periphery.

Low wages and incomes are an inducement to move to other regions. Migrants continue to leave Oaxaca and Chiapas. Here we meet a classic dilemma facing peripheral regions around the world, not just in Mexico. *Within* nations, migration to richer central regions is, by definition, unavoidable, precisely because they are regions and thus without economic borders. Migration is necessary if the poor are to better their lot. Labor mobility is also a necessary condition of efficiently functioning markets. Yet continued out-migration can further weaken a region's capacity to develop. How can the Mexican south ever hope to compete if its young continue to leave for the north, further bolstering the north? The specter of a self-reinforcing spiral in which rich regions grow richer and poor regions poorer is a real possibility in Mexico, although hopefully not inevitable.[40]

Lessons from Europe and North America

This bi-continental journey allows us to introduce other considerations into our simple template, notably the role of borders and physical geography.

Where the center (fountainhead) emerges will generally be the result of a combination of physical geography (water, soil fertility, etc.) and unique events (where the settlers landed, where the king chose to build his capital, etc.).

More than one center can emerge. In North America, at least two economic centers have emerged, one on each coast. The presence of a second coastline strategically located for trade with other growing economies was a determining factor. Continents or nations that open up to more than one strategically positioned coastline will normally have less geographically polarized economies than nations that have only one.

Larger culturally homogenous and economically integrated (inhabitable) spaces will produce bigger centers. The bigger the circle—in our stylized template—the bigger the central place will be and the higher the fountain will gush. Where goods, capital, and people can move freely, cities are able to grow unimpeded to their technologically feasible upper limits. New York and Los Angeles would not exist at their current sizes had the United States not emerged as a vast unified continental nation with a high degree of geographic mobility.

Taking Europe as a counter example—plus indulging in political fiction— imagine for a moment that World War I had not happened, that the Habsburg and German empires had remained intact, and that trade and migration had remained as free as it was before that calamitous war. In all likelihood, Vienna would perhaps have a population of 6 million today (rather than 2 million) and Berlin might have emerged as Europe's largest city, possibly some 10 million or higher (rather than 3.5 million).[41] One can also speculate what this might have meant for the possible emergence of a Hamburg-Berlin-Prague-Vienna economic corridor and the possible subsequent eastward shift of the Blue Banana. But this is an accident that never happened.

The introduction of international borders distorts the free flow of people and capital, allowing national centers to emerge. In Europe and in Mexico, national economic centers have emerged—generally around capital cities— independently of continental centers, giving rise to competing fountainheads, a reflection of the traditionally stronger role of the state in shaping economic geographies than in the U.S. and Canada. National centers and continental centers may pull economic activity in different directions. In Sweden, Stockholm pulls economic activity towards the center of the nation, while Europe's Blue Banana pulls it south. The outcome is not unlike a tug of war between competing players. In nations outside the continental center (Mexico, Poland, Spain, etc.), the pull and the dispersal effects of the continental center (the fountain's spray) will favor regions located on borders closest to it. If the border region also houses a major urban center, the advantage is amplified as in Nuevo León (Mexico) and Catalonia (Spain).

Borders can change the value of a location, transforming a bad location into a good one, and vice versa.[42] In Canada, were it not for the U.S. border, Toronto would probably have evolved into a much less central city, certainly not the corporate center it is today. Such examples are useful for understanding what might happen if borders weaken. The most northerly counties of New York State are among its poorest. Seen from the U.S., they are clearly peripheral. But Plattsburgh (population about 20,000), one of the larger towns in the area, is a stone's throw (about 100 kilometers) from Montreal, across the Canadian border. Were the border gone, it would probably have developed into a small but dynamic manufacturing center like many similar-sized cities near Montreal on the Canadian side, catching the spray from Canada's second largest center.

Nations with large, dry, or otherwise inhospitable regions will have large, sparsely populated spaces, which produce peripheries or act as separators between centers. Western Europe, with the notable exception of Scandinavia, has very few such empty spaces; but they are an important feature of North America's geography.

The regional impacts of economic integration (freer trade) between neighboring nations will depend both on their geography and on the initial income gap between them. Where the initial gap is major—as in the U.S.-Mexico case—the resulting shift in resources within the poorer nation may widen the internal rift between central and peripheral regions. In this unhappy scenario, peripheral regions such as Chiapas, eastern Poland, and eastern Slovakia are seemingly condemned to eternally lag behind other regions, which brings us to the mechanics over time of regional disparities in wealth, the question to which I now turn.

4

Why Is the Geography of Wealth More Unequal in Some Nations?

[T]he Industrial Revolution brought the world closer together, made it smaller and more homogenous. But the same revolution fragmented the globe by estranging winners and losers. It begat multiple worlds.

DAVID S. LANDES (1998)

The persistence within rich nations of significant income differences between places seems to fly in the face of basic economics. After all, if the potential for earning a living is much greater in one place, people will move there up until the moment when the difference disappears. There is much truth in this statement, but only up to a point, as we shall see. Regional income disparities are here to stay. To understand why, we need first to understand the mechanisms that caused regional inequalities to arise in the first place. What happens afterwards? Is there a predictable happy ending? Should we expect income disparities between central and peripheral places to widen or to lessen over time? The answer is not the same for all nations.

On the Use of the Word *Disparity*

Not everyone will have the same definition of what a happy ending would entail. Is it balanced growth where all regions obtain a fair share of national employment or rather a world in which welfare differences between regions will have disappeared? The two are not necessarily the same. Regional disparities can be viewed from different perspectives. Indeed, it can be argued that my use of the word *disparity* already betrays a bias, but I shall not go into that.[1] A region can be viewed as being less prosperous because it has comparatively fewer activities or, alternatively, because its citizens are on average poorer than the rest of the nation. Although the two—size and wealth—are related, as I have repeatedly suggested, they do not *necessarily* go together. Southern Italy is visibly poorer than the rest of Italy, but it is hardly devoid of economic activity. On the other hand, the great dry interior of North America is sparsely settled, but not all its places are poor.

Which of the two should primarily concern us: the size of the local economy—its absolute growth or decline—or the standard of living it provides for its citizens? In the end, the ultimate measure of success must be the economic welfare of the local population, whether measured by income or otherwise, and that is the yardstick I have been using and shall continue to use. Throughout this book, I have used wealth as a synonym for income or product per person or for other measures of material welfare. However, the size of the local economy and the potential wealth it can generate are related, and therein resides the problem. Is regional income equality possible without, as well, a more equal, or balanced, distribution of economic activity? Can the first disparity be addressed without also addressing the second?

The positive relation between wealth and size is almost always true when one looks at a static portrait. At any given moment, the largest cities and the most densely settled areas will, as a rule, exhibit the highest incomes. However, this does not inform us about the direction of the relationship *over time*. Should we expect income disparities between regions to widen or to lessen? Will the centers continue to grow richer and peripheral places continue to lag behind?

The key issue revolves around the long-term effects of capital flows and, especially, of migration on the gap between poor and rich regions. It is at this point that things start to become muddy and that arguments often take on an unfortunate ideological turn. In simplistic terms, for some commentators on the left, the free flow of capital and people will almost always exacerbate differences,[2] while for others on the right, such free flows will over time lead to greater income equality. There are elements of truth to both points of view. There is also ample evidence to support both. Data can be garnered to show that national economic growth has over time led to greater regional income equality and, alternatively, that it has generated greater inequality.[3] Among scholars, the debate on the regional consequences of economic growth is by no means over.[4] The evidence, on balance, tends to favor the optimists. Over time, regional welfare differences do in general tend to decrease. But, before concluding too hastily, an excursion into economic theory is in order.

Why Regional Disparities Happen—and Should Eventually Disappear

Imagine two regions at the outset of the Industrial Revolution. The first region is more densely settled—in part because its soil is more fertile—and has larger cities. This is the nation's historic *center*. The second, located on the *periphery* of the nation, is less densely settled and has smaller cities. The major trade routes, dating from before the Industrial Revolution, converge on the chief city in the center. Let me also assume—no economic reasoning is possible without some initial assumptions—that the income difference between the two regions is fairly minor at the outset. By "fairly minor," I mean that the difference between the two regions is not sufficient to cause anyone to move from one to the other. In addition, migration is costly because transport infrastructures are rudimentary. The two regions, predominantly rural, provide comparable standards of living to the great majority of their respective (largely poor) populations, although marginally higher in the center. In both regions, living conditions are still fairly primitive with high mortality rates. In short, no significant disparity exists.

What will cause a significant disparity to emerge between the two? The answer, unsurprisingly, is economic growth. We know that rising incomes produce a change in consumption patterns, with a shift over time towards goods produced in cities. The most centrally located cities are favored, as technological change allows for ever greater scale economies and ever lower transport costs. The growing weight of agglomeration economies also favors production points in around the larger cities. All this we know already. The crucial point is the impact of this transformation on the relative demand for labor in each region. The shift in consumption patterns will with time produce an increase in the demand for labor in the central region compared to peripheral regions. The type of goods and services that are increasingly consumed can be more efficiently produced in the center; investors will open plants there to meet growing demand. Employers in the center will call for more labor. Wages will rise there compared to peripheral regions. The disparity is born.

The spark that set off the wage disparity is economic growth. This, economic theory tells us, is entirely as it should be in a market economy. Wages are signals (prices, as economists would say) that point to the direction in which resources should move. In this case, higher wages in central regions mean that the national economy would gain if labor moved there from peripheral regions. The goods that are increasingly demanded are more efficiently produced there. Seen in this light, regional wage disparities are a good thing, for they signal to workers in the periphery that they should move. We do not need economic theory to tell us that people, as a rule, move from poorer to richer areas and not the other way around. But how will this affect wages in each region? The answer is straightforward if we apply simple economic reasoning, sticking to supply and demand. Workers leaving the peripheral region will reduce the local supply of labor, which should raise wages. Similarly, labor coming into the center will increase supply there, depressing wages. This is standard textbook economics. When supply decreases, prices rise; when it increases, prices fall. Immigration should drive down wages, which is very much the popular perception (which does not mean that it is entirely wrong). But immigration can also have the opposite effect. As the saying goes, it all depends.

Staying with standard textbook economics, migration is a good thing on two counts. First, it allows resources (labor, in this case) to be reallocated to where it is most needed. Migration is a necessary lubricant for a growing economy. Economies in which labor is mobile and moves freely will grow more rapidly. Second, migration, by adjusting labor supply to labor demand, allows wage (and/or unemployment) rates to be equalized among regions. Out-migration from poor regions raises local wages, while in-migration into rich regions depresses wages there. In short, migration is good both for growth and for equality. Wages—and thus also incomes—will equalize between the central and peripheral regions when sufficient labor has migrated between the two to reestablish a new balance between supply and demand. The disparity will have been erased and, as such, there will be no need for further migration. A new economic equilibrium will have been attained, which maximizes national income. Thus viewed, regional disparities are essentially temporary disturbances on the route to greater prosperity. How temporary is another matter.

This is a very condensed presentation of what I have called the standard economics perspective. The surprise is that it is not far from the truth, despite its simplicity and the displeasure it undoubtedly triggers among those—generally to the left of the political spectrum—who distrust markets. The evidence, insofar as data is available, suggests that long-term economic growth does indeed lead to a reduction in regional income differences. Consistent data series on the evolution of regional income disparities over long time periods are hard to come by, because of changing statistical standards, wars, and boundary changes, especially in Europe. Fortunately, data exist for the United States and for Canada (figure 4.1). The results are unequivocal.[5] Regional income disparities have fallen dramatically in both nations over the last century. Both nations, especially the United States, have a tradition of high labor mobility, certainly much more so than most European nations. It is difficult to argue that migration, on balance, had a detrimental effect on the long-term evolution of regional income disparities. We know that the twentieth century was marked by a massive out-migration—often African-Americans—from the traditionally poor American South to the industrial cities of the Northeast and the Midwest, which goes a long way in explaining the sharp reduction in regional inequality, particularly for the period between the 1920s and the 1960s. The reduction in disparities in the U.S.

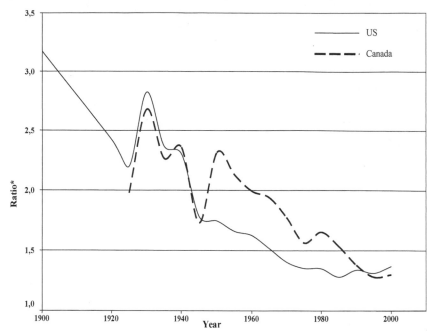

FIGURE 4.1. Evolution of regional income inequality (ratio of per capita income in the two richest states/ provinces to that in the two poorest): United States (1900–2000); Canada (1925–2000)

prior to the 1920s, on the other hand, has more to do with the filling up of the West, where labor was scarce and demand high. In both instances, these are straightforward cases of supply adjusting to demand.

Migration is not the only factor that explains the decline in regional income disparities.[6] Both the United States and Canada witnessed extraordinary economic growth during the twentieth century. Each economy became progressively more integrated as railways, highways, telephone lines, air traffic, and—more recently—high-speed Internet connections criss-crossed the nation. People, goods, information, and capital move far more freely today than a century ago. The American and Canadian experience can thus hardly be used as an argument against the virtues of economic integration. The western European experience since the Second World War, although for a shorter time period, points in the same direction. Income differences between the first member nations of the EU (formerly the European Economic Community)—the most ambitious economic integration project in modern times—have fallen sharply since the 1950s. Per capita income levels in Germany and in France, for example, are today pretty much the same. Regional income disparities *within* western European nations declined significantly between 1950 and 1980, the period of most rapid growth and integration, during which the continent's transportation infrastructures were not only rebuilt but also greatly expanded.[7]

In sum, it is difficult to argue—based on North American and western European experiences—that economic integration, labor mobility, and economic growth do not over time promote greater income equality between regions. The positive relationship between national economic growth and greater regional income equality is further illustrated by the sudden upsurge in inequality in both the U.S. and in Canada during the Great Depression of the 1930s, which then fell again just as abruptly following the rapid expansion of both economies with the beginning of the Second World War.[8]

A short caveat is in order. Regional income equality (or inequality) must not be confused with personal income equality. My comments on the equalizing virtues of economic integration and growth are limited to inter*regional* income disparities, which tell us nothing about inter*personal* income differences. The two types of inequality are not necessarily related. The United States is an admirably equal nation—considering its immense size—as measured by (per capita) income differences between regions; but the United States is also a notoriously unequal nation when measured by income differences between individuals.[9] I shall not pursue the subject any further. I raise it, mainly, as a reminder of the risks of drawing false inferences from data.

Returning to our two regions, let us do a fast forward to modern times. In the two centuries it took to complete the transition—demographic and economic—from an agricultural to an industrial society, the central region has grown impressively, the home now of great cities and the seat of most large national and international corporations. The peripheral region has also grown, but at a considerably slower rate; many of its young have—year in and year out—continued to migrate to the center. In the first decades after industrialization took off, the income gap between the two regions grew to alarming proportions, as the expanding factories in the center demanded ever more labor, driving up wages. The income gap was such at one point that whole cohorts of young left the farms of the periphery for the great industrial cities of the center. But the story has a happy ending. Over time, as society as a whole became progressively richer and the economy truly integrated, the income difference between the two regions eventually subsided, putting an end to the need for migration. Both regions now enjoy comparable standards of living.

WHY REGIONAL DISPARITIES DON'T DISAPPEAR

If the happy ending just described is the general rule, then there is nothing to be concerned about, and not much more to write about either. Over time, with sustained economic growth, coupled with properly functioning markets, regional income disparities will disappear or at least be reduced to manageable proportions. Although this statement may seem overly sanguine, it is not wide off the mark for the majority of today's industrialized nations. Regional *income* disparities continue to exist in industrialized nations—we shall shortly see why—but they are no longer a burning policy issue in most cases.

Jobs and public infrastructures, not personal income,[10] are more often the primary policy concern. For the mayor of a small town in northern Sweden or Saskatchewan faced with the closure of the town's only hospital, it is scant solace that regional income disparities are today fairly minor. What the mayor may have forgotten is that the community's current predicament is in part the outcome of past disparities in income and earnings. The small size of the community, its capacity to generate jobs and sustain infrastructures, is the outcome of decades of out-migration, which brings us back to the relation between (community) size and wealth.

Regional disparities in income (or product) per person will never totally disappear. Disparities endure in all industrialized nations, although at levels below those of the past. Regional income (or product) disparities have stabilized in most industrialized nations since the 1980s. However, more recently, disparities have begun to grow again in some nations,[11] which has given rise to much soul searching by members of the regional policy community, especially in the EU.[12] In Italy, per capita product in Lombardy—in which Milan is situated—is more than twice that for the south, a ratio that has hardly budged over the last twenty-five years. In Britain (recall chapter 1), regional disparities have remained equally stubborn over the last quarter century. Recent evidence suggests that wage inequalities have widened between London and the rest of Britain.[13] Why then should regional income disparities persist and even increase in some nations?

There are several reasons why disparities will never totally disappear even under the best of conditions. First, full wage equalization should only be expected for workers with similar qualifications in similar occupations or industries. Since different regions will have different industrial and occupational mixes, it is entirely normal that differences in *average* wage rates should exist between regions. Second, equalization applies to *real* incomes once cost of living differences have been considered. Obviously, nominal wages will be higher in New York, so are prices, especially for housing. Third—and most important—is the cost of migration. Moving between regions is not without cost for individuals or families, especially if the move is between distant or culturally different places. For an individual or family to move, the poten-

tial gain has to be sufficient to cover the cost. The costs are not only monetary: leaving friends, finding new ones; changing schools for the children;
and adapting to a new environment. The wage difference has to be fairly substantial for a person to pack up and leave for another region. And, the older
the individual, the greater the incentive needs to be. The reader can ask him-
or herself: "How much would I need to be offered to move to a town or city
located at the other end of the country?"

The fact that migration is not without monetary and psychological costs
means that some level of disparity is normal. In Canada, a very large nation,
most earnings differences—even between big and small places—fall within
the 20 to 25 percent range and have stabilized at that level over the last two
decades.[14] This is probably as good a reference point as any, suggesting that
most observed regional income disparities in industrialized nations are not
cause for concern.[15] The "normal" functioning of the market does, however,
not fully explain the persistent income gap between the north and south of
Italy or between the north and the south of England. Britain has, arguably,
western Europe's freest labor market. Neither the pull of London nor the
negative clusters that plague the Midlands and the north offer a sufficient
explanation. Other, more fundamental, economic forces are also at play.

THE RICH GET RICHER — CUMULATIVE CAUSATION

An alternative way of interpreting reality exists, which has historically been
associated with left-leaning economists and other thinkers unhappy with the
outcomes produced by free markets. Contrary to standard economic reasoning, free markets and economic integration, it is argued, increase inequality.
A half century ago, Gunnar Myrdal, a Swedish economist and Nobel Prize
winner, published *Economic Theory and Underdeveloped Regions*,[16] which
remains a classic. Myrdal's concern was as much with underdeveloped nations as with regions, but his basic line of reasoning, enriched by successive
authors, applies equally to both. The crux of Myrdal's argument is "cumulative causation." Elements of cumulative causation were already present in
my earlier arguments on the cumulative effects of infrastructure investments,
which over time reinforce the initial natural advantage of central regions.

The argument can be taken one step further. As the center, over time,
sucks in the best talents, builds up the best universities, and increases its
demographic weight within the nation, what is left of the periphery will over
time become more and more marginalized. At some point, the inequality in
resources, human and otherwise, will be such that the periphery will cease
to be an interesting location for industry. It will be too far from major mar-

kets, too poorly provided with advanced infrastructures (laboratories, airports, etc.), and with too few people to be a profitable location for anything
of worth. Once the periphery falls below some (population) threshold, its
continuing decline becomes inevitable and irreversible. Cumulative causation acts both ways: while an upward spiral stimulates growth, a downward
spiral spells decline. As the saying goes, nothing succeeds like success; but by
the same token, nothing fails like failure.

This rather pessimistic—but by no means totally unrealistic—view of the
cumulative consequences over time of the free movement of labor and capital
has, I have stated, been historically identified with the Left, distrustful of free
markets and globalization. However, this cumulative, self-reinforcing view of
the impact of migration on growth has entered mainstream economic thinking, due in large part to the writings of two American economists, Robert
Lucas (also a Nobel Prize winner) and Paul Romer,[17] the principal pioneers of
what is called *endogenous growth theory* or, sometimes, *new growth theory*.[18]
As in the case of Myrdal, their initial focus was on explaining development
differences between nations, but their arguments are perhaps even more con-
vincing when applied to regional economies. Lucas and Romer provide an
intellectually powerful explanation of why immigration, under certain conditions, will push productivity and wages up and not down.[19] Their argument
follows from an important insight: the law of diminishing returns does not
apply to human capital.

To explain how this works, I shall return to our two regions. Based on
simple supply and demand, the influx of labor into the center should push
wages down. However, simple observation tells us that this is not what is happening. New York, London, and Paris continue to draw in migrants from
around the world. Yet wages in those cities have not fallen compared to other
places. Our perspective starts to change once we consider not only the quantity but also the quality of labor and how workers interact to create value. Let
us suppose that demand for labor in the center is primarily for highly skilled
workers: electrical engineers, fashion designers, computer programmers,
financial analysts, etc. Imagine a rapidly growing software firm looking to hire
skilled electrical engineers. Will the arrival of a bright new engineer reduce
the productivity (and thus wage) of other engineers? It should in theory, if we
reason only in terms of supply and demand. But not if we remember how the
interaction of workers—the constant flow of ideas—affects productivity. We
have come back full circle to Alfred Marshall's quote of more than a century
ago on the benefits of agglomeration. Once this is understood, it no longer
automatically follows that the arrival of new workers will drive wages down.
It all depends on how new workers affect productivity and innovation. Their

impact might well be positive. Two clever programmers working together are more productive than each working separately. The same reasoning applies to almost any occupation that requires a modicum of skills and imagination. This idea is so simple and the conclusion so obvious that it is difficult to understand why it took so long to enter mainstream economic thinking.

Knowing this, let us continue our journey and see how this now plays out for the possible evolution of wage disparities between central and peripheral regions. The fact that migration involves costs has important consequences for *who* migrates. It is not generally the poorest who migrate. It takes at least a minimum of resources and ability to move to a distant city. Also, migrants are concentrated in the young-adult age group. Psychological cost of migration is lower for the young, more able to adapt to a new environment, and the period over which they will reap the benefits of their move longer than for an older person. After thirty-five, when a person is well-established, married, with a mortgage and all rest, migration becomes a much more difficult proposition. Persons with higher levels of education also have a higher propensity to migrate than those with less education. Migration, in a word, is "selective," to use the term favored by demographers. This means that those who leave are proportionally more educated, younger, and perhaps more dynamic— though this is difficult to measure—than the remaining population.

We are now ready to run the scenario again, following the initial spurt in demand for labor in the center, which in turn sparked the original wage disparity. Workers leave the peripheral region for the center. The supply-and-demand effects, which favor wage equalization, are operative. But we can now add in the cumulative causation effects, which act in the opposite direction. The cumulative impact over several years of selective migration into the center causes productivity to rise further, relative to peripheral regions. This in turn produces a new increase in the demand for labor in the center, pushing up wages again, and drawing in new migrants, setting off a another cycle of productivity increases, wages increases, and in-migration. This self-perpetuating cycle of in-migration and rising productivity can go on for a long time, judging by the experience of the world's great cities. If whole regions are the benchmark, then the process is even more open-ended. Should we expect California or the south of England to one day cease being regions of net in-migration?

At the other side of the scale, the continued outflow over time of educated, working-age migrants from the peripheral region leaves it not only with a population whose relative weight has shrunk, but also one that is less educated and with a higher dependency ratio than the rest of the nation.[20] As long as migration continues to be selective, especially with respect to education, migration will cause the human capital disparity between the two regions to widen. The loss for the peripheral region is compounded if education is locally funded. Its citizens, already poorer than the center, will be paying taxes to educate young people who, after graduation, will migrate to the center.[21] There is no necessary end in sight to this regional brain drain. At end of this continuing cycle of selective migration, it is entirely conceivable that cumulative causation succeeds in overwhelming the supply-and-demand effects. The predictable outcome is a regional wage disparity that remains stable or even widens over several decades.

Why Regional Disparities Are Higher in Some Nations

After this journey into economic theory, let us take a second look at real regional disparities, of which we had a foretaste in chapter 1 (recall table 1.1). Where does this tug-of-war between the forces of regional equality (standard supply-and-demand economics) and inequality (cumulative causation) leave us? The first predicts regional equalization over time while the second predicts the opposite. Both processes are continually at work. Which is more powerful at any moment in time will depend on several factors, one of which is a nation's level of development.

Regional disparities are, we saw, generally more acute in developing than in developed nations. In India, per capita product in the states of Maharashtra (which includes Mumbai) and Haryana (which neighbors Delhi) is five times that of Bihar, India's poorest state. In Mexico, the state of Nuevo León and the Federal District are, respectively, four and six times richer, by the same measure, than the state of Oaxaca. The champions of regional disparity are Brazil and China.[22] Per capita product in the state of São Paulo is six times that of Maranhao and fourteen times that of Ceara, two states located in Brazil's poor northeast. In China, Shanghai province is nine times richer than Gansu, by the same measure, and thirteen times richer than Guizhou, located respectively in the northwestern and southwestern parts of the nation.

The standard economics explanation remains entirely satisfactory. We should expect nations in the early stages of development to have higher regional disparities. The economic space of a poor nation is typically less integrated than that of a rich nation, precisely because it is less developed. Anyone who has traveled or attempted to transact business in a developing nation understands this. Transportation infrastructures are rudimentary and often poorly maintained. Financial markets are most often embryonic and business regulations erratic, all of which constitute obstacles not only to capital formation and investment but also to spatial mobility. The adjustment mechanisms predicted by standard economic theory cannot do their work, at least not in full. Trade, migration, and capital formation (and mobility) are all held back by what is still an incomplete economy.

Some forty years ago, the American economist Jeffery Williamson, in an article that has since become a classic,[23] suggested that the relationship between development and regional inequality takes the shape of a bell-shaped curve, with disparities rising during the first stages of economic growth, up to a limit, and then descending back down again as the nation becomes progressively richer. Taken as a broad-brush representation of reality, Williamson's curve is probably correct. It seems entirely reasonable that disparities should increase during the first stages of growth when the difficult transition from a rural to an urban society is in full swing. By the same token, we would expect disparities to increase more rapidly in poor nations that are growing most rapidly, which explains, at least in part, the widening of disparities in China and in India. In China, the process is compounded by the fact that migration was artificially held back for many years.

If Williamson and the standard economics explanation are exact, then we should expect regional disparities to eventually fall in India, China, and other developing nations whose economies are growing. The experience of the United States, Canada, Japan, and western Europe certainly leads to that conclusion. The recent history of South Korea provides additional cause for optimism. No nation has developed and urbanized more rapidly. Its story is truly amazing.[24] At the end of the Korean War (1953), South Korea was one of the world's poorest nations, with a GDP per capita comparable to that of Haiti. A generation and a half later, South Korea is, by any measure, a developed nation. South Korea completed the full transition from an overwhelmingly rural society (80 percent rural) to an overwhelmingly urban society (80 percent urban) within a mere forty years (1950–1990), a transition that took over a century in the United States and most other industrialized nations. Within one generation, South Korea's rural population fell by some 13 million, from 19 million in 1965 to 6 million thirty years later,[25] the sign of a remarkably mobile and adaptable population. Regional income disparities fell significantly over the same period and are now at levels comparable to that of Japan, among the lowest in the industrialized world.[26]

How confident can we be that South Korea's path will be followed by others? Only partly. Several factors contributed to South Korea's achievement, not always present in other nations. The first is the homogeneity of Korea's population. Korea is one of the most ethnically and culturally homogenous nations in the world. No real internal cultural barriers to movement exist, which means that the psychological costs of migration are less. Social cohesion and, by the same token, a collective capacity to adapt to change are easier to achieve in a land where customs, values, and patterns of behavior are much the same everywhere. China and especially India are, by comparison, much more diverse societies. Second, Korea is a fairly small and compact nation. Migration is never over very large distances. We should normally expect disparities to be greater in larger nations, although the U.S. and Canadian experience suggest that this need not necessarily be so. Also, Korea is a peninsula where no place is ever very far from the sea, although its mountainous terrain remains an obstacle to trade. There is no vast natural periphery.

In part because of South Korea's cultural homogeneity, compactness, and small size, development rapidly coalesced around the nation's largest city. Economic activity is highly concentrated in greater Seoul, which accounts for close to half of national GDP. Development outside of Seoul is largely concentrated along a northwest-southeast corridor linking Seoul with Pusan, the country's second largest city, at the southern tip of the Korean peninsula. Although economic activity in South Korea is highly concentrated, it is not limited to only one side of the country.[27] The lesson to be drawn from South Korea is that high disparities in the spatial distribution of economic activity do not *necessarily* spell high welfare disparities.[28] This outcome was possible precisely because South Korea is such a compact and homogenous nation, with an almost complete absence of internal barriers to migration, trade, and interaction, and a manifestly highly adaptable population. In this, South Korea is indeed an exception.

WHY REGIONAL DISPARITIES ARE LOWER IN INDIA THAN IN CHINA

Standard economics and Williamson's bell-shaped curve are of little use when searching for an explanation of differences between nations at similar stages of development. Nations at comparable levels of development should, in principle, exhibit comparable levels of regional disparity. There is, for example, no a priori reason why disparities should be so much higher in China than in India.[29] No fully satisfactory explanation is possible. However, recalling the lessons from Europe and North America, each nation's position on the world map and the location of their respective economies offer a possible explanation.

The economic center-periphery divide is more difficult to overcome where it is superimposed on a geographic divide between two geographic halves of a nation—east/west, north/south, etc.—as distinct from divides based essentially on urban-size and density differences. In the latter case, several centers will exist as magnets for migrants and investment. If the various centers are situated in different parts of the country, the distance to be overcome for potential migrants or investors will be less, both psychologically and geographically, than if they had to decamp to an entirely different part of the nation.[30] One would expect the transition from the land to the city to be easier to achieve if the rising industrial centers are not located too far away (as in South Korea).

The above is essentially a version of the small nation argument, adapted to big nations. A large nation with several competing centers is in effect reproducing the conditions of a small nation. Let us look again at China and India. The Indian subcontinent is basically a very large peninsula in which large stretches of the nation open up onto the sea with several large port cities well poised for international trade: Mumbai, Calcutta, and Chennai. Each side of the subcontinent opens up to dynamic trading partners. The west coast, with Mumbai, points towards Europe, while the east coast, with Calcutta and Chennai, points to Japan and the emerging economies of east Asia. The three cities, the three largest in India (save Delhi), are located in different parts of India, rather than being bunched together. Delhi, the second largest city (National Capital Territory, to be precise), is located in yet another part of India. Delhi had already been the capital of previous empires. Its historic importance has its roots in its strategic location between the Aravalli Hills to the southwest and the Yamuna River (on whose banks it sits), which enabled it to dominate the old trade routes from northwest India to the plains of the Ganges. Bangalore, India's fifth largest metropolitan area—with a population of about 6 million—and a growing high-tech center, is situated in yet another part of the nation. Located on a plateau, Bangalore has a milder climate than most other southern Indian cities, which recommended it to British colonial administrators and has continued to attract migrants from all parts of the nation.

In short, India's unique natural geography plus a few historical accidents have produced a surprisingly balanced economic geography with several competing centers located in very different parts of the nation. This is not unlike the U.S. Yet I do not wish to push the analogy too far. India's poorest states form a vast swath of territory in the north-central part of the nation, jammed, as it were, between the economic centers of Mumbai, Delhi, and Calcutta. This is not the kind of periphery we have encountered so far, usually situated on the geographic margins of nations (or continents) or in comparatively sparsely settled territories. It would be difficult to argue that Bihar, India's poorest state, suffers from a particularly peripheral location, situated in the densely populated Ganges lowlands between Delhi and Calcutta. This suggests that the reasons for the greater poverty of the north-central states, compared to the rest of India, must be found elsewhere. India is a very diverse nation with deep linguistic and cultural divisions. The north-central states largely coincide with the Hindi-speaking heartland, which is perhaps a coincidence.[31] If cultural and linguistic differences are a factor, then India's regional disparities are akin to national differences in development. This also suggests that the disparities between Indian states would be lower were it not for the presence of cultural and linguistic differences.[32] On the other hand, linguistic and cultural boundaries allow competing centers to flourish, as we saw in Europe and Canada.

China's geography is different. Located at the eastern end of the Eurasian continent, China looks to the sea in only one direction. China is, as it were, the replica of Europe, facing in the opposite direction. China, however, lacks the Mediterranean. As such, it is an even more extreme example of a nation (a quasi-continental nation) with one seafront and one (principal) direction for international trade.[33] It should thus not come as a surprise that development is highly concentrated, in this case along an arc following the east coast from, roughly, Beijing in the north to Hong Kong in the south. A comparison with Europe's Blue Banana is not unwarranted, with the major difference that the Rhine forms the spinal cord of Europe's economic heartland, while China's recent economic growth has largely clung to the coast, with inland extensions along the Yangtze and Yellow River waterway systems. The Chinese economy is being pulled in one direction, towards the sea, analogous to the pull which the north exerts on the Mexican economy. In both cases, the national economy is being pulled in the direction of its principal trading partner or partners. China is different in that there is no countervailing force comparable to that of Mexico City and Mexico's central plateau. China's three largest urban conurbations—Shanghai, Beijing-Tianjin, and Hong Kong–Guangzhou—are all on the east coast.

Inland development is by no means absent. Chongqing, located at the head of the Yangtze River system, is situated more than a thousand kilometers from the coast. However, the overall picture is that of a unidirectional, lopsided economic geography, in which one part of the nation is clearly favored over the rest. Coastal regions, precisely because they are gateways for trade— but also for ideas—have also generally been more open to change and foreign ways.[34] According to a recent Bank of Finland study, some 80 percent of foreign direct investment is concentrated in ten coastal provinces.[35] Those same provinces accounted for over 85 percent of China's exports in 2002.[36] In short, China's geography—not least its location on the world map—has tended to favor the coastal provinces and cities, whether it be via the pull of foreign trade, the flow of ideas, direct foreign investment, or institutional change. It is difficult not to make the connection between the unidirectional evolution of the Chinese economy and its very pronounced regional disparities.

Brazil, the other large developing nation historically plagued by high regional disparities, equally exhibits a unidirectional development pattern, in this case with a sharp south-north divide. São Paulo and Rio de Janeiro, the two largest cities, together with the richest states, form a solid wealthy block in the south. In a continental context, the more developed Brazilian south is part of South America's continental economic center on the Atlantic (the southern mirror of North America's megalopolis), which stretches roughly from Buenos Aires, Argentina, to Rio de Janeiro. In Brazil, the south-north divide is compounded by differences in climate and geology, which meant that the Brazilian northeast—much like the antebellum American South— developed a plantation economy founded on slavery, which inevitably left its mark, not only on the racial makeup of the population but also on local traditions and customs, not to mention an unfortunate legacy of soil erosion. When an economic divide becomes as entrenched as in Brazil, there is a strong possibility that it will also over time become a de facto cultural divide, further entrenching the difference. In such cases, it is difficult to separate causes from consequences.

The distinction I have made between center-periphery relationships with two players (one periphery, one center) and with several players also provides a useful template for comparing industrialized nations. Italy, which historically has among the most persistent regional disparities in western Europe, is almost a carbon copy of Brazil, in which the south-north coordinates are reversed. The chief difference is the presence of Rome in the middle, which somewhat softens the divide. Nonetheless, Italy's north-south divide manifestly cuts the nation into two economically and, some would also say, culturally distinct halves. Economic divides of this type (whether in Brazil or Italy) produce more intractable regional disparities than those founded on more diverse center-periphery patterns.

Only time will tell whether the high disparities currently observed in China will become equally entrenched. I will return to China in chapter 7. China is still in the first stages of the rural-urban transition—migration is in full swing—while Brazil and Italy have largely completed their transition (both are 80 percent urban). At the risk of oversimplification, one might say that China is an example of an incomplete transition, while Brazil and Italy are examples of stalled or failed transitions, with respect to the (expected) evolution of regional income disparities.

WHY THE KNOWLEDGE ECONOMY MIGHT CAUSE
REGIONAL DISPARITIES TO WIDEN

There is no evidence that regional disparities are universally widening in industrialized nations. The evidence for Japan and Canada, for example, points in the direction of lessening disparities.[37] But, here again, different national conditions will produce different results. The widening of regional income disparities in some nations, especially in Europe, calls for further explanation. It is at this point that cumulative causation comes fully into its own, for neither standard economics nor geography can provide a full explanation of why disparities should have widened in a number of industrialized nations.

The explanation, in a nutshell, is that the increasing returns argument carries more weight in knowledge-rich economies. The impact of increasing returns, in determining whether local wages will rise or fall, very much depends on the industrial composition of the economy. In economies where few industries rely on highly educated workers, we would not expect increasing returns to outweigh the standard supply-and-demand effects.[38] In economies based on brainpower, the opposite will often be true. We may reasonably assume that the number of industries subject to increasing returns has grown. In the knowledge economy, it is entirely plausible that the cumulative growth effects may in many instances overpower the more traditional supply-and-demand effects of in-migration. The more educated and skilled people a place attracts, the more productivity will rise. If brains are the primary rare resource that drives growth, the more a place can accumulate the better.

This view of the world in which brains (imagination, innovation) drive local economies has become somewhat of a mantra among urban growth gurus in recent years. Richard Florida, whom we already met in chapter 1, has built an entire growth strategy around it, in which he proposes his recipe for attracting what he calls the "creative class." Florida has been highly successful in marketing his message. Almost every town and region has its strategy for attracting young educated professionals. Every city today aspires to be a magnet for talent and brains, or however one to wishes to designate this lucky group. In the end, whether Richard Florida's recipe for attracting brains is effective is immaterial. What matters is that this game necessarily implies winners and losers. Migration, let us recall, is selective by its very nature. If one place attracts brains, another place necessarily loses them.

What then matters is where modern knowledge-intensive industries locate. If location is systematically skewed towards certain places, the probability of producing self-reinforcing wage disparities grows. We know that knowledge-intensive industries are normally drawn to the largest urban centers for two complementary reasons: production requires frequent face-to-face contacts, and transport costs of the product (images, music, text, advice, etc.) is almost zero thanks to IT. Combining the two—agglomeration pressures on the production side and low transport costs on the consumption side—it is easy to imagine a self-reinforcing cycle in which the most dynamic industries are subject to increasing returns and concentrate in the largest cities, drawing in skilled labor, further driving up productivity and wages, in turn drawing in yet more skilled labor. In this scenario, wages will continue to grow more rapidly in knowledge-rich locations as long as the cumulative growth effects of in-migration continue to outweigh other effects, which can be a long time. It is no coincidence, among major U.S. metropolitan areas, that the highest per capita personal incomes are found in the Greater Boston and San Francisco Bay areas, leaving aside the leafy Connecticut suburbs of New York.[39]

In short, the mechanics of regional growth are changing as brains replace brawn, putting an even greater premium on size and corresponding accumulations of human capital. Only a few places will attain the necessary size. However, the scenario described above need not automatically lead to entrenched regional disparities. It very much depends on how the centers that draw in brains are distributed over the national landscape. True *regional* disparities are more likely to unfold where such centers are concentrated in one part of the nation, which fairly describes the situation prevailing in Britain, where both the first and second rules of regional growth—size and location—are pulling in the same direction.

Why Are Regional Disparities More Difficult to Overcome in Some Nations?

The time has come to return to the four golden rules of regional growth. The interplay between the first two will in part determine why regional disparities are more persistent in some nations than in others. No two nations are exactly the same. In no two nations do size and location play out in the same manner. This is where we reconnect with real geographies. The economic center—the fountainhead in figure 2.5—is rarely located exactly in the middle of a perfectly round nation. Nor in reality does trade and direct investment solely converge on one national economic center. The direction of trade and investment flows with the outside world—with continental centers—will also influence the economic value of their respective locations.

In Britain and China, we saw, size and location both favored the same parts of the nation, in contrast to India where the forces of location—driven by trade—and size pulled the economy in several directions. We can now reformulate these lessons to make a more general statement. Region disparities in wealth will be more acute and more persistent where the forces of size and of location overlap to favor the same part of the nation. The extreme case—recalling figure 2.5—is one in which the fountainhead sits at, say, the westernmost edge of the circle (nation) and the nation's chief trading and investment partner is situated to the west of the nation. The eastern half of the circle (nation) now constitutes a vast periphery beyond the reach of the fountain's sprays. This extreme scenario, although hypothetical, is not totally imaginary.

In the following paragraphs, I have grouped nations into three classes depending on how the two first laws of regional growth interact, going from those to where we would expect disparities to be the most stubborn to those where we would expect regional disparities to be less of a concern. This way of looking at national economic geographies will allow us, among other things, to understand why the U.S. and Britain are almost two polar opposites and why regional development is not, and likely never will be, a major national policy issue in the U.S., but is in Britain and likely will remain so.

UNIDIRECTIONAL GROWTH

In nations characterized by what I call unidirectional growth, both laws of regional growth pull economic activity in the same general direction. These nations have one clear favored area of economic growth and a clearly identifiable less favored periphery. Aside from Britain, Ireland and Slovakia are examples in Europe.

Ireland is indisputably the greatest success story of the European Union, proof that the reduction of trade barriers does indeed—certainly in the great majority of cases—promote economic growth. The Republic of Ireland, traditionally one of western Europe's poorest nations, has not only caught up with the rest of the continent, but has surpassed it. The republic today has one of the highest per capita incomes in western Europe. This is no mean achievement. All of Ireland has benefited from the expansion of the national economy in the last decades, but some areas have benefited more than others. Growth has tended to concentrate in one part of the country, in Dublin and the eastern half of the nation. The location of Dublin on the east coast— facing the European heartland—reinforces the natural eastward pull of the Irish economy. The result has been a widening gap between the dynamic east, centered on Dublin (and to a lesser extent on Cork and Waterford), and the less dynamic counties on the west coast such as Mayo, Sligo, and Clare. Ireland now has a regional problem, so to speak.[40] Dublin has become one of the most expensive cities in Europe, while the western half of the republic remains sparsely settled with no city even remotely comparable to Dublin. Limerick and Galway are less than one-tenth of Dublin's size.

The Slovak case on the other side of the EU is almost the mirror image of Ireland; we need only reverse east and west. Slovakia's economy is being pulled slowly westward as it integrates into Europe. However, Slovakia is at a much earlier stage of development. We can only hope that Slovakia meets with same economic success as Ireland. If Slovakia's economy grows rapidly in the coming decades, we can predict with a fair degree of certainty that growth will be highly concentrated in and around Bratislava, the nation's capital and largest city, in the extreme western end of the nation (only 50 kilometers from Vienna). We may similarly predict a widening gap between the economic fortunes of the favored western part of the nation and the less favored eastern periphery. Here is a regional problem in the making.[41] The principal change that might redress the economic fortunes of eastern Slovakia would be a dynamic Ukrainian—and also Russian—economy, making the east a dynamic trade destination, comparable to western destinations. This does not seem terribly likely at the time of writing. Slovakia's integration into Europe will most probably amplify regional differences—certainly during the first decades—until such time when a new equilibrium is attained.

A major difference exists, however, between Ireland's recent regional evolution and Slovakia's probable future evolution. Ireland's rapid economic expansion occurred during a period when birth rates were still relatively high, meaning rapid population growth and a young population. Ireland is somewhat of an exception in Europe in this respect.[42] Slovakia, although poorer, has completed its demographic transition much earlier, meaning slow—indeed zero—national population growth. The shift east of Ireland's economy in and around Dublin did not—with some exceptions—translate into massive population losses in the western parts of the republic, only slower growth; Limerick and Galway have continued to grow, although less so than Dublin. In the Irish case, it would be an exaggeration to speak of a spiral of regional decline fueled by falling populations in the periphery, although this might conceivably occur in the future. Ireland may well have the good fortune of being sparred the predicament of an intractable national west-east divide. The decentralization of industry driven by high costs in Dublin is taking off at a moment in time when mid-sized cities in the west still have relatively young populations. Neither Galway nor Limerick are all that far (about 200 kilometers from Dublin), meaning that they stand a reasonable chance of capturing a larger share of Ireland's future growth.

Viewed from afar, such optimism seems less warranted for Slovakia's east-ern periphery.[43] Slovakia is—hopefully—entering a period of rapid economic expansion at a moment in time when its population has all but ceased to grow. Since growth is unidirectional, this inevitably means population decline for losing regions in the east as Slovakia's economy shifts west. Under conditions of zero population growth, one region's gain is another's loss. In Slovakia—as well as Hungary and Poland—the potential for population decline in less favored regions is compounded by the attraction of rich EU regions in neigh-boring Austria and Germany. I would venture that the number of Slovak, Polish, and Hungarian restaurants in Vienna, Munich, and Berlin has grown exponentially in recent times.

This brief incursion, admittedly somewhat conjectural, into the good for-tunes—or not—of Ireland and of Slovakia provides a useful lesson on the dangers of sweeping generalizations on the regional impacts of globalization. There are no universal outcomes. The outcomes will be different, as we saw in the Mexico-Europe comparison, not only because nations are at different stages of development but also because of differences in the internal geog-raphy of regional growth. The probability that globalization—economic integration—will accentuate regional differences is higher for unidirectional nations.

I also put Canada in this class, which may surprise the reader. After all, Canada's three largest urban centers are situated in very different parts of the nation: Vancouver in the west, Toronto in the middle, and Montreal further east. Growth is occurring both in the traditional Ontario-Quebec industrial heartland and in the west. Yet Canada is a good example of the overlap of the first and the second laws of regional growth. The three major urban cen-ters, although separate from each, are all located at a short distance from the U.S., the dominant trading partner. Both the forces of urban concentration and of trade are pulling in the same direction, towards the south. The basic difference with the simpler Slovak case is that the favored part of the nation does not come in the shape of one contiguous zone, but rather is the sum of a limited number of favored regions. The periphery is easy to identify: those parts of Canada farthest from major U.S. markets and lacking a major urban center. The principal exception is Alberta, a growing region neither because of location or of urban size, but because it has a particularly rich resource endowment—oil—the third law of regional growth.

Back to Britain. The UK does not totally fit the description of a unidirec-tional nation. The first and second laws of regional growth are indeed pulling the economy in the same direction: towards the south. However, it is an exag-geration to say that the first law *exclusively* pulls activity towards the south.

Manchester, Leeds, Liverpool, and Newcastle have not been wiped off the map, not to mention Glasgow and Edinburgh even farther north. These are all great cities by European standards.[44] Their economic woes are not solely or even primarily the result of poor location but of their negative industrial legacy as we saw in chapter 1. *Location* cannot be changed. Manchester cannot be moved south. But the effects of negative clusters should wear off at some point in time. After so many decades of relative decline, there is reason to hope that the worst is over, that size will again start favoring the growth of urban-centered regions in the north of England. Growth has been healthy in recent years in Yorkshire in and around Leeds and York. But this is proof, yet again, that location matters, for Yorkshire lies on the east coast of England, facing Europe.

A BRIEF JOURNEY TO AFRICA AND BEYOND

The vulnerability of unidirectional nations is bad news for most west African nations. All those lying along the Atlantic coast between Morocco and Cameroon find themselves with roughly similar economic geographics.[45] Their largest and most dynamic urban centers are located either directly on the coast or near it—in general, in the nation's southern tier—in contrast to the less urbanized or less developed interior. Nigeria is the exception with several large urban centers in the north: Kano, with about 3.7 million inhabitants, is the largest, but still far behind Lagos in the south, with about 10 million inhabitants.[46] In all these nations, the largest city is also the chief port and gateway to the rest of the world. Both trade and the forces of urban concentration pull economic activity—such as it is in these poor nations—in the same direction, towards the coast. The integration of these nations into the world economy—globalization—will almost certainly accentuate the divide between the favored coastal and coastal-oriented parts of the nation and the less favored areas of the interior.

In west Africa, increasing regional differentiation is more than simply an economic problem. In many cases, the growing economic divide is superimposed on an ethnic or religious divide. With the exception of almost totally Islamized countries such as Senegal, the divide between the coast and the interior also corresponds, roughly, to the divide between Christianized and Animist parts of the nation and those—generally farther inland—that are Islamized. This, as any student of Africa knows, does not facilitate political stability. Nigeria fought a bloody civil war not so long ago, compounded in this case by the fact that the southeastern region, which attempted to secede, was not only largely populated by one ethnic group but also had major oil reserves. The Ivory Coast is—at the time of writing—in the grip of a quasi civil war, which more or less divides the nation between the more European-ized and Christianized south, nearer the coast, and the rest of the nation fur-ther north. The nations of Africa have enough problems as it is, not the least of which is a legacy of totally absurd boundaries (in most cases) that do not follow cultural or ethnic lines. The interplay of economics and geography has dealt them an additional bad hand, certainly in west Africa. The laws of eco-nomic geography introduce an added divisive factor in nations already diffi-cult to govern. If my analysis is correct—and I hope it is not—then the uni-directional nature of economic development in many African nations signals an intensification of internal divisions in the future.

Nations characterized by unidirectional growth have—I have suggested—the greatest potential for creating national divides, where large parts of the nation feel left out. This bodes ill for other developing nations as well. Most North African nations would qualify as unidirectional, as do several South American nations besides Brazil, notably Peru and Argentina. In Asia, Thai-land and Turkey equally share some of the traits of unidirectional growth. In all cases, the forces of urban concentration are pulling development in the same direction as the forces of trade and globalization, the perfect recipe for creating aggrieved regions. One of the most extreme cases is Mozambique, already one of Africa's poorest nations. Mozambique's capital and largest city, Maputo, sits on the border with South Africa, Africa's economic powerhouse, and by far its chief trading partner and source of investment. The port of Maputo is a natural outlet to the sea for the Witwatersrand urban conurba-tion—Johannesburg and Pretoria—and as such an almost extra-territorial extension of the South African economy. The result is an economic geog-raphy in which almost all development, such as there is, is concentrated in the southern tip of the nation, around Maputo, leaving the rest of the nation to wonder if the fruits of development will ever reach it.[47]

BIDIRECTIONAL GROWTH

In nations characterized by what I call bidirectional growth, the forces of economic integration—globalization, trade—are pulling in a different direc-tion from the forces of agglomeration. Such nations are the theater of a tug-of-war between the pull of the historical national economic center—con-verging in general on the national capital or largest city—and the pull of the nation's chief trading partners. Examples in Europe are Spain, Hungary, Swe-den, Poland, Austria, and Italy. Mexico is a prime example in the developing world. The tug of war between two magnets is of some consequence for the geography of wealth, for it means that the club of potentially favored places covers a wider area than it would if there were one dominant magnet.

Mexico illustrates this point very well. Were it not for the pull of the U.S. market, most of northern Mexico would have remained peripheral and undoubtedly much poorer. Everything would have been centered on Mexico City and the Central Plateau. The existence of two poles tugging at the Mexican economy improves the growth potential of places—otherwise remote— situated *between* the two. The cities of Torreón and Saltillo, to take two examples, would probably be impoverished backwaters were it not for their location on trade corridors between the Mexican heartland and the United States. Both today are mid-sized industrial cities. This of course, as we saw, is of little solace to places situated beyond the Central Plateau, on the other— southern—side of Mexico. This brings home a second characteristic of bidirectional nations. The location of the national economic center—generally the capital—will largely determine the size of the periphery. In Mexico, since Mexico City is located pretty much in the middle of the nation, this leaves a large part of the nation—the south—lying outside the potential corridors of trade and interaction with the United Sates.

In a nutshell, for any nation, the shorter the distance between the national economic center and the trade partner border, the greater the area that will find itself left out. A comparison of Italy and Austria illustrate this point. Rome lies in the middle of the Italian boot, giving rise to an almost continuous band of high income areas between it and Italy's northern boundary. As in Mexico, this leaves a considerable part of the nation—the south—lying outside the corridors of trade. This is the less favored part of Italy. Now look at Austria. Vienna lies at almost the extreme eastern end of the republic, about as far as one could wish from Austria's western boundaries. Austria's economy has been drifting westward over the last fifty years, ever closer to the European economic heartland, a shift compounded by the virtual cessation of trade with the east while the latter was under communist rule. Were it not for Vienna, Austria's eastern provinces would undoubtedly have fallen into a period of almost irreversible stagnation. Imagine if Innsbruck in the west—not Vienna—were the national capital and largest city; such a scenario would have produced a case of extreme unidirectional growth, leaving most of the nation outside the corridors of trade. Fortunately for Austria, this is not the case. Because Vienna is located at the *other side* of the nation (far from its principal trade partners) very little of Austria can be said to be truly peripheral. Austria's good fortune—from a regional development perspective—will undoubtedly continue into the future. The reestablishment of trade links with the east—with what was once Vienna's natural trading area—is reinvigorating the Viennese economy and that of surrounding places. Most of Austria today finds itself between two powerful mag-nates, a true case of bidirectional development.[48]

In Poland, the location of Warsaw in the eastern party of the country equally serves to reduce the potential area of the periphery: the eastern prov-inces bordering on former Soviet lands. The less favored regions to the east and northeast of Warsaw still cover an important swath of territory. However, we may reasonably predict that the majority of Polish regions—that is, those located *between* Warsaw and the German border on corridors of trade with the west—are well poised for future growth.[49] The city of Poznan seems par-ticularly well positioned, located about halfway between Warsaw and Berlin on the principal road and rail corridor linking the two.

Viewed through the same template, there is good reason to be optimistic about the future evolution of Germany's regional economies. Berlin—Ger-many's reborn capital—is located in the extreme eastern part of the nation. As Berlin reclaims its role as the nation's largest city, it should increasingly become a magnet for economic activity, with positive effects for surround-ing places. At the time of writing—2008—the negative legacy of the former GDR[50] still had a profound dampening effect on the economic performance of East German *Länder*. This is not surprising, a mere two decades after the collapse of the GDR. I believe that the effects of that legacy—some forty years of communist rule—will eventually wear off. When that happens, Germany will find itself with a remarkably balanced economy, with few real peripher-ies. The area north of Berlin—basically, the *Land* of Mecklenburg—would be the closest thing to a truly less favored region. But this is a small corner of Germany. With many strong economic centers dispersed across the nation—Hamburg, the Rhine-Ruhr conurbation, Munich, Frankfurt, Berlin—Ger-many should in the end come to resemble what I call a model of multidirec-tional development, to which I now turn.

MULTIDIRECTIONAL GROWTH

In nations falling in this group, development is being pulled in several direc-tions at once. An important factor is often the absence of *one* dominant trad-ing partner, pulling commerce in only one direction. No one side of the nation is the side best poised for trade. Prime examples are India, discussed earlier, and South Africa.

South Africa bears some resemblance to India in that it is a quasi-peninsula with a coastline that opens up to several trading partners. South Africa's second and third largest cities, Cape Town and Durban, are ports located on almost opposite ends of the nation. Cape Town, at the tip of Africa at the meeting of the Indian and Atlantic oceans—hence its name—has historically looked to Europe, while Durban on the Indian Ocean looks more to Asia. Unlike China—where development is almost exclusively drawn to the coast—South Africa's principal economic center is located squarely inland, many hundreds of kilometers from the sea. The reason the great urban conurbation of what is now Gauteng Province—Greater Johannesburg—sprung up on the Veldt, South Africa's vast grassland plateau, is related to one of the many "accidents" that keep popping up in this book. In this case, the "accident" was gold. Were it not for the discovery of gold at the end of the nineteenth century, Johannesburg would most probably not have passed the stage of a small rural town.[51] The Boer War (1899–1902) might not have happened either, and southern Africa's history might have evolved differently—for better or for worse, no one can say. But gold was discovered and Johannesburg, together with nearby Pretoria (the national capital), emerged as the economic and political heart of the nation. This has given South Africa an economic geography characterized by three economic magnets—Gauteng, the Western Cape (Cape Town), and Durban, each pulling in a different direction. This does not mean that South Africa does not have less favored peripheries. The dry, sparsely populated northwest, as well as the former intentionally neglected Bantustans such as Transkei (Eastern Cape) and KwaZulu remain problem areas.[52] However, the multidirectional nature of South Africa's development has meant that its peripheries are more circumscribed and hopefully less entrenched than they otherwise might have been. On the other hand, the legacy of apartheid has left an imprint on South Africa's economic geography that will not be easy to erase.

Why the United States Is Different

The most eloquent example of multidirectional growth is the United States. The U.S. is special not only because of its bicoastal geography and immense inhabitable space and internal market, but also because of the absence of a dominant direction of international trade. The U.S.'s chief trading partner is Canada (to the north), now closely followed by Mexico (to the south), while the east Asian tigers draw trade to the west and Europe to the east.[53] Each destination accounts for only a relatively small share of American GDP. The outcome is a nation with no real entrenched peripheries. The U.S. has close to fifty metropolitan areas with populations over 1 million. The most striking feature of regional growth in the U.S. is the variety of reasons for which different regions—located in very different parts of the nation—are growing and will undoubtedly continue to grow.

One of the reasons is the distance between the largest urban centers and trading partners, giving rise to corridors that cross almost the entire nation, in turn creating numerous *in-between* places. This is nowhere more evident than in the regional evolution of the American population.[54] Between Texas and Illinois—in essence, between Monterrey (Mexico) and Chicago—growth is concentrating along a corridor that roughly follows highway I-35 and crosses the cities of San Antonio, Austin (of high-tech fame), Wichita (aerospace), and Kansas City. The relatively low-wage area of northeast Arkansas (the Ozarks) and neighboring Little Rock, also growing rapidly, are within easy reach of this corridor. Its breadth is in part a result of the distance separating the industrial Midwest—centered on Chicago—from the emerging industrial centers of Mexico.

Another growth corridor is the southern projection of the U.S. coastal megalopolis. Here also, the line of expansion generally follows the interstate highway system, connecting urban centers. I can think of no better illustration of the continuing weight of the forces of agglomeration than the emergence of this southern extension of the coastal megalopolis. Its emergence is a direct product of the forces of urban concentration that initially fueled the creation of the coastal megalopolis. We know that size—above a certain threshold—creates counter pressures that drive low- and mid-tech firms to search out lower cost locations. The South—specifically, this stretch of the South—was well poised to capture the fruits of dispersal: cities of different sizes, relatively low wages, the absence (in general) of negative clusters, good transportation links, and water. The apparel industry, once almost totally concentrated in the New York area, has moved most of its production facilities to the South (fashion design and marketing have remained in New York). The textile industry, historically rooted in New England, is now largely concentrated in the Carolinas and neighboring states. Much light industry, such as electronics mainly, but also furniture, has since followed.

The crowding out of industry from the coastal megalopolis overflows into several parts of eastern Pennsylvania and in northern New England (Maine, New Hampshire, and Vermont). Indeed, the entire coastal stretch from Maine to Georgia, which shifts slightly inland in the South, is an elongated urban corridor in the making, interspersed here and there by rural areas. Perhaps, at some future date, economic geographers will refer to a single 1,500-kilometer megalopolis stretching from Boston to Atlanta,[55] encompassing not only the great urban centers of the Northeast, but also North Carolina's Research Triangle and Charlotte, as well as parts of Virginia and Tennessee. The essential point is that crowding out, explained earlier, which has allowed growth to disperse from its initial center, occurred because places farther out *had* the attributes needed to attract industries in search of lower costs. This is different from Britain where the Intrusive Rentier Syndrome continues to haunt many urban centers north of London.

The dispersal of manufacturing from the great industrial cities of the Midwest has also spread over a wide area. We met Interstate Highways 75 and 65 in chapter 1, which mark out the area of dispersal of the automobile from Detroit. The chief beneficiaries are, again, small and mid-sized cities—recall Greensburg. Here again the presence of a well-connected network of small and mid-sized cities to which manufacturing industries *could* move was a prerequisite. Staying in the Midwest, it is no accident that the most rapidly growing large cities (Chicago aside) are those that do *not* have a negative legacy of heavy industry: Minneapolis–St. Paul, Indianapolis, Grand Rapids, Columbus, and Kansas City. The Minneapolis-Chicago corridor is on the whole growing more rapidly than the old Chicago-Cleveland-Pittsburgh corridor. That could change as the old Rust Belt cities of the Midwest progressively shed their negative industrial legacies.

I will only briefly mention a last (but not least) attribute that makes the U.S. different, since it will feature prominently in chapter 6: the abundance of places that offer the pleasures of surf, sea, sun, or mountains. The difference is not so much in the fact that the U.S. has sun and beaches—so do Spain and Italy, for example—but in their location relative to the economic centers of the nation. The American Sun Belt, stretching from Florida to California, lies at almost the polar opposite side of the nation from the historical centers of industrialization in the Northeast and Midwest, thus pulling growth in yet another direction, facilitated in the twentieth century by technological progress (air-conditioning, the eradication of tropical diseases, etc.). Miami barely existed in 1900; Los Angeles, Houston, and Dallas–Fort Worth have all seen their populations grow a thousandfold or more since. This, again, is different from Britain, where climate is pulling in the same general direction as size and location.

LESSONS FROM THE U.S.-UK COMPARISON

The contrasting economic geographies of Britain and the United States send an important message: it is not because a law of economic geography is valid that we should expect it to automatically produce the same results everywhere. Here we have an excellent example of the constant balancing act between general rules and particular circumstances: how the workings of the same fundamental forces in the end produce different results. In both nations, economic growth over time has—as would be expected—meant urbanization, the emergence of great urban conurbations and the concentration of activity in particular regions. The laws of urban concentration and of location are operative in both nations. But the resulting economic landscape is very different. In Britain, the forces of agglomeration and of economic integration (into Europe) act together to pull economic activity towards the same part of England, compounded by London's continued place as a global financial center, in turn further compounded by the negative industrial legacy of the north and its even colder climate. The outcome has been a sharp rift between the north and the south of England. One would thus expect British politicians and academics to be concerned with regional policy, as indeed they are, and perhaps to take a more pessimistic view of the regional consequences of globalization.

Most American academics and commentators would probably take a quite different perspective, precisely because America's economic geography has turned out differently, and not because the laws of economic geography do not apply in the United States. The outcome has been a surprisingly balanced geography of economic growth. The United States truly has multiple centers pulling growth in different directions, often for quite different reasons. Although pockets of poverty persist—notably in Appalachia and in the Deep South—and population decline in much of the dry North American interior is probably irreversible (more on this in chapter 6), no overriding regional issue, analogous to that in England, has emerged in the United States. Issues of regional development—often hotly debated in the UK and in Europe—are surprisingly absent from the American academic and political scene.

The greatest achievement of the U.S.—from a regional-equality perspective—is without a doubt the economic resurgence of the South, cursed in the past not only by the legacy of slavery and by cultural isolation, but also by its distance from the main corridors of industry and trade. That resurgence, we saw, is in large part the outcome of the dual mobility of labor (which flew north) and of capital (which flew south in search of lower-cost locations). But the peculiarities of the American political system also played a role, as we shall see shortly, yet another example of how particular circumstances keep affecting outcomes.

THE STRATEGIC VALUE OF PERIPHERIES AND THE RESURGENT SOUTH

The bureaucracy aside, the location of defense facilities is essentially determined by strategic considerations and by politics. My own city, Montreal, is a case in point. Montreal is the center of Canada's aerospace industry. Why

Montreal? Nothing initially predisposed it to become a center for designing and constructing airplanes in the 1940s. No great inventors in the field were born there. No great industrial pioneer in the industry—on the model of Henry Ford in Detroit for the auto industry—stemmed from there. Montreal had no particular labor force advantage. The reason Montreal developed an aeronautics industry is war, the Second World War to be exact. Canada entered the war in 1939 together with Britain, which needed a location for assembling warplanes that was out of reach of German aviation and submarines (even Halifax was somewhat risky on that count), but also close enough so that the warplanes could be delivered to Britain without too many stopovers (Toronto was too far on that count). Thus was born the aviation industry in Montreal. Many of the earliest firms were British-owned. Montreal had the additional advantage—certainly over Halifax—of proximity to the U.S., lowering assembly costs for warplanes with American content. Most airplane construction in Montreal today is for peaceful purposes, but the origins of the industry lie in war and strategic considerations.

The location of defense facilities (military bases, military schools, missile sites, defense research laboratories, etc.) is also guided by politics. This is nowhere truer than in the United States. It is sometimes half jokingly said that America's regional development policy is its defense program. Because of the way the U.S. political system works—in which the smallest states carry the same weight in the Senate (two senators) as large states—defense spending is more geographically balanced than it would otherwise be. A second feature of the U.S. system tends to more richly reward those states or congressional districts that systematically vote for the same party—that is, for the same senators or congressmen—since committee chairmanships are allotted on the basis of seniority. The chairman of a Senate or House committee is a person of some influence. The most sought-after chairmanships are those that concern appropriations and spending. Military expenditures are by far the most important items of direct on-the-ground spending in the U.S. federal budget that are not territorially preordained.

In the past, these two features of the U.S. political system have tended to favor smaller states and especially the states of the Old South. Here, we meet again the after-effects of slavery or, to be more precise, of the American Civil War (1861–1865). Not only in Europe does history keep popping back up, sometimes in the oddest places. The victorious North in the war was led by a Republican President (Abraham Lincoln). After the war, the defeated South[56] long harbored a grudge against the Republican Party. As a result the former Confederate States repeatedly elected Democratic senators and congressmen—the so-called "Solid South"—for more than a century, well into

the 1960s. Thus, southern representatives in both houses tended to monopo-
lize the most lucrative chairmanships. The South, in a significant way, lost
the war but won the peace. The outcome is that the South was well-served
by federal spending, and no more so than in the area of national defense,
which in large part explains the important presence of military bases and
other defense establishments across the South.

Purely strategic considerations have played less of a role in the location of
defense installations in the U.S. than in most nations, due to its continental
character, protected by two oceans—although less so today—and with two
non-threatening nations on its borders. It would be difficult to argue that
Canada and Mexico pose a military threat to the United States. Thus, borders
have played only a minor role in the location of military installations. However, strategic considerations are not totally absent. The growth in the twentieth century of Denver and nearby Colorado Springs cannot be understood
without reference to their strategic location in the middle of the continent at
the foothills of the Rocky Mountains. The area is home to NORAD (North
American Aerospace Defense Command), the U.S. Air Force Academy, the
U.S. Air Force Space Command, missile defense and satellite control installations, as well as several defense-related research establishments.

In Europe, where neighbors had the unhealthy habit of invading each
other well into the twentieth century, strategic considerations dominated
until very recently. The aerospace industry is, again, a case in point. It is no
accident that the cities of Bordeaux and Toulouse in southwestern France—
the home of Airbus—are major aerospace centers. Historically, the military
threat came from the northeast, first from Germany and then from the Soviet
Union. Bordeaux and Toulouse are about as far as one can imagine in continental Europe from a hypothetical western front, which fortunately never
came to be, leaving aside the Iberian peninsula, which was out of the picture
for technological and political reasons.[57]

Strategic advantages, it is useful to recall, depend on politics, and can thus
also be lost if the political climate changes. Plattsburgh in northern New York
State on the Canadian border, which we met earlier, was home to a U.S. Air
Force base until recently, a logical location for intercepting incoming enemy
(Soviet) projectiles or aircraft from the north. With the end of the cold war,
the base closed, and Plattsburg's population declined sharply during the
1990s, but has stabilized since. The defense industry is perhaps the prime example of an industry for which being peripheral can be an advantage, where,
in short, the first two rules of regional growth do not apply, a useful reminder
that every rule has its exceptions. But, like all advantages, it can be won
and lost.

WHY REGIONAL DISPARITIES ARE SO ACUTE IN LITTLE BELGIUM

Politics can overturn geography in other ways. Belgium's unusually high differences in wealth between places have as much if not more to do with internal politics than with geography.[58]

In terms of wealth (GDP per person), Belgium is essentially cut in half along an east-west line, with the south—Wallonia—systematically poorer than the rest of Belgium. In addition, the Brussels region in the center of Belgium has one of the highest per capita GDPs in Europe, higher even than Greater London or Paris. In short, within this very small nation we find regional wealth differences among the highest in the industrialized world.[59] The negative industrial legacy of Wallonia is not sufficient to explain this curious outcome. For this, we need to consider other factors: the presence of a language boundary separating Dutch-speaking Flanders from French-speaking Wallonia, public policies that have constrained the growth of Brussels, and Brussels' role as the capital of the EU. None of these taken alone would have been sufficient to produce Belgium's peculiar economic geography; it took the simultaneous interplay of the three.

Belgium is a very small country by any measure, barely the size of Vermont. We saw that its southern Walloon provinces suffer from a severe case of the Intrusive Rentier Syndrome. At the same time, the northern Flemish provinces have seen their economies thrive. Per capita GDP in the province of Antwerp is almost twice that in the less fortunate province of Hainault. Were we in the U.S. or Canada, many workers and their families in Hainault would have left for Antwerp. This has not happened. The city of Mons in Hainault is less than a two-hour drive from Antwerp. But it might as well be on another planet. Belgium is divided by what is arguably the most watertight language boundary in the world, certainly within one nation. South of a line that separates the country along an east-west axis, *everything* must be in French; above that line, *everything* must be in Dutch—signs, publicity, schools, public services, etc. Perhaps the most symbolic measure was the expulsion in the early 1970s of the centuries-old French-speaking (originally Latin) Catholic University of Louvain from Flanders to Wallonia. The French-speaking faculties were transferred to a new location just south of the language boundary, appropriately baptized *Louvain-la-Neuve* (literally, New Louvain). In a word, the separation between the two halves of the nation is total.

Why this seemingly inflexible application of linguistic separation? The story is complex, and an unbiased telling of it is probably impossible. In a nutshell, the Dutch-speaking Flemings have developed an almost obsessive fear of assimilation, of the Dutch language being overwhelmed by French. History gives some support to those fears. Until not that long ago—until roughly the late nineteenth century—the sole administrative language of the Belgian state was French. The language of the business, cultural, and political elites in Flanders was French. These assimilated Flemings—pejoratively called *Franskiljons*—were an object of particular contempt by Flemish nationalists. Repaying the compliment, the French-speaking elites considered the Dutch spoken by the Flemings a vulgar rural dialect far from the *real* Dutch spoken in the Netherlands and thus not worthy of being learned. Linguistic grievances and animosities run deep in Belgium.

Historical grievances have a nasty habit of lingering on long after the original causes of the grievance have disappeared. Looking at Belgium today, an outside observer might wonder why language is *still* an issue. The Flemings appear to have won on all counts: Dutch has not only been totally rehabilitated, but French has been literally banished from the land of Flanders. On top of that, fate has dictated that French-speaking Wallonia—once the nation's industrial powerhouse—would slide into decline while Flanders would prosper. Demography has also favored the Flemings, who are now the majority in Belgium and dominate national politics. The tables have been turned. The Flemings, who were once a linguistic and economic minority, are now the majority. To add insult to injury—for French-speakers—the French language no longer has the drawing power it once had. Young Flemings today prefer to learn English as their second language.

Yet the language issue remains. Seen through Flemish (nationalist) eyes, the fight against the encroachment of French is not over, which brings me to Brussels. Brussels—officially bilingual although essentially French—sits in the middle of Flanders, surrounded by Dutch-speaking communes (municipalities). Allowing Brussels to expand is anathema to Flemish nationalists, for it would mean ceding a piece of historically Flemish territory to French-speakers. That is the issue. For Flemish nationalists, Brussels epitomizes everything that went wrong in the past. Brussels was once a Flemish city; many of its citizens are assimilated Flemings.[60] For nationalist Flemings, Brussels is—to put it brutally—a machine for assimilating Flemings. Therefore, Brussels must be contained.

The result has been a complex set of provisions to contain the suburban growth of Brussels into the surrounding Flemish countryside. A young French-speaking couple choosing to move to the outer suburbs—officially in Flanders—forfeits its rights to French-language services and French-language schooling for their children. The situation is in reality somewhat more complex, with constant political battles over the status of French in the officially Flemish outer suburbs of Brussels. These linguistic skirmishes act as a highly efficient brake on suburban expansion. Brussels' exceptionally high wage and housing costs are in part the outcome of the constraints placed on its growth, compounded by the growing demand for housing generated by EU personnel. The exceptionally low product per capita in Wallonia is primarily the legacy of negative clusters, compounded by the constrained space in which labor can move.[61] Finally, the Walloon-Flemish split has made it difficult to develop national policies focused on the depressed regions of Wallonia.[62] The Belgian story is the mirror opposite of the U.S. story on at least one point: where artificial constraints exist on the movement of people, differences in wealth between places will be more acute and more persistent. On the other hand, such constraints can act as a barrier to out-migration, thus stemming population decline. Few things in local economic development are black and white.

Cities and National Economic Growth:
An Asymmetrical Relationship

For contemporaries, there seemed to be no connection between the mainly urban man-
ufactories and the great increase of poor in the countryside.

KARL POLANYI (1944)

The emphasis all throughout this book on the positive relationship between
size and wealth easily leads to the conclusion that cities, especially big ones,
automatically *create* wealth. It would be very convenient if things were that
simple. The seven pillars of agglomeration inform us that firms are, as a rule,
more productive in urban settings and thus able to generate greater wealth.
True. But this does not really inform us about the long-term origins of economic growth and wealth creation. Great cities existed in ancient times—
Rome, Alexandria—without spawning an Industrial Revolution, neither did
the great cities of Aztec Mexico or Ming Dynasty China. Clearly, there is
more to wealth creation than agglomeration.

The growth of wealth and the growth of cities go hand in hand, about that
there can be little argument. The problem, as so often is the case in the social
sciences, is the direction of causation. Which causes which? The relationship
between increasing wealth and city formation is fairly easy to document and
to explain. In a nutshell, it is the story of urbanization since the Industrial
Revolution. Earlier, I observed that size and location came to matter more
because people and firms, in ever greater numbers, were now able to move
and to choose where to establish themselves, freed from the tyranny of the
land and of insurmountable transport costs. What I have left unexplained is
why people felt obliged to leave the land, why job opportunities and wages
began to shrivel in the countryside.

Causation in the opposite direction is far more difficult to establish. Does
growth in share of the population living in cities in turn provide the necessary conditions for further wealth creation? I shall briefly consider the
evidence. This examination from both ends, so speak, of the relationship
between urbanization and national economic growth will allow us to better

understand why the relationship between cities and the origins of wealth is not straightforward, but also why the experience of today's urbanizing nations is different from that of industrialized nations, which urbanized many decades earlier. For that, we need again to go back in time.

A Short History (and Explanation) of Urbanization

The exodus from the land to the city was a signal that a new era was about to begin. Life on the land, as noted earlier, was the normal lot for the overwhelming proportion of mankind before the Industrial Revolution. The proportion of the world's population living in cities remained below 5 percent for most of history. Even during the zenith of the Roman Empire and of the Ming Dynasty in China, it is doubtful that city dwellers ever accounted for more than 10 percent of the total population. The predominance of urban life is a very recent occurrence. As recently as 1900, our planet was still 90 percent rural.

Today's industrialized nations were the first to witness the shift to cities. The progression of urbanization in the United States is fairly typical. In 1800, less than 10 percent of the U.S. population lived in urban areas. Today the figure is 80 percent. The movement to cities is today largely over in industrialized nations. In the first nations to urbanize—Great Britain, Belgium, and the Netherlands—urbanization levels have reached 90 percent and even higher. The transformation from overwhelmingly rural to overwhelmingly urban societies is complete. All this has occurred in a fairly short time span.

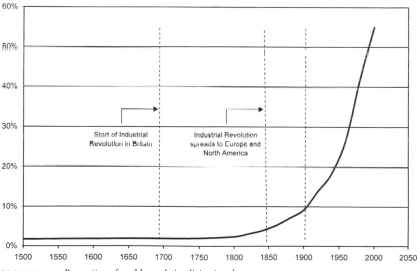

FIGURE 5.1. Proportion of world population living in urban areas, 1500–2050

The rapidity of the transformation has been especially impressive in east Asia. Japan, still massively rural less than a century ago, completed the cycle from rural to urban in a mere two generations, going from 80 percent rural in 1925 to 80 percent urban some seventy years later.[1]

Today's developing nations are undergoing a similar population shift with varying degrees of intensity. In India in 1950, shortly after its independence, the proportion of city dwellers was 17 percent; the figure has since risen to 30 percent (2005). In China, the share of the population living in urban areas has progressed constantly over the past twenty-five years, going from 20 percent in 1980 to perhaps 40 percent in 2007, a proportion we may expect to see rapidly grow in the future. Only the poorer nations of Sub-Saharan Africa — as well as other very low income nations such as Nepal — have continued to remain massively rural. For most of the rest of the planet, urbanization is an irreversible movement.

These trends will be familiar to most readers. But why did populations suddenly seek to flee the land? The short answer, of course, is the Industrial Revolution, but this is not sufficient. We need to look deeper into the meaning of economic growth[2] to understand why that revolution and the era of increasing wealth that followed triggered an irreversible exodus from the land.

A WORD ON THE MEANING OF ECONOMIC GROWTH

Few things are certain in economics. However, the positive relationship between national economic growth and urbanization can be asserted with a high degree of certainty.[3] Economic growth, especially in its early stages, necessarily produces urbanization. The passage from a majority rural society to a majority urban one is in sum an unavoidable outcome of economic growth. To explain why this is so, I must first define what exactly is meant by economic growth.

Economic growth is often used as a synonym for economic development. I use the two terms interchangeably. Most of us intuitively understand what is meant by economic growth and development. More "developed" societies are wealthier than "less developed" societies. Economic growth is, in short, the process by which wealth is created. However, a more operational definition is needed for this chapter. The now standard definition proposed by the American economist Simon Kuznets a half a century ago is entirely adequate: *a sustained increase in real per capita product or income.*[4] Like Kuznets and most development economists, I will use the term *economic growth* only with respect to nations, as distinct from places, communities, or regions. It is worthwhile taking a moment to reflect on Kuznets's definition of economic growth.

Why a sustained increase? In short, because economic development can only be said to be genuine if it results in a long-term, irreversible rise in incomes and material welfare. This is to distinguish true economic growth from short-term cyclical upswings in incomes, attributable for example to sudden jumps in the price of a natural resource. Incomes in Saudi Arabia rise and fall with the price of petrol. This is not the same as a rise in incomes founded on sustained increases over many decades in the productive capacity of the Saudi economy. Why the word *real* in Kuznets's definition? Simply to indicate that income growth must be adjusted for inflation in order to be real. If a family's income doubles, but prices do also, then there has been no real improvement in its material welfare.

Finally, why per capita income or product? The answer is the same as for regions and communities. The ultimate yardstick of growth is the welfare of individuals and households, not total income generated. It is of little comfort to the average Indian that India's Gross National Income is greater than that of the Netherlands, since the Indian total must meet the needs of over 1 billion people, while the Dutch total is distributed over a mere 16 million inhabitants. Income per person in the Netherlands is about fifty times higher than in India.[5]

The Kuznets definition, widely accepted today, only considers material or economic welfare. The principal reason is the absence of alternative, agreed-upon measures of welfare. For most people, per capita income (or product) continues to be the yardstick by which a nation's level of development is judged. This measure is not without its limits, even from a purely economic perspective. Since it is an average figure for a whole nation, it does not tell us *how* income is distributed among individuals. Income distribution might be very unequal. The United States and Norway have about the same per capita income (2005 figures), but the distribution is more unequal in the former. The poorest 10 percent of the population receives 1.8 percent of national income in the U.S. compared to 4.1 percent in Norway. Thus, even though per capita income is about equal in the two nations, the poor are better off in Norway. Official data only counts income (or production) derived from market transactions, duly registered with the appropriate authorities (via tax forms, payroll data, sales slips, etc.). Informal or illegal income (and production) is not counted, resulting in an underestimation of true income, especially in developing (poorer) nations, where much economic activity takes place outside the formal market. It also means that non-market activities such as housework, cooking, washing, and painting are not included.

Official income and product figures do not explicitly integrate environmental considerations such as cleaner air, purer water, and better sanitary conditions. In the vocabulary of economists, income and product data measure *flows*—everything earned or produced in a given year—not stocks. The value of fish (in the oceans), forests (standing), minerals (in the ground), and the air around us is not taken into account. However, environmental improvements such as cleaner air are, in general, positively correlated with rising incomes. On the other hand, economic growth can also inflict environmental damage, of which global warming and a depleting ozone layer are among the more spectacular examples. Such environmental risks are not counted in official income and product data

These measurement problems should not make us lose sight of the dramatic improvement in living standards since the inception of the Industrial Revolution. Economic historians such as Paul Bairoch, David Landes, and Angus Maddison have attempted to measure its magnitude.[6] World per capita product in the year 2000 was some twenty-two times higher than in 1850, compared with barely a doubling over the previous 150 years[7]. These dry statistics—which remain estimates—are the expression of a veritable revolution in the material condition of mankind, reflected also in declining child mortality, increased life expectancy, as well as transformations in the manner in which societies govern and organize themselves.[8] Bradford DeLong estimates that some three-quarters of world consumption today is spent on products that simply did not exist in the early 1800s.

This dramatic improvement in the material welfare of mankind is, of course, very unevenly spread over the planet. The continuing disparity between rich and poor nations remains one of the great challenges facing the world community. To cite but two data: income per person in Tanzania is some sixty-six times less than in the United States (even after adjusting for cost-of-living differences); income per person in Malawi is about forty-three times less than in the United Kingdom.[9]

CHANGING CONSUMPTION PATTERNS

Why should rising incomes produce urbanization? The first part of the answer is actually quite simple. When household incomes increase, consumption patterns change. Some 150 years ago, a Prussian economist by the name of Ernst Engel (no relation to Friedrich Engels) observed that the share of household expenditures spent on foodstuffs (he studied 153 families) fell systematically with income. This has since become known as Engel's law. Simply, the share of household (or individual) income spent on food will decline as income grows. A person can eat only so much (at least most people). If one's income doubles or triples, it does not follow that one will eat two or three times as much. The kinds of food one purchases will undoubtedly change, and one may in fact spend more on food (in absolute terms), but the *share* of total expenditures going for food will fall as a general rule.

The result of this change in consumption patterns is a steady decline in the share of expenditures on food. In 1870, over 50 percent of expenditures by American households went for food. Some 130 years later that percentage had fallen below 10 percent, and is still falling.[10] The relationship between income levels and foodstuff expenditures can also be illustrated by comparing poor and rich nations. Thus, while foodstuff expenditures accounted for respectively 9 percent and 11 percent of household expenditures in Canada and Britian, they took up some 40 percent of household expenditures in Pakistan and 48 percent in Nigeria.[11] As incomes rise, consumers spend proportionally more on items such as automobiles, entertainment, travel, health care, education, telecommunications, and other non-food products. The consequences for the composition of overall national demand (for goods and services) are not difficult to infer. As a nation's real per capita income grows, foodstuffs will represent an ever-decreasing share of national demand.

The first building block for explaining urbanization is now in place. The declining share of agriculture-based products[12] in national demand means that the demand for labor in agriculture (and related sectors) will also fall, *relative* to the demand for labor in other sectors of the economy that produce the goods and services that consumers increasingly want. If, for example, the demand for secondary education is growing more rapidly than the demand for foodstuffs, then the demand for teachers will grow more rapidly than for farmers. Consequently, wages will rise more rapidly for teachers. This again is a simple matter of supply and demand. As the wages of teachers continue to rise relative to that of persons working the land, newcomers into the labor market (generally, the young just out of school) will be tempted to go into teaching rather than into farming.

Thus begins the movement out of agriculture, whether into teaching, manufacturing, or other occupations for which demand is growing more rapidly, and for which wages, correspondingly, are also growing more rapidly. If the speed at which consumption patterns are shifting (from food to non-food products) is greater than the ability of workers to react (by changing occupations), then the income gap between workers on the land and other workers will grow, with the former becoming relatively poorer compared to workers in other occupations. Herein, in a nutshell, lie the origins of the income gap between those working the land and those working in cities. The chief culprits, in a manner of speaking, are our tastes. Incomes in the countryside would rise, if we all decided to eat much more, hardly a desirable solution.

As long as we continue to consume, in ever-increasing proportions, products that are produced in cities—be they CDs, novels, or computers—the demand for labor in the city will continue to grow faster than on the land. This does not mean that *total* spending by households on food falls as nations grow. We do eat more. In the United States, total consumer spending per person on food is some 50 percent higher today in real dollars than a century ago. What matters is the change in the proportion of income spent on food. But the story does not end here. Another factor is pushing workers off the land, compounding the effects of relative falling demand for foodstuffs.

RISING LABOR PRODUCTIVITY

Rising labor productivity is at the heart of economic growth. Very simply, more can be produced with the same amount of labor or, alternatively, the same amount with less labor. In 1930, it took, on average, an American farmer twenty hours to produce one hundred bushels of wheat, using the most advanced technology of the time. By 1975, a farmer could do the same work in five hours.[13] In other words, labor productivity quadrupled. It has not stopped growing since.

The relationship between productivity and per capita income can also be illustrated by comparing rich and poor nations today. The average value of agricultural production per agricultural worker (2000–2002 figures) was about $40,000 for the United Kingdom, and $50,000 for the United States compared to about $400 for India and $700 for Nigeria.[14] In other words, the average British farmer produces about sixty times more than a Nigerian farmer and a hundred times more than an Indian farmer or agricultural worker. What lies behind these differences in agricultural productivity? The answer can include a myriad of factors: improved and new crops, better land management techniques, widespread use of fertilizers, more and better farm machinery and equipment, better storage and distribution facilities, a better educated and informed rural labor force, etc. The list of factors that underlie productivity differences is almost endless.

The higher productivity of farmers and agricultural workers in richer nations does not necessarily mean that the farmers in, say, Britain work harder than farmers in Nigeria. In fact, the contrary is often true. The higher productivity of the British farmer (or worker), in addition to the factors already mentioned, also depends on the surrounding social and institutional environment: the presence of adequate transportation infrastructures needed to bring the farm's produce to market; the quality of other infrastructures such as electricity, water, and waste facilities; but (and perhaps most impor-

TABLE 5.1. Share of Labor Force in Agriculture: Selected Nations, 1900, 1950, 2000

Industrialized Nations	1900 (%)	1950 (%)	2000 (%)
Germany*	35	24	3
Belgium	20	12	3
Canada	42	20	3
Spain	—	50	7
United States	38	13	3
France	43	30	2
Italy	60	42	6
Netherlands	30	20	3
Japan	70	49	5
United Kingdom	9	5	2
Sweden	40	21	3
Switzerland	30	16	4
USSR/Russia	80	45	12

Developing Nations	1900 (%)	1950 (%)	2000 (%)
Egypt	70	65	29
Morocco	—	67	50
China	—	70	48
India	—	74	60
Argentina	31	25	8
Chile	—	34	14
Colombia	—	57	30
Mexico	70	61	20
Peru	—	58	23

*West Germany in 1950.

tant) the proper functioning of a modern state, ensuring public order, the rule of law, and the respect of contracts. The British farmer may not realize how much of the farm's productivity is dependent on conditions not directly related to his or her personal efforts, but this does not lessen their importance. The origins of productivity differences between nations run very deep, leading back into the historical foundations of national institutions and cultures, a point to which I shall return shortly. If productivity differences were easy to explain—and especially to remedy—then there would be no more poor nations, and there would be no more need for institutions such as the World Bank or for foreign aid programs.[15]

Returning to the relationship between economic growth and the decline in the demand for agricultural labor, two forces are now combining to push labor off the land: falling relative demand for food and rising labor productivity on farms. Close to half the Canadian labor force was employed in agriculture in the year 1900 compared with 3 percent today. The evolution is much the same in other industrialized nations (table 5.1). Most developing nations have already entered the stage of declining shares of employment in agriculture. China has seen the share of its labor force in agriculture fall from 70 percent in 1950 to 48 percent in 2000. In nations that have finished urbanizing, the share of employment in agriculture has stabilized in the range of 2 to 3 percent. In other words, a mere 2 to 3 percent of the labor force on the land is sufficient to meet the needs of local (and export) demand for foodstuffs.[16]

Urbanization Is an Outcome of Economic Growth (Not the Other Way Around)

Increases in income per person need not be very large to set off urbanization. The shape of the the relationship between GDP per person and urbanization (pictured in figure 5.2), first rising sharply then flattening out as incomes reach a certain level, tells us that significant increases in urbanization levels can occur at fairly low levels of income.[17] Nations such as Nigeria, still in the early stages of development, exhibit urbanization levels approaching 50 percent. Three conclusions follow: 1) disparities in income and in labor demand between the countryside and the city are sharpest during the early stages of development; 2) populations react fairly rapidly to these disparities; and 3) once urbanization has taken off it will continue, at least for some time, carried by its own momentum.

Urban/rural income differences are generally much greater in developing than in developed nations, for reasons explained in the previous chapter.

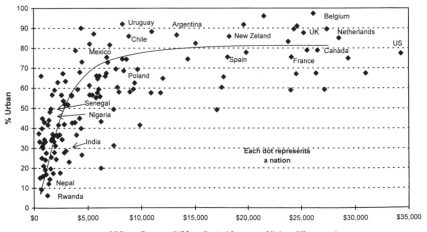

FIGURE 5.2. Relationship between GDP per person and urbanization levels

Wages in manufacturing in China were in the late 1990s more than double those in agriculture; in India the ratio was close to four to one.[18] By comparison, manufacturing and agricultural wages were close to equal in the majority of industrialized nations, which largely explains why rural-urban migration is coming to an end in industrialized nations. Wage disparities such as those noted for China and India are a signal that the national economy would gain if more workers moved from agriculture to industry. Higher wages in manufacturing mean that labor can be more productively employed there than in agriculture. A shift from agriculture to manufacturing will contribute to economic growth. Average incomes will rise.

Does the positive impact on incomes of a shift in labor from agriculture to manufacturing mean that urbanization is a *cause* of economic growth? Only in part. The contribution of urbanization to economic growth is essentially "allocational" and not "dynamic," to use the language of economists.[19] Rural-urban migration is an adjustment to the changes in demand and productivity unleashed by economic growth, whereby labor is reallocated from less to more productive uses. The rural exodus will continue as long as rural-urban wage differences persist, a signal that the adjustment is not yet over. Once the reallocation (from rural to urban) is completed, the contribution of urbanization has ended.

A corollary of the preceding paragraph is that the relationship between economic growth and urbanization must eventually weaken and even break down beyond a certain point. The curve on figure 5.2 starts to flatten at urbanization levels of nations such as Mexico and Poland, meaning that further increases in income (or product) will translate into only minor additional increases in urbanization (and vice versa). This is entirely natural, for once urbanization is in the 70 percent to 80 percent range (or higher) it cannot go much higher. Taking an extreme case, it is highly implausible that future income growth in Belgium would foster further urbanization since that nation is already 98 percent urban. Economic growth in Belgium, no longer has anything to do with urbanization. The effects of urbanization lie in the past.

Why have I gone off on this rather technical tangent? I wish to dispel any possible confusion as to the direction of causation. The evidence that economic growth produces urbanization is indisputable. But a causal relationship in the opposite direction—urbanization producing economic growth—is far less certain.[20] There is little evidence that higher levels of urbanization lead subsequently to higher growth. No statistical relationship exists between initial levels of urbanization and subsequent growth.[21] Nor is there any evidence that *nations* will grow faster because they have big cities. It is worth keeping this in mind when considering the relationship between urban size and *local* economic growth (I shall return to this point at the end of this chapter).

A brief look at Sub-Saharan Africa and South America is instructive. The southern cone nations of Latin America—Chile, Argentina, and Uruguay—have among the highest urbanization levels in the world—above 80 percent—higher than many industrialized nations. Yet their incomes per capita are far lower, barely a quarter on average of that of the United States.[22] Their high levels of urbanization are in large part the result of earlier periods of prosperity and export-led growth (notably wheat and beef in the case of Argentina and Uruguay), which led to a rapid expansion of urban centers in the first half of the twentieth century. However, the high levels of urbanization for the time were not sufficient to ensure subsequent economic growth comparable to that of today's industrialized nations. Economic growth continued, but slowly and in spurts. Urbanization continued as well, carried in part by its own momentum, terminating in today's high levels, but without comparable high levels of income.

In Sub-Saharan Africa, the comparatively advanced levels of urbanization of many nations, attained at fairly low income levels, have not necessarily improved their chances for future growth.[23] We saw that urbanization takes off at relatively low income levels. If the movement is indeed partly irreversible, then we should not be surprised to find cases of economically slow-growing or stagnant nations with comparatively high levels of urbanization. An urbanization level of 30 percent—not unusual in Africa today—is very high compared to past historical experience. A case can be made that urbanization in parts of the developing world has been artificially accelerated by international aid. Aid can stimulate urbanization in two ways: 1) by artificially increasing incomes, provoking the consumption effects described earlier;[24] and 2) by artificially reducing demand for *local* agricultural labor in cases where aid comes in the form of food. The latter, although generally undertaken with the best of intentions, can serve to undercut local food producers. The real impact of aid on urbanization is probably minor.

Deforestation, soil erosion, and war can also accelerate the exodus from the land. All are—unfortunately—realities in Africa and elsewhere in the developing world. Indeed, some nations may well be over-urbanized compared to what objective economic criteria would warrant. Were such forced urbanization beneficial to economic growth, then we would expect the lot of such nations to improve accordingly. There is little evidence that this is what is happening in Africa or elsewhere.

CAN URBANIZATION BE STOPPED?

For nations not yet fully urbanized, the exodus from the land will continue to be chiefly driven by shifting consumer demand—towards urban-produced goods—and by increasing agricultural productivity. This raises the question of whether urbanization is stoppable in nations whose economies are growing.

"The fatal irreversibility of urbanization" is how Karl Polanyi (92) put it more than sixty years ago in his classic work on the social origins and consequences of the Industrial Revolution. His evaluation is no less true today. No nation in recent times has been able to industrialize without seeing its agricultural labor force decline and without a corresponding population exodus from the land to the city. But does this mean that urbanization is truly unstoppable? The answer is an unequivocal yes. Urbanization is impossible to stop in growing economies. Once economic growth takes off, governments have no (or little) control over the speed at which urbanization occurs. Let us ponder the policy implications of this statement.

In many of today's developing nations, the desire to slow down the rural exodus is entirely understandable and, some might be tempted to add, laudable. Rural-urban migration entails high social and personal costs. Anyone who has witnessed the squalor and horror of the slums and shanty towns of the metropolises of the third world cannot fail to empathize with the plight of poor rural migrants in the city. Surely, wouldn't they be better off if they had stayed on the land? How can anyone confronted with such abominable living conditions possibly maintain that these slum dwellers are better off in the city? Yet this is indeed the case. Surveys carried out in third world cities have time and again arrived at the same conclusion: in almost all cases, individuals who had left the countryside for the city stated that their condition had improved.[25] This conclusion is perhaps difficult to accept, but in the end the prevailing conditions in the countryside determine the relative attractiveness of the city. By almost any measure (health, employment opportunities, sanitation, educational facilities, etc.) conditions are generally far worse in rural areas.[26] Why this is so for employment opportunities should by now be obvious. People move to where the opportunities are, even if such opportunities may appear terribly inadequate to today's western observer. People move because they believe they and their children will be better off. Were they worse off in the city, they would move back to the countryside.

It should thus come as no surprise that attempts to slow down or to stop urbanization have failed miserably. The impact of measures to suppress rural-urban migration, in cases where they have been able to do so, has simply been to artificially hold down urbanization for a certain time, leading to even greater rural-urban income disparities and an explosion of urbanization once the measures are lifted. This is largely what occurred in China during the 1990s and beginning of the twenty-first century, where rural-urban income differences grew rapidly following the liberalization of the Chinese economy. This does not mean that liberalization is to blame for rising income disparities, but rather that the previous (planned economy) regime kept necessary adjustments from being made. The best analogy is that of a boiling pot. One can, given sufficient downward pressure, keep the lid on the pot for some time. But, at some point, resistance becomes impossible and the lid flies off, releasing a flood of steam. The forces driving urbanization are not unique to capitalist economies. What we have said about the impact of shifting consumer demand and rising agricultural productivity equally holds for socialist economies. Households in China, no less than in Britain or Japan, will increasingly demand urban-produced goods and services as their incomes rise.

The most common effect of policies aimed at holding back rural-urban migration is the creation of a black market. Perhaps the best proof of the irrepressible nature of urbanization is the persistence of rural-urban migration even under conditions where such movements are officially illegal. In the old Soviet Union, internal movements were strictly regulated via the use of internal passports. This did not prevent a healthy black market from developing in official "permissions," local residence permits, and housing allocations, allowing (well-connected) rural migrants to settle in Moscow and other large cities. At the other end of the political spectrum, the story of pre-1990 apartheid South Africa provides an even more vivid illustration. Under apartheid (which, literally translated, means *separateness*), the infamous influx controls were explicitly conceived to keep black Africans out of cities; in essence, to keep the core of South Africa's cities white. The majority of black Africans, who were officially considered to be residents of rural, "independent" Bantustans, were required to carry passbooks, severely limiting their right to live elsewhere. Yet, despite the apparent efficiency of the South African authorities at the time, black Africans continued to flow into the cities in ever growing numbers, creating so-called "townships," often illegal on paper, driven by the growing demand of the cities for labor.[27] The growing, unstoppable need of South Africa's cities for (black) labor was a major factor in bringing down apartheid.

In many developing nations, migration into the city continues despite the absence of legal land on which to settle. Indeed, a large proportion of urban dwellers in the world's poorest cities live in areas that are not legally recognized as such—which is why the tem *squatter settlement* is often applied—

with no recognized property rights or civil administration. Much third world urbanization takes place under what can only be called black market conditions, where land and dwellings are informally traded, with little legal protection for those involved.[28] That the rural exodus nonetheless continues in the face of such constraints is further proof of the irrepressible nature of the forces driving urbanization.

RURAL DEVELOPMENT PROGRAMS WILL NOT SLOW DOWN URBANIZATION

Trying to stop people from moving to cities will not work, certainly not as long as opportunities are more plentiful in the city than in the countryside. Then why not improve living conditions in the countryside as an antidote to urbanization? Improving conditions in rural areas is an entirely laudable objective, worthwhile pursuing in its own right. In developing nations, living conditions are in general far worse on the land than in the city. However, rural development programs—aimed at helping the rural poor—will not necessarily slow down the exodus to the city. Indeed, it is not impossible that rural improvement may accelerate urbanization. There are two reasons for this. First, if such programs succeed in raising rural incomes (certainly a good thing), then the impact on consumer spending will be the same as that described earlier. Richer farmers, like the rest of the population, will spend proportionately less on food and proportionately more on urban-produced goods, thus indirectly fueling the forces of urbanization.[29]

Second, rural development programs necessarily seek to help poor farmers to improve their productivity. The more successful such programs are, the more they will fuel urbanization for reasons that should now be self-evident. The more productive farmers are, the fewer of them are needed. The chief exception to this rule is where agricultural production is exclusively (or largely) exported, and where increased productivity allows local farmers or other primary producers to capture a larger share of the world market. Such cases are not infrequent, but this does not negate the general rule that rising agricultural productivity stimulates urbanization.[30] Rising agricultural productivity stimulates urbanization in another more indirect manner. Modern agriculture is increasingly founded on a wide array of urban inputs, ranging from fertilizers to agricultural machinery to advanced distribution, transportation, and marketing facilities. Modern agriculture relies on a broad range of services (financial, technical, and scientific), which are provided, as a rule, by firms located in cities. In sum, the demand for (urban-produced) intermediary inputs will grow as agricultural productivity rises.

Rural development initiatives, especially in developing countries, often focus on education, which again is entirely laudable.[31] However, better rural education will often accelerate migration to the city, for the skills acquired can be more productively put to use in the city. It is entirely normal that a young rural lad or lass fresh out of school, having acquired numerical and perhaps computer skills, should look to the city, since he or she knows that such newly learned skills are in demand there. Education opens the door to higher incomes in the city. The young and the more educated are generally the first to leave, as noted earlier in our discussion of the mechanics of regional disparities. Those who stay are the least educated.[32] Indeed, without wishing to sound cynical, one of the most effective ways to keep people on the land is to keep them ignorant, hardly a policy to be recommended. This unpleasant truth is one of the recurrent dilemmas in rural and local development in general. One of the most effective means of lifting the poor in remote rural regions out of poverty is to improve their education. But, at the same time, this may produce an increased exodus to the city, leaving those who stay behind little better off. I shall return to this dilemma in other chapters, for it is not limited to developing nations.

Is Urbanization Different in Developing Nations?

Many readers must be asking why there is such squalor in third world cities if the link between economic growth and urbanization is so strong. Surely, something must have gone wrong. Cities in Sub-Saharan Africa such as Lagos and Kinshasa, with respective populations of about 10 and 6 million, surpass most western European cities in size, but with little to show in the way of higher standards of living. Greater London's population in 1841, with the Industrial Revolution in full swing (at the time the world's largest metropolis), was barely 2 million,[33] far less than Lagos or Kinshasa today. It would be difficult to argue that the economies of Nigeria and the Congo are in full swing at the time of writing; yet they have given rise to cities far larger than those of Europe or North America during the early stages of industrialization. Why has today's urbanization created such huge—seemingly unmanageable—cities in the heart of nations that are clearly still in the very first stages of industrialization? Surely, urbanization in today's developing nations is unlike that witnessed by Europe, North America, Japan, and Australasia some generations earlier?

Urbanization in today's developing nations is both the same and different from that which occurred decades or centuries earlier in today's industrialized nations. Let me begin with the similarities. On the whole, the forces

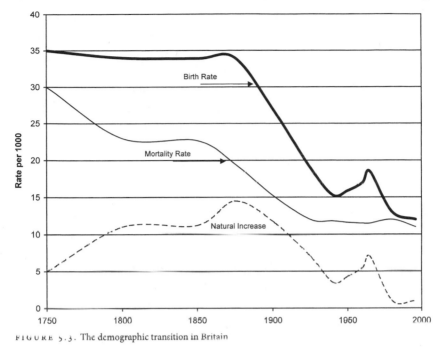

FIGURE 5.3. The demographic transition in Britain

driving urbanization (as described in the previous sections) are the same, notwithstanding the caveats on the impact of remittances, foreign aid, soil erosion, and conflicts. Today's developing nations are urbanizing for the same fundamental reasons as those that caused North America and western Europe to urbanize. However, there are also two fundamental differences, which are not related to the forces driving urbanization, but rather have to do with the *magnitude* (or size) of the populations affected and with the local *institutional context* in which urbanization takes place. Let me begin with magnitude: why are the urban populations so much bigger today than a century or so earlier?

Third World Cities: Victims of Progress?

Urbanization is not the only inevitable transformation flowing from economic growth and modernization. Sociologists and demographers use the term *demographic transition* to refer to the process (over many generations) by which a society moves from a situation of high birth rates with high mortality rates (and low life expectancy) to a situation of low birth rates with low mortality (and high life expectancy). Most industrialized nations have today completed the transition. Mortality among newborn infants, a frequent occurrence not so long ago, has all but disappeared. Average life expectancy, which was in the range of 40 to 50 years at the beginning of the last century, is now in the range of 75 to 80 years in most industrialized nations (generally higher for women). Birth rates have fallen dramatically everywhere. Figure 5.3 illustrates the transition over time for the United Kingdom, the first nation to industrialize. In 1750, the UK had both high birth and death rates. As sanitary conditions and medical science improved over time, the death rate declined, with the most dramatic drop between about 1850 and the 1920s. The birth rate followed, with a sharp decline after 1850 (note the baby boom in the 1950s and early 1960s). The rate of natural population increase—the difference between the birth and death rates—first rises then falls, peaking in the late nineteenth century in the UK. This was the period during which the British population grew most rapidly, with a maximum of about 1.4 percent growth per annum.

How can we explain this transition, which reflects a dramatic change in the child-bearing behavior of women? The fall in the death rate, as noted above, is not difficult to explain, the result of improvements in sanitation, medicine, nutrition, and living conditions in general. The birth rate is more intriguing. We see that the birth rate remained very high (by today's standards) until the 1850s, even though death rates had already begun to fall. There is a time lag between the moment that improvements in health are introduced, especially as they affect infant mortality, and the moment that women decide to have fewer children. This is entirely understandable; behavior patterns ingrained over many centuries do not change overnight. Throughout human history (that is, until the Industrial Revolution) birth rates have been high, a rational reaction by women—and their spouses—to the hard reality that few children would survive beyond the age of five. Women risked their lives, for giving birth was a hazardous proposition in those days, to bring five, ten, or fifteen children into the world so that two, five, or six might survive. Urbanization also contributed to the fall in birth rates since children, useful as labor on farms, are less so in cities. Like urbanization, the change to small families marks a major break with the past.

The British experience is fairly representative of other industrialized nations. Let us look at a developing nation. Figure 5.4 gives similar information for India.[34] At the turn of the last century, both birth and death rates were very high, meaning almost zero natural growth. However, since 1900, death rates have fallen systematically, but birth rates only began to fall significantly after the 1960s, meaning a steadily rising rate of natural increase until the 1960s, peaking at an annual maximum growth rate of about 2.6 percent. Thus, the natural rate of growth during its peak was considerably higher in

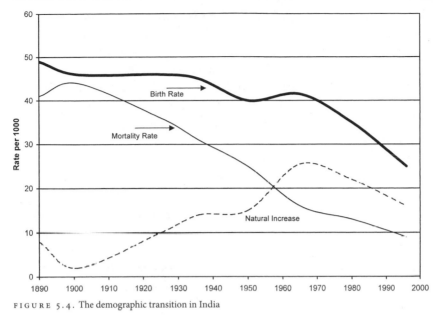

FIGURE 5.4. The demographic transition in India

India than in the UK. Why the difference? The explanation does not lie in the different behavior of Indian women. Indian women, like their British sisters before them, are giving birth to ever fewer children. Indeed, it can be argued that Indian women have been even more prompt to react to changing conditions than their British counterparts a century earlier. A century elapsed (1750–1850) before British birth rates began to fall significantly, while Indian rates began their descent some sixty years (1900–1960) after mortality rates started to decline. Birth rates have been steadily declining in almost all developing nations. That is not where the difference lies. Women in developing nations are not behaving very differently from women in today's developing nations a century or so ago

The difference lies in the evolution of mortality rates. Since the 1960s, the mortality rate in India has been similar to that of the UK and recently even somewhat lower, due to India's more youthful population. Between 1980 and 2000, infant mortality and child mortality—under five years of age— have been halved, though still above rates in industrialized nations. Over the same period, life expectancy has gone from 53 to 63 years, which is quite high by historical standards.[35] Stated differently, modern science and medical advances make it possible to reduce the risks of infant and child mortality (and of giving birth) fairly rapidly, even under conditions of low economic development. Compared to what occurred in Europe or North America a century ago, the risk of dying (from disease or other factors) has fallen much more rapidly in today's developing nations. If we were to compare today's developing nations with industrialized nations a century ago, we would discover that both groups had about the same birth rate; but that mortality rates in developing nations today are well below that of industrialized nations a century earlier.[36] The inevitable result: populations in developing nations today are growing much more rapidly than in today's industrialized nations a century earlier.

Developing nations are, in a sense, the victims of progress. They are urbanizing at a moment in time when their populations are growing rapidly, thanks to progress in medicine and other fields. Urbanization in the past in today's industrialized nations occurred under conditions of much slower population growth, leading to comparatively smaller cities and slower rates of urban expansion. The consequences for the magnitude of urban growth can be significant. Let us consider a hypothetical example. Nations A and B start with a population of 10 million and a similar urbanization level (20 percent); thus with an urban population in each nation of 2 million. Both urbanize at the same speed over the next twenty years (to 30 percent urban), which is another way of stating that the underlying process is the same in the two nations. Over the twenty years, nation A grows by a quarter to a population of 12.5 million. Its urban population now stands at 3.75 million, somewhat less than double twenty years earlier. Nation B, however, has grown to a population of 20 million. Its urban population has tripled in twenty years, now 6 million. Nation B, which might be compared to a developing nation today, has both a bigger urban population and a higher rate of urban population growth, although it is urbanizing at the same speed as nation A.

The story does not end there. Progress in sanitation, engineering, and public administration have removed the constraints that existed in the past on city size. Before the seventeenth century, cities were generally unhealthier than the countryside because of the greater risk of infectious disease. In 1841, recalling the London example, the technology and know-how simply did not exist to successfully manage a city of more than 2 or 3 million people. Electricity had not been invented. Intra-city transport was still largely dependent on the horse and carriage (with attendant sanitary risks) and on walking, severely limiting the geographical size of the city. Today, by contrast, we are able to manage urban agglomerations with more than 10 million people (and even higher), although admittedly not always with ideal conditions, as the presence of metropolises such as Lagos, Cairo, Calcutta, and São Paulo attests. Today's developing nations are facing a double challenge. Not only are their cities growing more rapidly than those in the past, but—for comparable levels of development—they are also growing to sizes unheard of before. No wonder many developing nations find it difficult to keep up, and no wonder that infrastructures lag behind. Cities nonetheless continue to expand, often under abominable conditions, proof yet again—as if more were needed—of the irrepressible nature of urbanization.

Christine Kessides, an economist at the World Bank, nicely sums up the dilemma of developing nations: "African countries are *not* [her emphasis] urbanizing faster than other countries have, and the distribution of urban population among large and very small cities is *not* unusual for their level of development. That said, the absolute rate of urban growth is historically unprecedented and a challenge for urban management."[37]

The Difference between the Foundations of National and Local Economic Growth

Before ending this chapter, a brief look the institutions that allow markets to function properly is in order. Looking at institutions will further help us to understand the difference between the experience of developing nations and the experience, decades earlier, of today's industrialized nations, and also to understand the difference between the foundations of national economic growth and the foundations of regional growth.

In industrialized nations, the existence of markets and appropriate institutions is taken for granted. It is assumed as a given, to use the language of economists. Indeed, institutions are hardly mentioned in most textbooks on regional or urban economics.[38] This is entirely understandable, since the institutions that ensure property rights and the respect of contracts—to take two examples—are so deeply engrained in our social fabric and history that we tend to forget that they are the result of a long historical process, whose roots go back to ancient Greece and Rome, and perhaps even further. However, such historical amnesia (probably involuntary) sometimes leads economists—generally on the right of the political spectrum—to falsely assume that markets spring up "naturally," that the state is basically a nuisance that prevents the "free" market from flourishing in all its glory. Admittedly, this viewpoint has lost some ground since the demise of the old Soviet Union, when it became increasingly evident that markets would not spontaneously flourish once the old Soviet planning apparatus was dismantled. Much more was needed.

To be sure, what Olson (2000, 175) calls spontaneous markets will arise in the absence of a functioning public sector. The vitality of the informal sector in many cities of the developing world bears witness to this. However, these are limited markets where the costs of doing business are high, due in large part to the absence (or deficiency) of a wide range of what economists call "public goods"[39]: contract enforcement, regulation of financial institutions and land markets, property rights, public safety, macroeconomic stability, etc. *Laisser faire* (translation: to let be or to let do), often used to describe market economies, is very far from the reality of modern market economies. There is nothing "free" about modern markets. Markets, if they are to function properly, need an arbitrator who sets and enforces the rules and ensures that the playing field is properly maintained. That is the role of the state and its institutions.

The need for a functioning state becomes even greater as a society urbanizes. Cities require more public services and supervision than the countryside. Some hundred years ago, Howe (1915, 4) observed: "The city can only live by co-operation, by co-operation in a million unseen ways. Without co-operation for a single day a great city would stand still." Howe then goes on to describe the myriad of new public services, hitherto unfamiliar, needed to make a "modern" city work. Collective (public) goods such as street lighting, sidewalks, sewage systems, streets, and public parks must be collectively financed. The provision of those services presupposes the existence of a functioning state (national, regional, local), an institutional environment where people are accustomed to paying taxes and those that spend tax revenues are accountable (or, at least, acceptably honest). The full realization of the economic benefits of urbanization requires institutions and institutional changes for which history has prepared some societies better than others.

This is nowhere truer than in the implementation—on the ground—of urbanization. Urbanization requires that pieces of land change from one use to another. Land that was once agricultural is now used for housing or industry. This generally means the exchange of property from, say, a farmer to a developer. All this is entirely ordinary and functions smoothly in societies where private land ownership is the norm and where the contractual arrangements for buying and selling land are historically grounded.[40] However, where this is not so, where communal landholding is the norm, for example, urbanization will proceed much less smoothly. The clash between the forces driving urbanization and local (communal or other non-market) landholding traditions can severely complicate the creation of real estate markets and, by the same token, make it difficult to raise local land taxes needed to finance urban infrastructures.[41] The absence of clear property rights not only complicates local finance, but also hampers the introduction of mortgages, preventing urban dwellers from using land or housing as an asset on which they might draw to invest in business ventures, education, or other endeavors.

In short: we cannot simply assume that markets *will* function smoothly, that, for example, a proper real estate market is in place that will allow changes in land use to proceed in accordance with the forces of supply and demand. This constitutes a major difference between the historical experience of today's rich nations and that of many developing nations. Some might also be tempted to add that the lack of appropriate institutions is the primary reason why many poor nations have remained poor. Much recent work in development economics stresses the role of institutions, which have become a catch-all for a broad range of attributes: laws and regulations, social values, forms of governance, etc.[42] That, in a nutshell, is also what makes nations different from communities, places, or regions. Institutions do not vary greatly *within* nations, certainly not to the extent that they differ between nations. Institutional differences cannot normally be invoked as the primary factor explaining regional development differences *within* nations.

The preceding paragraph leads me into one of the most hotly debated issues in economic geography: do cities *create* wealth or, rather, do they capture wealth whose ultimate foundations lie elsewhere? Mayors are fond of saying that their cities are engines of growth. I cannot blame them. The evidence, at first sight, seems irrefutable. We know that—*within* all nations—cities account for a disproportionate share of GDP and income (recall table 2.1). Nor do I need to repeat the strong positive relation—*within* nations—between city size and wealth. Yet it is not possible to demonstrate an equivalent positive relationship between national urbanization or city-size levels and *national* economic growth. How should this apparent contradiction be viewed? The answer lies in the difference between the mechanics of wealth creation at the local level and at the national level. The two are not on the same plane. Wealth creation at the local level will not happen, no matter how large the city, unless the necessary preconditions—whose foundations are grounded in society as a whole—are also present. Cities, just by being cities or being big, will not automatically create wealth.

An opposing school of thought exists, most eloquently articulated by Jane Jacobs,[43] who has consistently argued in her highly popular books that cities are the primary movers (causes) of national economic growth. Jacobs, who died in 2006, has become somewhat of a cult figure in urban planning circles. Her work is full of splendid insights and flashes on how to plan cities. I very much agree with her penchant for mixed, lively, cosmopolitan, and slightly chaotic cities. But I remain unconvinced by her economic arguments. It is difficult to argue with the proposition that cities are a *necessary* condition for economic growth. It is far more difficult to show that they are a *sufficient* condition. It would be so much simpler if economic growth could be kick-started, so to speak, by building cities, even superbly planned cities. Unfortunately, there is little evidence that this works. Well-functioning cities are an essential condition of economic growth, but so are a well-functioning state and an educated population.

The wealth of today's industrialized societies is the result of a historical transformation whose origins run much deeper than the territorial rearrangement of populations and firms. For Adam Smith,[44] the secret lay in properly functioning markets, which are by no means a foregone conclusion, as we saw. For David Landes,[45] going one step further back, differences in culture—which encompasses such attributes as value systems, religion, and institutions—are the primary factors underlying differences in national levels of economic development. For nations, Landes is undoubtedly right.[46] Going even further back, Jared Diamond[47] in his now classic work, *Guns, Germs, and Steel*, argues that the roots of our (western) values and institutions lie in the evolutionary result of climatic and geographic conditions that allowed certain types of agriculture and social structures to develop in certain parts of the planet and not in others.[48]

With this mind, let us take a second look at the positive relationship between city size and wealth. The relationship is in part misleading, that is, if economic history and national differences are ignored. Size matters *within* nations, but not necessarily between nations. Luxembourg City and Reykjavik both generate per capita incomes comparable to that of Greater New York, although a hundred times smaller. *National* conditions and prevailing technologies set the upper limits of the gains that can be realized from greater size (bigger cities). The upper limit for an Indian city will not be the same as for an American city of equivalent size. And, as was the case for urbanization levels, the productivity (wealth) gains that can be realized by greater size will taper off after some size threshold. That threshold is not fixed and will, again, depend on prevailing technologies. We should normally expect the threshold to grow as our capacity to manage large cities improves, thanks chiefly to improved (and cleaner) urban transport systems. For nations at comparable levels of development, the additional gains to be had from increasing the size of its largest cities size will in part depend on their current size. It is doubtful—given current technologies and urban management skills—that an increase in the population of Greater New York would significantly increase its potential to generate higher incomes.[49]

A comparison between Canada and Argentina is instructive. At the end of World War I, Argentina and Canada were at similar levels of urbanization. Buenos Aires, Argentina's largest city, was considerably larger than Canada's largest city at the time, Montreal, and undoubtedly as cosmopolitan and as sophisticated if not more so.[50] Both nations share an early history of agricultural export-led growth, roughly from 1880 to 1929. Before the Great Depression, income per capita in Argentina was not far below that of Canada. Since then, the two nations have diverged. Per capita income in Argentina today is about one-third that of Canada. In short, Argentina's initial advantage, which it continues to hold, of housing a large sophisticated metropolis, larger than any in Canada, was manifestly not sufficient to ensure a process of sustained income growth comparable to that of its northern sister. Other conditions were also needed.

In the end, people create wealth, not places. And people will only create wealth if all necessary conditions are present. Big cities can be one element—often a very important one—in creating those conditions. But cities are reflections of the societies that nurtured them, no more and no less. Harmonious societies will bread harmonious cites; violent societies will breed violent cities. The process of wealth creation is like a many-layered cake. The ultimate source is seldom purely local. And, in the porous world of regional economics, the sources of wealth can be won and lost. For the nation's largest city, the accumulation over many decades, even centuries, of human and physical capital will have given it an advantage over its smaller rivals for all the reasons given in chapter 2. However, for it to keep that advantage, it must continue to draw in talent and money. The image of cities as places that capture wealth—or, more correctly, the sources of wealth—is perhaps closer to the truth than the image of cities as the initial creators of wealth. The ultimate prize to capture is to be *the* place—the center—to which the most dynamic industries of the time converge.

Regional Growth in the Green and Gray Knowledge Economy

As the railroads made larger markets possible, they made larger enterprises possible as well. . . . Wherever they went, railroads brought economic activity in to being. . . . In Europe, the railroads connected existing cities. In America, in many cases, they mid-wived them into existence.

JOHN STEELE GORDON (2004)

The transition of today's industrialized nations from poor rural societies to rich urban societies has, we saw, been accompanied by profound changes, not the least of which is the potential of different places to generate wealth. Great cities arose where there were only small towns before. New regional disparities in welfare emerged, more persistent in some nations than in others. Brains have increasingly replaced brawn as sources of economic growth. Technological change has dramatically reduced communications costs and created new resources while making others obsolete. New technologies, as yet not invented, will in the future introduce new shocks, altering the relative advantages of different places.

In this chapter, I focus on two emerging trends in rich societies: hedonic regional growth, which, as we shall discover, often acts to increase the range of places that will grow; and zero sum growth, which, in contrast, increases the range of places that risk decline. Both are the outcome of the demographic transition and consequent slower population growth and graying of industrialized societies.

Hedonic Regional Growth

The combination of rising incomes and greater longevity is driving change in the geographic distribution of wealth. Each affects the manner in which individuals and families view their needs and display their preferences, in turn, affecting their life choices, not least their choice of where to live and work.

The fact that a growing number of people in rich nations have a *choice* constitutes in itself a minor revolution. For most of human history, there were few choices to make; staying or moving was very simply a matter of survival.

The massive move to the city during industrialization was not really a choice, which is precisely why urbanization was both predictable and irreversible. But today an increasing share of the population can truly choose. In terms of its impact on the geography of wealth, this perhaps is the most momentous change of the twenty-first century, already in evidence in the economic landscape of many nations. Places are growing simply because people want to live there and not because they have to be there to earn a living. I shall call this new form of regional growth *hedonic*, from the ancient Greek for "pleasure."

Hedonism is the doctrine that considers the pursuit of pleasure as the supreme goal in life. My use of the term is slightly broader. I use the word *hedonic* as shorthand for life choices that are not primarily motivated by economic considerations or, more precisely, that are not primarily aimed at increasing one's income or furthering one's career. Rather the prime motivation is more personal: greater happiness, peace of mind, comfort, beautiful surroundings, and (of course) pleasure. I call this the *hedonic imperative*, which in part drives all human beings, some more than others. A growing number of individuals in rich societies are guided by hedonic considerations when choosing a place to live, the predictable outcomes of a combination of higher incomes and longer life spans.

As individuals and families grow richer—as basic needs are no longer a concern—perceptions of what is important inevitably change. We saw in the previous chapter how urbanization was in large part the outcome of changing consumption patterns. By the same token, the *relative* importance of things other than income (money) should increase as incomes grow. This does not mean that money is losing its importance—by no means—but rather that the *relative* importance (compared to more dollars earned) of, say, a walk in the forest or a walk on the beach is presumably greater for richer than for poorer individuals, that is, for individuals who like to walk in the forest or on the beach. Thus, a young professional in a well-paying occupation (computer programming, corporate accounting, etc.)—fairly sure of landing a job almost anywhere—may well decide that he or she prefers to live in an environment where the sun shines and swimming is possible the whole year round even if it means refusing the highest wage offer. The individual—with a strong preference for the sun and the sea—may therefore decide to accept a job offer in San Diego, California, even though prospective employers in Chicago are willing to offer higher wages.

A second reason for the growth in hedonic-motivated choices is a direct outcome of longer life spans. Populations over sixty years of age are growing rapidly in all industrialized nations. A growing share of the population is made up of retirees. For retirees, the choice of a place to live is, in principle, almost entirely disconnected from income considerations. Whether they live in Florida or New Jersey (in the U.S.) or in Lille or Cannes (in France), retirees will still receive their pensions or other investment income. Stated differently, retirees are free to choose where they live without having to worry about where the money will come from. In the past, such a luxury, as it were, was reserved for the happy few: royalty, rentiers, and tycoons. Today, this is a mass phenomenon and a growing one, although the majority of retirees are not necessarily as rich as the royalty of yore. The emergence of this new, older population is a truly unique event in human history. Here we have a population—numbering in the millions in nations such as the U.S., Japan, France, and the UK—that is basically free to settle where it chooses. For retirees, there is little reason to believe that choices will be guided by traditional economic criteria. However, this does not mean that the rules of economic geography are canceled. Size and location continue to matter, but in different ways.

The range of choices open to hedonically motivated migrants will in the first instance depend on distance and on physical geography. A Canadian or Swede will obviously be hard put to find year-round sunny beaches, unless he or she is prepared to move to another country. However, technological change has considerably broadened the range of possible choices, opening up new places to hedonic growth where it would have been unthinkable before.

The twentieth century has seen momentous technological changes, which have made it possible to comfortably inhabit lands that before were thought generally uninhabitable. Because of its geography, the impact of these changes has been most profoundly felt in United States. Developed nations are as a rule almost wholly situated in cool, temperate, and well-watered zones. Indeed, this is one of the initial factors that favored their development in the first place. In the U.S., large parts of the nation fall outside the temperate zone, with humid tropical and subtropical regions in the Southeast and dry, hot, desert landscapes in the Southwest. Today, the humid Southeast— Florida plus nearby coastal regions—and the hot Southwest—Arizona, New Mexico, and Southern California—are among the fastest growing regions in the nation. The reason these places are growing is, obviously, that people have chosen to live there. But these choices were made possible—or at least greatly facilitated—by modern innovations in health, sanitation, irrigation, and internal climate control. Without the invention of air conditioning, Arizona would still be mostly empty. Without the invention of penicillin and other antibiotics and the introduction of modern public health measures, the Miami area would still be a malaria-ridden and disease-infested tropical nightmare. The interplay between technology and hedonic migrations needs to be kept in mind. This is nowhere truer than for temporary migrations, common among retirees. Florida and Arizona are, for example, home to many winter residents who return north at the beginning of spring, only to return south again at the end of fall. This mobility would not be possible—certainly more expensive—without the invention of the automobile and the airplane.

The hedonic imperative will not necessarily affect the two groups—retirees and young professionals—in the same manner, nor should we expect them to necessarily converge on the same regions, although they may overlap. I shall call the first group *gray migrants* and to the second *green migrants*.

Green Migrations: Sun, Surf, and Cafés

The group I am referring to has been abundantly characterized—and satirized—in the mass media. Most readers—certainly in North America—will know to whom I am referring when I speak of the Starbucks or caffè latte crowd. Or I might simply call them the new yuppies. Richard Florida prefers the term *creative class*.[1] None of these terms is totally satisfactory, but I believe the message comes across. These green migrants are, as a rule, young professionals—generally at the outset of their career—who place a high value on the environment (visual, cultural, natural, etc.) in which they choose to make their career. Generalizations are risky since tastes and preferences differ. Not all green migrants will have the same definition of what constitutes a quality environment. Some will place a high value on the buzz of big city life while others will prefer the more bucolic pleasures of a small university town.

BEAUTIFUL PLACES

The environmental factors that attract young professionals—indeed most of us—are entirely obvious and do not require long scholarly dissertations. Studies both in the United States and Europe have demonstrated the positive relationship between climate, physical geography, and population growth.[2] In the U.S., climate remains one of the best predictors of population growth.[3] The term *Sun Belt* says it all. Given the choice, most people prefer warm to cold weather and sunny to gray skies. The attraction of the sea—or other water surfaces—also seems universal. Mountains are generally preferred over flat land. The general movement south of the American population is thus entirely predictable and unsurprising, as is the movement towards shorelines and mountainous areas. There are very few coastal communities in the U.S. that are not growing. If, in addition, the community can offer a pleasant climate and mountains, as well, its attractive power becomes almost irresistible, which in no small part explains the continued rapid growth of the coastal parts of Oregon and Washington on the West Coast.

Climate and topography are not everything. It's worth repeating that hedonic choices remain very much a matter of taste. Minneapolis–St. Paul is the American Midwestern urban area with the highest proportion of college graduates, but also the region's coldest. *De gustibus et coloribus non disputandum.*[4] Big cities continue—and will continue—to attract large sections of the population simply because that is where interesting things are happening and where some people, especially the most educated, want to be. There is little reason to believe that this will change.[5] Simply looking at the U.S., big and exciting cities are certainly not lacking: New York, San Francisco, Chicago, and Boston, to name only a few, will continue to attract migrants from across the nation and around the world. And so will London, Paris, Toronto, Sydney, and all the other cities that offer the looked-for opportunities and lifestyles.

The professions and occupations I am talking about are inescapably urban, as should be abundantly obvious by now. Here, two additional factors come into play, one hedonic—the "character" of the city, so to speak—and the other less so—the presence of a university. The first is difficult to reduce to one word and also highly subjective, as all hedonic preferences must be. The images that come to mind are: scenic, old-world, charming, trendy, a place with sidewalk cafés and art galleries, plus an appropriate density of bicycle and jogging paths. Such attributes are difficult to measure, but some cities are visibly more blessed than others when it comes to architecture and to urban landscape. There is little doubt that the attractiveness of the San Francisco Bay Area and of Greater Boston—which remain America's dominant high-tech magnets—is not unrelated to the aesthetic quality of their urban landscape and the vibrancy of their urban street life, which rivals that of European cities. Without wishing to overdo the importance of this hedonic attribute—tastes differ, I repeat—it does give an edge to cities with a unique architectural heritage or with a particularly spectacular natural setting. In Canada, Vancouver, a magnet for immigrants from around the globe, is reputed for its bohemian lifestyle, innovative urban planning, and spectacular natural setting. Charleston, South Carolina, would probably have remained an economic backwater and perhaps even declined were it not for its superb antebellum architectural heritage, which is attracting a growing number of Yankees (northerners, in southern parlance).

Another way of making this point is with reference to opposites. Heavy industry and mining have the unfortunate trait of leaving behind terribly ugly urban landscapes. I've already talked about the Belgian Borinage area and the dismal industrial landscapes of the English Midlands. In the U.S., few Midwestern cities are celebrated for the quality of their urban landscape, Chicago's proud architectural heritage notwithstanding. With all due respect to Midwestern cities, beauty is not generally one of their trademarks. As in Europe's old industrial cities, the cities of America's Rust Belt have found it difficult to shake off their blue-collar image. Cities with a legacy of heavy industry or mining have in general found it more difficult to make the transition to the service-based knowledge economy, in part because of the greater difficulty of attracting young environmentally conscious professionals. The most successful towns and cities have often been those that were bypassed by the first Industrial Revolution, producing slower growth in the nineteenth century, but in turn allowing them to preserve their architectural heritage, especially in Europe. It cannot be a total coincidence that one of the fastest growing cities in England outside the prosperous south is the old cathedral city of York.

In Germany, the attraction of the warmer south, mountain landscapes, and towns that were able to preserve their historic centers—and which were not bombed out (or less so)—may also have played a role in the economic success since the Second World War of southern Bavaria, centered on Munich, and of the *Land* of Baden-Württemberg, centered on Stuttgart, which are home to much of Germany's high-tech industry. But the true role of climate, urban landscapes, and beauty is, I repeat, hard to establish. One often hears it said—at least in local economic development circles—that Barcelona's economic success is in part the result of superb city planning;[6] there is little doubt that Barcelona is a uniquely beautiful and well-planned city, with the not-inconsequential added advantage of the Mediterranean, nearby beaches, and a mild climate. Barcelona projects a positive image, the polar opposite of that of a rusting old industrial city. Yet Europe is full of beautiful old historic towns with magnificent piazzas, delightful neighborhoods, and tall cathedrals that have not become centers of the modern high-tech IT economy.

UNIVERSITY TOWNS AND RESEARCH PARKS

I now move to a second, less hedonic, attribute: the presence of a university or other institutions of higher learning. Here also, the evidence of a positive relationship with growth is fairly solid,[7] although we do run into the classic problem—in the social sciences—of circular causation. Do universities *cause* growth or, rather, are they a *result* of prosperous and dynamic societies? Researchers looking into the relationship between human capital (education levels) and local economic growth constantly run into this problem. Do educated populations *cause* growth or do they naturally *flock to* growing places and places with a greater growth potential? Sorting out the two is terribly difficult and may in the end be impossible. Here, I focus on the relationship between universities or other institutions of higher learning and the attractiveness of a place for green migrants.

Universities attract green migrants for at least two easy-to-understand reasons: they are major employers of green migrants, often the principal employers; they bring in students who, in turn, foster the type of lifestyle and services that make a city "hip," trendy, and all the rest. Other more indirect impacts—on entrepreneurial spin-offs, on innovation—are more difficult to rigorously demonstrate. However—and this is the main point—whatever (positive) aspect of the presence of a university one wishes to highlight, its impact on the local economy will ultimately depend on the size and the quality of the institution, compared, that is, to other universities elsewhere. All advantages are relative. Our ambitious young green migrant aspires to go to the city with the best universities, the best bookstores, the best libraries, and the best laboratories and research hospitals. Why settle for East Podunk, even if it's got a great liberal arts college and super sports facilities, if you can go to Boston? Which brings us back to the very beginnings of this book and why real estate prices are higher in Boston and in San Francisco than in East Podunk.

They matter for universities because universities are subject to agglomeration economies, perhaps more so even then most industries. Great universities are not created overnight, but are the result of decades, centuries even, of accumulated investments in human and physical capital. The Boston and San Francisco areas are home to what are arguably the four top universities in the United States today, and perhaps the world.[8] Boston and San Francisco are not the two largest urban areas in the U.S.; but they are major metropolitan areas—large by any standards—with populations well above the 5 million mark. Larger cities tend as a rule to have higher percentages of adults with university degrees. Two parallel processes are at work: more highly educated populations migrate into than out of big cities; bigger cities produce proportionally more university graduates because that is where institutions of higher learning are concentrated. In short, smaller places face an uphill battle if they wish to become centers of higher learning and magnets for university-educated young professionals. But it is not impossible, as we shall now see.

Location also matters. Many top universities, both in North America and in Europe, are located in fairly small towns, but *close to* a major metropolis. Examples abound: Princeton (between New York and Philadelphia); Yale in New Haven, Connecticut (near New York); Cambridge and Oxford Universities (near London); the University of Michigan at Ann Arbor (near Detroit);

Leiden in the Netherlands (near Amsterdam and The Hague); Heidelberg (near Manheim and Frankfurt) and Tübingen (near Stuttgart) in Germany. These places have the good fortune, as it were, of combining the advantages of size with the more bucolic pleasures of a small town. It is thus not entirely surprising that many research corridors—clusters of laboratories and high-tech firms and start-ups—have sprung up in areas between a large metropolis and a nearby university town. A large number of high-tech firms and laboratories in the south of England are located on the motorways linking London to Oxford or to Cambridge. Silicon Valley, the very symbol of the high-tech IT economy, originally developed along a corridor—the San Jose Valley—between Stanford University at Palo Alto on one end and the University of California at Berkley and downtown San Francisco at the other. The Valley—once the plum-growing capital of California—has since become entirely urbanized and integrated into the San Francisco Bay Metropolitan Area.

Once we understand the relationship between size, location, and hedonic factors for universities and research clusters, we can understand why certain initiatives have succeeded. One of the great success stories in local economic development planning is the research park at what is now called Sophia Antipolis (a play on the Greek "city of wisdom"), originally an agricultural zone in the south of France. The area now encompasses what is probably the largest cluster of IT firms, high-tech start-ups, university faculties, and research laboratories in France outside the Paris area. The idea was initially launched in the 1960s and, in the words of one of its promoters, was "to build a Latin Quarter in the countryside."[9] Aside from the undoubted political skills of those who made it happen, Sophia Antipolis combines two unique advantages: 1) it is located a few minutes' drive from the city of Nice and its university, and 2) it is on the French Riviera, a worthy rival in sum in terms of natural beauty—of California's Silicon Valley. As far as hedonic locations go, it's difficult to beat. What young professional would not want to move there?

Sophia Antipolis is located in what I have called the periphery, outside Europe's Blue Banana. However, the population of Greater Nice is close to 1 million, which is not insubstantial, plus home to France's second largest airport. The example of Sophia Antipolis demonstrates that a peripheral city need not be *very* large to become a magnate for young, "hip" professionals if—besides a decent university—it can offer *something else*. North Carolina's Research Triangle provides another example with a story not very different from that of Sophia Antipolis.[10] The Research Triangle, located again in a very pleasant setting, is a high-tech business park built around Duke University in Durham, the University of North Carolina at Chapel Hill, and North

Carolina State University at Raleigh. The combined population of Raleigh and Durham is close to 1.5 million, which again is not insubstantial. In the North Carolina case, the *something else* was probably not primarily its natural setting—it certainly helped—but also lower costs, both for real estate and for labor, compared to locations around Boston, San Francisco, and other major urban centers at the time.

Another city in the south of France, Montpellier, illustrates that a good natural setting, combined with a pleasant urban landscape, can sometimes overcome the constraints of size. Montpellier, with a metropolitan population of about 300,000, has developed into one of France's most dynamic university towns, with an emerging IT and high-tech cluster, a magnet for young researchers and professionals. Like Sophia Antipolis, Montpellier is located on the Mediterranean—the beaches are a few minutes away—and not far from the rolling hills and nature parks of the French province of Languedoc. For a mid-sized university town in the periphery to succeed, in sum, it must be able to offer something special—if it does not have the initial good fortune of being located close to a fairly large city—which, more often than not, is its natural setting. But not all peripheries can offer what the south of France has to offer.

Cornell, one of America's foremost universities, located in the small town of Ithaca in Upstate New York (not really close to anything), is an example of an institution that seemingly has had little impact. Cornell University provides perhaps the best example that a university *by itself*, even a very prestigious one,[11] will not automatically trigger an inflow of talent and economic growth, unless other factors are also present. Ithaca is the very model of an attractive university town with all the appropriate attributes: a bohemian lifestyle, liberal politics, a pleasant natural setting on the shores of Lake Cayuga. Yet Ithaca does not seem to have attracted much of an inflow of young professionals beyond the core group associated with the university. Ithaca has not—to my knowledge—spawned a major industrial research cluster. Perhaps this was a community choice; I do not know. The point is this: Ithaca is favored neither by size nor location. Its positive attributes, most notably the excellence of its university, have visibly not been sufficient to offset the disadvantages of distance from a large urban center.

UNLIKELY PLACES

Oulu in northern Finland is an exception to the rule, about as peripheral as one can imagine in Europe. One could hardly think of a worse location, just below the Arctic Circle, cold, far from everything, and with a small population. The population of Oulu is about 150,000 but has increased rapidly in recent times. Oulu also has a healthy high-tech sector. Why Oulu? Although the complete story is undoubtedly more complex, there are at least two reasons. The first is the University of Oulu. Finland is a small country—in population, not size—with about 5 million inhabitants. The University of Oulu, with some 15,000 students, is Finland's second largest, with strong engineering and science faculties. It is as if the largest concentration of universities in England outside London were located in Newcastle, the equivalent, as it were, of moving Oxford and Cambridge to the north. This is an exceptional situation, rarely encountered in other nations. The second reason, no less exceptional, is the dominant position within the nation of a single high-tech company, Nokia, the pioneer of mobile telephones. One may reasonably assume—although it would be difficult to prove—that this dominant position of Nokia within Finland facilitates policy coordination between government and industry, including on where to locate facilities. Nokia has located a number of its production facilities in Oulu. To come to the point: exceptional circumstances will produce exactly that, exceptions.

To illustrate the difficult-to-generalize interplay between natural setting, higher learning, and "accidents," let me present a last example: the city of Burlington in the state of Vermont. By any definition, Burlington is a small peripheral city. Burlington has a metropolitan population of about 170,000 (2000 census), located close to the Canadian border, some four hours north of Boston. But the Burlington area is also very prosperous with systematically low unemployment rates and a per capita income above the national average, in sharp contrast to the depressed areas of Upstate New York to the west. Burlington also has a burgeoning high-tech economy, specifically in the areas of computer components manufacturing, computer systems, and health care. What explains Burlington's apparent success? Like much of this part of America, the economic mainstays of the area were historically textiles and lumber, both of which have declined. The area's early period of prosperity was in the first part of nineteenth century before the railroads robbed Burlington—located on the shores of Lake Champlain—of its natural advantage for water-born commerce. In the decades that followed, northern Vermont remained an economic backwater, growing only slowly,[12] as befits a peripheral region. Then, in 1957, an "accident" happened: IBM, the largest computer company of the time, chose the city as the site for a new plant for the design and production of memory chips. Four thousand jobs were created; by 1980, the plant provided more than seven thousand jobs.[13] IBM remains the area's largest employer, but has since been followed by other IT firms. I do not know why exactly IBM chose Burlington in 1957, why it stayed, and why others have followed. However, my personal acquaintance with the area leads me to suggest that a mix of indefinable factors were at play.

What were these indefinable factors? First: *image,* even if I don't much like the term. Vermonters—sturdy New Englanders—have long had a reputation of being hard-working, frugal, and honest, the personification of the old Protestant work ethic. These are people who do not complain or waste time. But, at the same time, Vermont has acquired a reputation as a socially progressive and nonconformist place, willing to welcome eccentrics and unconventional lifestyles—within bounds, of course (as long as they don't upset the horses, as the Queen used to say). This apparently contradictory combination of strait-laced Protestantism and socially progressive politics recalls my earlier story of the hardy Scandinavian dairy farmers of Minnesota. And like the Minnesotans, the people of Vermont have a tradition of electing independent politicians. Since 1991, Vermont has elected the only independent congressman—Bernie Sanders, the former, openly progressive (socialist) mayor of Burlington—to the U.S. House of Representatives and then Senate (in 2006). Whether this unconventional electorate is a cause or consequence of the coming of IBM, it is impossible to say.[14] What can be said is that Vermont has become a magnet for a certain type of young professional. This lifestyle choice is visible in the urban planning of Burlington, unique among U.S. cities of comparable size. Burlington has managed to slow the proliferation of large shopping malls—which have destroyed main streets in much of small-town America—via a combination of zoning and other bylaws. Burlington's main street is a pedestrian mall on the European model, almost always lively, and which has visibly remained the heart of the town.

Burlington has two added advantages. First, it is the location of the University of Vermont, which although not one of the U.S.'s greatest universities, nonetheless gives the town the feel of a university town, with a substantial student population. Second, Burlington's natural setting, although not overly spectacular (these are not the Alps or the Rockies), is nonetheless very attractive, poised on the shores of Lake Champlain overlooking the Adirondack Mountains. One of the best known ski resorts in the Northeast, Stowe, is but a few miles away, as are numerous state parks, equipped for hiking, boating, and mountain climbing. Vermont has done a remarkable job of marketing itself as an environmentally conscious, nature-friendly state. It's the kind of place, in sum, to which environmentally conscious young professionals would normally be attracted. Whether all this really makes a difference in the end is difficult to say. But it is certainly preferable to a negative image of grime, crime, and sunset industries.

Finally—returning once again to the "all advantages are relative" refrain—

Burlington is not all that peripheral compared to other places. Burlington is not in South Dakota or in Newfoundland. It all depends on where one sits. Seen from New York—the home of IBM's head office—Burlington, Vermont, seems like a pretty sensible choice if one is looking for a small town (but not too small either) with a pleasant environment and a reliable workforce. And perhaps back in the 1950s, when northern Vermont was still a low-cost location, that little added fact might have made all the difference.

Much of what I have said in this section is speculative. Many professionals and businesspersons are undoubtedly turned off by the caffe latte–sipping, bicycle-riding crowd and are looking for precisely the opposite kind of environment. Many modern high-growth industries are not necessarily in search of trendy, unconventional environments. What in the end could be more typically conservative than corporate accountants, investment bankers, and corporate executives? For many young professionals and aspiring executives, the epitome of hedonic success, certainly in North America, is a large suburban home with an equally large swimming pool and an even larger stable of expensive automobiles and other playthings. A well-paying job and a shot at a suburban château may be the deciding factors. How else can one explain the impressive growth of metropolitan areas such as Atlanta and Dallas, which, despite their undeniable qualities (including warm weather), cannot be said to be particularly beautiful or artsy? If young professionals are drawn to these cities—and they obviously are—it is certainly not because of their lively downtowns and bohemian lifestyle.

I may be making too much of what in the end is a minority—some would say "elite"—phenomenon.[15] Not only do tastes differ (and change), but the number of people who can truly choose where to live and work is probably quite small. Few people of working age can truly choose freely where to live without also taking job and career opportunities into account, which inevitably brings us back to size. If no jobs are on offer, if no business opportunities exist, young graduates will not come, no matter how beautiful the natural setting or how well planned the area is. The chain linking green migrants and jobs can never be totally cut. It is on this point that gray migrants, to whom I now turn, are different from other migrants. For gray migrants, the chain has been cut.

Gray Migration: Golf, Châteaux, and Boardwalks

Gray migrants—retirees—are the most rapidly growing population group in industrialized nations. We have barely begun to feel the full impact of this rising gray tide. Not all, of course, are sufficiently independent of means or sufficiently mobile to be able to freely choose their region of retirement. A growing number are, however, and their choices can have a profound effect on the economy of regions. Incoming gray migrants are the equivalent of an export industry for the region that receives them. These retirees spend money in the community—on health services, real estate, entertainment, food, etc.—that was earned elsewhere. A retiree from New York living in Miami who buys locally grown oranges is contributing just as much to the local economy as the Florida farmer who exports oranges to New York. Gray migrants provide a local economic base in the same manner as any other industry; they bring money into the community.

THE RISE OF RESIDENTIAL ECONOMIES

In more technical terms, we are witnessing the birth of an entirely new local economic base, founded on private and public transfers (i.e., unearned income, so to speak). The money coming into the community is not in return for a good or a service that a local firm is selling to the rest of the world because it can produce it more cheaply, but because people coming from elsewhere have chosen to spend their savings, investment income, or pension benefits there. The French economist, Laurent Davezies, has coined the term *residential economies* to describe these new local economies.[16] Davezies documents the gap between income generated in the Greater Paris region and income spent in other places, generally in the south or west of France. Concretely, what Davezies observes is the income earned by, say, a Paris fashion designer who chooses to retire (or semi-retire) to a coastal village in the south of France, where he ends up spending most of his income, perhaps commuting back to Paris from time to time. Another example would be a New York banker who buys a condo in Boca Raton,[17] where he spends most of his time and income, although flying back to New York now and then to close a business deal.

Residential economies are true examples of places capturing wealth rather than creating it. It is not entirely accurate, however, to say that all the wealth so captured is unearned. A place blessed by natural beauty and good weather may also have put a considerable effort into creating a pleasant environment, attractive to gray migrants. Urban planning, public security, libraries, and other public services are all things that communities can and do control. Fierce competition exists between beautiful places. However, without the right initial natural attributes, even the best-planned places will have difficulty attracting and holding gray migrants. In the end, the real good that the place is selling was produced by nature and not by man.

The places favored by gray and green migrants will often be the same, not only because both are in search of beauty and pleasure, but also because the dividing line between the two is often fuzzy, as in the case of our commuting New York banker or other semi-retirees still at work. Green migrants may eventually become gray migrants. Some young working-age migrants will choose their region of work with an eye, also, to retirement. Why not kill two birds with one stone, as it were, and choose early on in one's career a place where one would like to live out one's life? The longer we live, the more important that "eye on retirement" will become in making residential decisions, even earlier in life. It is impossible to separate out the hedonic imperative from other considerations: proximity to family, proximity to (insured) health services, career possibilities after retirement, etc. Nonetheless, the rise of residential economies—fueled by the hedonic imperative—is a powerful force pushing populations and their wealth in certain directions.

The impact of the rise of residential economies on the relative success (or not) of places will be most profoundly felt in nations with significant climatic and topographic differences, specifically, those that have regions attractive to both green and gray migrants, which brings me back to France.

FRANCE'S HEDONIC GROWTH CRESCENT

France is a nation truly blessed by geography.[18] Lying entirely within the temperate zone, it nonetheless has a broad range of climates, going from the cool, damp, and often gray north to the dry and sunny south. Almost all of French territory is inhabitable and useful for agriculture or grazing. France borders on two majestic mountain ranges: the Pyrenees to the southwest and the Alps to the southeast. France has two long and attractive shorelines: the Atlantic to the west and the Mediterranean to the south. In between, the countryside is made up of a variety of landscapes, generally flatter in the north and hillier in the south. The French have over the centuries added to the natural attractions of the landscape, dotted with picturesque villages, châteaux of various dimensions, well-planned towns, and (in the south) well-manicured vineyards. France had the additional good fortune that few of its great historical cities or towns were bombed during the Second World War. Most of its rich architectural heritage is intact and has been well maintained. France's rich agricultural legacy, with its wide variety of produce, dairy products, and wines, undoubtedly contributed to the development of a culinary tradition that has few rivals. Anyone who has had the good fortune to visit a farmer's market or to dine out in France will know what I mean.

For the hedonic migrant, whatever his or her pleasure—be it fine cuisine, the café life, châteaux, the sea, or the mountains—France, specifically the west and the south of the country, has much to offer. The first to be affected are the French themselves. The French population of retirement age—retirement sometimes starting at fifty or fifty-five years of age—has been systematically moving to the southwest and south. When added to the pull, related earlier, of several attractive university towns—Toulouse, Bordeaux, Sophia Antipolis, Montpellier, etc.—the pull of this part of France becomes almost irresistible, France's California and nearly as big. I call this France's hedonic growth crescent (or *croissant*), a large arc-shaped territory that stretches, roughly, from Brittany in the west to the Italian border in the southeast, following both shorelines, interrupted by the Pyrenees, and culminating in the French Alps and the French Riviera. We may reasonably predict that this part of France will continue to witness population growth in coming decades. This is the heart of what Davezies calls *residential economies*, fueled by green and gray migrants fleeing Paris and the cold French north, bringing their wealth with them.

The pull of France's hedonic growth crescent is not limited to the French. It also exerts a powerful attraction on gray migrants from nations to the north: the Netherlands, Germany, Scandinavia, and the United Kingdom, an attraction considerably facilitated by membership in the EU. Spanish, Italian, and other southern European regions exert a similar attraction on northerners. However, France's hedonic growth crescent has advantages that make it particularly attractive to non-French gray migrants. A major advantage is location, which in this case we might call the *grandchild factor*. For all sorts of reasons, not the least of which is the desire to see one's grandchildren from time to time, retirees will—given the choice—prefer a location that is closer to home over one that is farther away. French hedonic destinations are closer, certainly for the British and the Dutch, than most alternative destinations. A second factor, more difficult to define, which notably affects British gray migrants, is cultural and historical proximity, in large measure a consequence of geographic proximity. The west and the south of France have long been playgrounds of British elites, long before gray migrations became a mass phenomenon.[19] The tradition of buying up châteaux in the Bordeaux—vineyards included—has long historical roots. In addition, the British must be one of the last peoples in the industrialized world—English Canada excepted— where French is still the preferred second language taught in school, precisely because they already speak English (Spanish has long since replaced French in the U.S.). In short, France for many Brits is less "foreign" than Italy, the Iberian peninsula, and certainly the Balkans.[20]

France's hedonic growth crescent is, in sum, founded on a combination of advantages. Viewed from a regional growth perspective, this makes France a very lucky country, for that crescent of growth almost exactly coincides with France's historical periphery—those parts of the nation furthest from the Europe's Blue Banana. These have traditionally been among the poorest regions, especially those lying in the southwest. Hedonic regional growth is in the process of eliminating France's center-periphery divide. Green and gray migrants are pulling the French economy in the opposite direction from Europe's Blue Banana, producing a more balanced pattern of growth and wealth. In France, the hedonic imperative is working to reduce regional income disparities. By the same token, it could be argued that there are now two classes of local economies in France: those that serve to generate wealth—notably, in and around Paris—and those that capture wealth, due largely to the good fortune of their natural geography.

The analogy with the U.S. will certainly not have escaped the reader. In the U.S. also, hedonic regional growth—powerfully aided by technology—has played a major role in reducing regional income disparities and in widening the range of places that can aspire to attract talent and money. In the U.S., as in France, the impact of hedonic growth on regional disparities has been largely positive because hedonically blessed places were for the most part located in the periphery, at the opposite end of the nation from the initial fountainheads of economic growth. In both cases, the popularization of long-distance transportation (now affordable by most)—air travel in the U.S. and high-speed trains in France—has enabled hedonic peripheries to attract green and gray migrants who wish stay in touch with the center. And, as in France, the hedonic regions of the U.S. are favored destinations for gray migrants from neighboring nations—Canadians in this case—bringing home yet again the importance of proximity (both real and cultural) for hedonically motivated residential retirement choices.

THE RELATIVITY OF HEDONIC ADVANTAGES

The importance of geographic and cultural proximity means that many gray migrants will move within a relatively restricted area or seek out cultural enclaves—artificially generated, so to speak—where they can feel at home. Both because of proximity and old historical ties, German-speakers (Germans and Austrians) will often prefer the Adriatic coast of Slovenia and Croatia, where German remains widely spoken and where a good Wiener schnitzel is never far way. Sometimes, gray migrations can lead to tensions, especially where one culture—the gray incoming one—threatens to overwhelm the local culture or language. The move south of German Swiss into the Italian Swiss canton of Ticino continues to preoccupy the local Italian-speaking population. Gray migrants are also sensitive to local political conditions, understandably so. One does not invest one's life savings in an apartment or house in a place where the currency might collapse or the police turn unfriendly. For northern Europeans, this gives an additional edge to French (as well as Iberian and Italian) destinations, compared, for example, to possible Balkan or North African alternatives.

The quest for security and cultural affinity—added to simple geographic proximity—will mean that many, if not most, gray migrants will prefer to stay within their nation's borders. In Britain, the most rapidly growing places outside the London suburbs are mainly concentrated in three areas: along the southwest coast (Cornwall, Devon, Dorset), eastern Wales and Hereford, and East Anglia. These are all very pleasant areas, characterized by shorelines, rolling hills, or rural farmlands and—within the British context—somewhat (although not much) more clement climates. All these regions lie in the southern tier of the nation, which comes as no surprise. In the case of Britain, we saw that the hedonic imperative is pulling populations in the same direction—towards the south—as the pull of the center: London. In nations where peripheral regions are also the coldest or otherwise unattractive to gray migrants (as is often the case in Canada and Scandinavia) the hedonic imperative will further weaken those regions that are already the weakest.

The British example highlights, yet again, the importance of proximity. All the "green" destinations listed above, though not falling directly within the Greater London area, are never very far from London. This cannot only be attributed to what I called the "grandchild factor," but also to the desire not to move *too* far from one's former place of employment and residence. As noted earlier, several reasons may motivate gray migrants not to move too far away: health care, the desire to maintain social and business contacts, or, simply, the desire to stay in touch and go back from time to time to old familiar places. The business link should not be underestimated, even for some gray migrants. In many professions—writing, consulting, teaching, etc.—a form of semi-retirement is not uncommon. The job link is there, but not on a continuous basis, meaning that the green-gray migrant may need to go to the big city only once a week or less. The Internet has made this even easier, including for non-retired persons in similar professions, which do not require a daily presence at one's place of work (they remain a small minority, however).

In most industrialized nations, one will find clearly identifiable hedonic growth sheds within roughly a two-hour drive of major metropolitan areas, places whose most visible characteristic (besides their natural setting) will be high real estate prices and concentrations of secondary residences. Geography is the prime determinant in this case. The region must have something to offer—lakes, mountains, the sea, etc.[21] The most rapidly growing part of the province of Quebec is the Laurentian Plateau north of Montreal, famed for its lakes and mountains, a growth increasingly fueled by retirees. Around New York, the seaside communities of Long Island and the mountain hideaways of the Catskills play the same role. Hedonic growth areas of this kind, within easy reach of large urban centers, are consistent with the first two laws of regional growth, as I am sure the reader has already spotted. Such regional growth, although hedonically motivated, is a natural outgrowth of urban concentration. The larger the urban concentration, the wider will be the potential range of hedonic destinations: the fountainhead will gush higher and the sprays go farther. However, the hedonic imperative means that growth *within* central regions will shift to places with attributes that gray and green migrants find attractive.

The importance of proximity means that—like so many other advantages—hedonic advantages are relative.[22] For hedonic advantages, relativity is in part the result of national boundaries. As noted earlier, many gray migrants will absolutely want to stay within the bounds of their national state. Canadians who permanently leave the country lose their health insurance benefits after six months, which is why the many hundreds of thousands of retired Canadians who "live" in Florida migrate back north every spring. Not all barriers to international gray migration are as stringent, but national boundaries do limit the options of potential migrants. Thus, a place may have an indisputable advantage within its home country because of its natural setting but which is not exceptional when compared to other nations. Cornwall, in the southwestern tip of England, has no rival in Britain in terms of its natural setting and, correspondingly, is one the most rapidly growing areas. But landscapes of equal spectacular beauty can be found in northern Spain, which have not necessarily generated corresponding above-average growth *within* Spain. The Okanagan Valley in British Colombia is another example. The Okanagan resembles numerous areas in the neighboring states of Washington and Oregon. In the U.S., it would most probably have gone unnoticed. Yet, *within* Canada, it is exceptional: a sunny and dry valley with lush orchards and vineyards with a deep azure lake surrounded by snow-capped mountains. Kelowna (population: about 150,000), the commercial hub of the region, is one of the fastest growing middle-sized cities in Canada.

Summing up: geography will largely determine which places gain and which stand to lose from the rise of the hedonic imperative. In France and the U.S., the impact is, on the whole, positive, widening the range of places that can hope to capture the fruits of economic growth, often revamping the economy of historically peripheral places. In Britain, the impact is quite the opposite, further strengthening the already strong south of England. The principal difference between France and the U.S. is that the hedonic-driven development of America's Sun Belt owes more to technology, notably the eradication of tropical deceases and the invention of electricity and air conditioning. The role of technology in changing regional fortunes allows me now to turn to tourism.

Size and Location Also Matter for Tourism

Tourism is arguably the clearest expression of an economic activity founded on the pursuit of pleasure. In fact, the dividing line between tourism and gray migration is fuzzy, except for the age factor. The example of the Canadian snowbirds—as these retirees are popularly called—who flock down to Florida or Arizona each winter only to migrate back north in the spring is a case in point. Are they tourists or migrants? The dividing line with green migrants is no less fuzzy. Second homes—on the sea, in the mountains—are not only limited to retirees, but often purchased with an eye on retirement. Should we consider a young New York or London professional who owns a condominium in Florida or the French Riviera, and spends a good part of the year there, a migrant or a tourist? By the same token, is a German shopper who crosses the Rhine to buy cheese and wine in Strasbourg, but also stops to admire the local cathedral, a tourist or not? Or is a Japanese executive who travels to Paris for a conference, but spends several days visiting museums, a tourist or a business traveler? It is not always easy, in sum, to separate tourism from other pursuits.

Tourism, for this reason, does not feature in most industry classifications used by national statistical agencies. I shall limit the use of the word to true temporary migrations—travel, in other words, for the purpose of pleasure, entrainment, sports, or other pursuits not linked to career concerns. For tourism to provide a solid economic base, a place must be able to generate a constant stream of travelers. Such places are rare outside large urban areas and locations close to them. Such that do exist are generally founded on a unique attribute or event. In Europe, Lourdes in southern France and Santiago de Compostela in northwestern Spain are examples, which might be more properly called religious tourism. Venice and Salzburg might also qualify—in both cases, tourism is probably the city's principal economic base—but neither of these are truly peripheral places. Only rarely does tourism provide the principal economic base for regions located far from large metropolitan markets. The challenge facing all tourist developers outside large urban centers is the generation of a *steady* stream of tourists over several months of the year. An attraction that only brings in tourists for one season can seldom sustain a regional economy. This puts peripheral regions in cold or very hot climates at a disadvantage, although heat seems to be less of disincentive—in part thanks to air-condoning—than the cold. The need to provide multi-season attractions gives an edge to places in mountainous regions that can offer the conditions both for hiking and other nature activities in the summer and for skiing in the winter.

Proximity to large urban markets remains the main constraint. For tourism, the first rule of regional growth can be reformulated to read: for two comparable tourist attractions, the place closest to the center will be favored. This is a simple restatement of the law of intervening opportunities, too often forgotten by over-optimistic tourist developers. The Pyrenees have wonderful conditions for skiing and hiking, but the Alps are closer to major European markets and will thus be developed first. By the same token, the fact that there are no intervening opportunities—for skiing or for mountain hiking—between Paris and the foothills of the French and Swiss Alps gives the mountain resorts there a competitive advantage. The ski and summer resorts of Stowe (Vermont) and Lake Placid (New York) are profitable—although these are peripheral locations—because there are few intervening opportunities between them and the huge megalopolis market to the south. If the Rockies were equally close, neither resort would have survived, yet another example of the "everything is relative" theme. From a regional growth perspective, the crucial point, however, is the limited impact of these two resorts on the surrounding economy. Both, although successful, can hardly be said to have generated a broad economic base sufficient to sustain an entire regional economy. Stowe and Lake Placid remain small islands within their regional economies. Upstate New York around Lake Placid remains a largely depressed area. Further west, the well-known Rocky Mountain resort of Aspen in Colorado—even more peripheral—is another example. Despite its success, Aspen remains a small village of about 5,000 inhabitants.

Most major tourist developments are located within easy reach of at least one rich urban market. Market proximity is essential in order to reduce risks in what is a very volatile industry. Tastes are fickle. Fashions change. An international crisis can bring an abrupt end to foreign visitors. Tourist expenditures are luxury goods, the first things to go during an economic downturn. Tourism is rarely a solid base on which to build a whole economy. By locat-

ing close to a large urban market—within driving distance—firms dependant on outside visitors can draw on two different markets: local weekend
and second-home tourists, and non-local and foreign tourists. Canada's three
largest mountain resorts are located within driving distance of a major urban
area. Mont-Tremblant is close to Montreal; Banff is near Calgary; Whistler is
close to Vancouver. Proximity to a large urban center provides two additional
advantages that are by no means inconsequential: access to a major international airport and the possibility of combining the attractions of the city and
the mountains. Both advantages are examples of scale economies, which provided the first pillar of agglomeration in chapter 2.

The role of airports in modern tourism illustrates, yet again, the importance of technology. Technological change has allowed places—before
unimaginable—to become tourist destinations. Tropical tourist destinations—be they in the Caribbean, the Indian Ocean, or the Pacific—all owe
their existence to innovations in medicine, sanitation, and transportation
technology. But technological change, especially in transportation, can also
cause places to lose advantages they once had. Deauville on the Normandy
coast and Saratoga Springs in Upstate New York are examples. With the
arrival of the railroad, both became chic destinations in the nineteenth century for the Paris and New York elites of the time, respectively. Although
still respectable tourist destinations, both have long since been abandoned
for sunnier and more glamorous destinations by the Paris and New York
jet sets. Changes in tastes—thermal baths are no longer the rage—and the
emergence of mass tourism have contributed to the change in fortunes of
Saratoga and Deauville, but the airplane is the principle culprit. Other once-
fashionable destinations such as Brighton (south of London) and Atlantic
City (south of New York) have gone through a similar cycle. But these are
squarely located at the centers of their respective national markets. Tourism,
like any other service activity, will naturally first seek out locations at the center of the market.

Revisiting the Rules of Regional Growth

Can we make plausible predictions about the regions or places most likely to
grow in the future or, alternatively, those most likely to decline? The time has
come to revisit the four golden rules of regional growth. We are now able to
expand our initial descriptions:

1—*Size matters.* The positive relationship with wealth will be enhanced
where large urban areas also share the following attributes:

- They are part of a wider network of interconnected large, mid-sized, and small cities.
- They have a positive industrial legacy—a diversified industrial base, including knowledge-rich services and small and mid-sized firms.
- They have an above-average proportion of highly educated workers, plus at least one top-notch university.
- They are hedonically blessed by nature or by architectural heritage.

2—*Location matters*. In addition to being well-positioned for trade, the potential of a place to generate (or capture) wealth will be enhanced if the following is true:

- It is located in a hedonically blessed part of the nation.
- A border or cultural barrier bestows an advantage, reducing labor and capital outflows and/or providing captive markets.
- It is located at the center of a growing part of the nation or continent.

3—*Costs matter*. Costs or unique advantages can counteract (or reinforce) the effects of size and location:

- Hedonic endowments can offset the negative effects of small size and distance, providing no equally endowed intervening places exist.
- A resource advantage can have a lasting positive wealth effect, but only if the Intrusive Rentier Syndrome is avoided.
- A negative industrial legacy or other feature that raises costs can undo the advantages of size or location.

4—*Exceptions abound*. Fortunate (or unfortunate) accidents come in many shapes, we have seen: border changes, technological breakthroughs, politics, etc. For smaller places, they may come in the shape of a charismatic individual—a mayor or a businessperson—who at a crucial moment in its history made a difference. Few things are more difficult to predict than the birthplace of the next great inventor or entrepreneur.

No place, city, or region will score well on all the attributes of growth.[23] It is highly unlikely that one region would hold a monopoly, that is, be number one on all attributes *compared* to others. If one region were thus blessed, the pull of that region would be almost irresistible. It can be argued—as I have—that the south of England, precisely, holds such a monopoly *within* in Britain. *Within* the U.S., the San Francisco Bay Area probably comes close. It does well on all elements of size and location. True, it is not *the* biggest urban area in the U.S., nor does it lie in a multi-city network comparable to the East Coast megalopolis. But it is arguably the only major U.S. urban region (popu-

lation over 5 million) that is at the same time hedonically blessed, education-
ally blessed, and propitiously located for trade with the world's most dynamic
economies. This goes a long way in explaining why the San Francisco Bay
Area has the highest per capita personal income of any major U.S. metropolis, and is likely to stay on top (or close) in the foreseeable future.

A comparison with Chicago is instructive. Although Chicago has been
doing well in recent years, it has nonetheless grown less rapidly than San
Francisco and generated lower per capita incomes.[24] Chicago, although large,
does not do terribly well on several attributes of size and location. Although
the city itself has shed much of its old heavy industry, a large number of cities
that are part of its natural market area continue to be plagued by negative
clusters, which in turn translates into a generally slower growing greater
region (the Midwest). Chicago is a successful city in what is otherwise a slow-
growing region. Chicago is well-located within *its* region; but that region is
not terribly well-located within the United States, certainly not if we add in
hedonic considerations. Chicago provides an eloquent demonstration that
the success of a great city depends in part on the strength of the region of
which it is the center. A great city can only grow so far if its natural market
area is not growing. The future growth of Chicago is, in other words, inextri-
cably linked to the future of the Midwest and its success in finally shedding
its negative industrial legacy. However, there is not much that can be done
about Mother Nature. Chicago will always be colder than San Francisco, and
Lake Michigan, despite its undeniable attractions, will never match the maj-
esty of the Pacific and Big Sur.

Archipelagos of Growth

The Chicago example within the Midwest demonstrates that growth or
decline is rarely the lot of an entire region or part of a nation, that is, of every
single community in it. Most of the American South—seen as a region—is
growing; but this has not prevented population declines in parts of small-
town Louisiana, Mississippi, and Alabama.[25] Although most of Canada east
of Quebec City is witnessing population losses, growth continues in and
around mid-sized urban centers such as Halifax and Moncton. The appropriate image—for growing or for declining regions—is that of archipelagos of
growth or decline, made up of constellations of growing (or declining) places,
interspersed with declining (or growing) places. The positive attributes of size
and location must be interpreted as probabilities. The sudden replacement of
oil by a new renewable fuel would, for example, drastically alter the fortunes
of many parts of Texas and Alberta, currently well-poised for growth. The

more specialized—or smaller—a place is, the greater the probability of accidents and of unpredictable events.

Size, location, and hedonic attributes must always be put in context. In Europe, Italy provides a good example.[26] The hedonic imperative is fairly useless for explaining differential regional growth in Italy. It is difficult to argue that any part of that architecturally and scenically blessed land is not hedonically favored. The above-average growth of the northern-middle part of Italy, centered on the regions of Emilia Romagna, Lombardy, and Venice, is due in each case to a particular mix of circumstances, which defy easy generalizations. The much-heralded success of Emilia Romagna—sometimes called the Third Italy (*Terza Italia*)—is essentially grounded in a particular environment of small and middle-sized firms in mid-sized towns (Bologna is the largest city, population about 750,000) with a long artisan tradition of skilled workmanship and mutual assistance. The Emilia story has given rise to numerous writings and scholarly works extolling the virtues of trust, cooperation, and flexibility.[27] These, of course, are positive virtues. But local industrial cultures and traditions—the fruit of many centuries of learning and trial and error—are exactly that, *local*, and difficult to replicate.

Others, however, have argued that the Emilia model, far from being a model to emulate, is representative of much that is wrong with the Italian economy today.[28] It worked well as long as the Italian economy was relatively protected—in no small part via recurring devaluations of its currency—and organized around personal, political, and family relationships. This is no longer the case in today's centrally regulated European Union with a common currency. The small and mid-sized family-owned firms—the backbone and pride of the Emilia economy—are singularly ill suited, it has been argued, to compete in today's globalized knowledge economy, which places a premium on size and on investments in R&D and worldwide marketing. Whether this criticism is founded, I am not equipped to say. However, it does bring out an important point. A way of doing things that worked well in one epoch or in one context may not work in another.

But the rules of regional growth can never be totally overturned. The growth of northern Italy in general—at the risk of repeating the obvious—has its roots in location and in size (Milan) and in a rich network of small and mid-sized cities. Nor is it entirely accidental that the slower-growing regions of the north are Piedmont with the city of Turin, home to the Italian automobile industry, and Liguria—Genoa is its largest city—with an industrial legacy around metallurgy and shipbuilding. In Italy as elsewhere, regional growth or decline is always the outcome of the interplay between general forces, whose impact we are able to predict, and unique stories, which are, by definition, unique. And, as the Emilia story reveals, what may be true in one epoch may not be true in another.

Equally intriguing in Europe is the formation of what appears to be a growth archipelago linking southern Germany, western Austria, and north-eastern Italy, which I shall call the Munich-Bologna corridor. The emergence of this Munich-Bologna corridor is not so surprising once one combines the continuing pull of Europe's Blue Banana for Italian and Austrian regions, the density of mid-sized towns, the relative absence of negative clusters, and the hedonic advantage of southern Bavaria within Germany. I do not wish to overstate the degree of integration of this corridor. The Alps remain a powerful barrier to commerce. Trade and travel between the two sides of the Alps is largely funneled through one passageway: the Brenner Pass.[29] However strange this corridor appears—fueled by different factors on each side of the Alps—it does suggest that the Blue Banana is progressively expanding towards the southeast.[30] If so, this is good news, for example, for the Austrian city of Innsbruck, as well as for much of northeastern Italy.

The shift south of activity and populations has led some scholars to suggest the emergence of a Mediterranean growth corridor along an east-west arch linking eastern Spain, southern France, and northern Italy.[31] Whether one uses this representation or a Munich-Bologna corridor, both suggest that the hedonic imperative is in the process of transforming the economic geography of Europe no less than that of North America. But the pull of the sun should not be overstated. All of Europe and America is not about to move south. Both in Europe and in North America, northern coastal regions—up to certain latitudes at least—continue to attract populations. The coastal towns and villages north of Boston continue to grow and the German *Länder* bordering on the North Sea—not very sunny places—continue to display above-average population growth. In both examples, growth may have as much, if not more, to do with the proximity of a dynamic large city, Boston in the first case and Hamburg in the latter.[32] The population growth of the Rhine-Main conurbation and around urban centers such as Amsterdam, Madrid, and Prague clearly has more to do with the continuing attraction of size than with hedonic preferences.

GROWING SMALL CITIES (CLOSE TO THE CENTER)

Perhaps the best illustration that the rules of regional growth need always be put in context is that they should not be read the same way for big cities as for small and mid-sized ones. For larger cities, rule 1—size matters—is unambiguous. For smaller places, it conveys the message that proximity to size is an advantage. Smaller cities within easy reach of a large metropolis have, we saw, a greater probability of attracting economic activity. "Within easy reach" is, of course, an elastic criterion that, again, depends on context. Two hours from New York does not have the same significance as two hours from Kansas City, just as an hour from London does not carry the same weight as an hour from Glasgow. In most cases, the maximum distance from a large city—beyond which the chances of growth diminish significantly—will be in the one- to two-hour (driving time) range.

However, proximity to a large city can also have exactly the opposite effect. The impact will be different depending on the town's initial economic base. For most manufacturing—notably mid- and high-tech industries—proximity is a definite advantage. On the other hand, if the town's primary function is that of a service center for a surrounding market area, then proximity to a larger (competing) center becomes a negative attribute. Distance, in this case, becomes a positive attribute, acting as a protector for its local market.

The advantages of a positive industrial legacy obviously also hold for smaller places, favoring towns with a tradition of small and mid-sized firms and a history of light industry, services, workmanship, and good labor relations. This positive attribute, however, contains an internal contradiction. If—as in the Greensburg example—the town succeeds in attracting a large plant, it then ipso facto becomes a company town, with the inherent risk of what I have called the Intrusive Rentier Syndrome. There is no easy way out of this dilemma. All clusters—industry specializations—carry, so to speak, the seeds of their own destruction. No cluster is eternally positive. However, the risks are tempered—as the Italian Emilia example demonstrates—if the cluster (the industry) is founded on a network of interrelated small firms, rather than on a single large employer.

That low land and labor costs are an essential condition for attracting industry need not be repeated. However, this advantage only holds if labor (and land) costs are lower for a comparably skilled workforce. The effectiveness of lower wages is influenced by the skill and educational characteristics of the local labor force. If—and this a rare *if*—a low-wage small town *also* has a highly skilled and educated labor force, then its attractive force increases correspondingly, including possibly for high-tech industries. This usually means the proximity of a technologically oriented university. High-tech growth corridors—recall the Oxford-London example—often develop between university towns and a nearby large metropolis. But the cost advantage—for land, labor, and infrastructures—remains a crucial parallel attribute. Why else would high-tech firms wish to locate outside a large urban area, which is their natural habitat?

I turn again to Canada to illustrate the different paths that mid-sized cities can take. I begin by considering two cities that are close to a major metropolis, and then consider a mid-sized city which is in the periphery, far from major markets. Guelph (population 117,000) lies about 100 kilometers west of Toronto; Drummondville (population 69,000) lies about 100 kilometers east of Montreal.[33] Both have grown more rapidly than their respective provinces in recent years, although Guelph's growth has been more vigorous. In both cases, average earnings—a good indicator of wage rates—are below those of the nearby metropolis.[34] Both are on or near major trade corridors: Guelph is near highway 401, which links Toronto with the U.S. Midwest; Drummondville is on highway 20, linking Montreal with eastern Canada. Both are primarily manufacturing centers, as one would expect, with fairly comparable economic structures grounded in a broad range of mid-tech industries; notably, food processing, various types of machinery and metal products, transportation equipment (mainly auto parts in Guelph), consumer electronics, and textiles (in Drummondville).

There are, however, also major differences between the two cities. Guelph is located in the center of a growing region (southern Ontario) near Canada's largest city; while Drummondville is located to the *east* of Montreal, in a region where many communities are already losing population. Guelph, unlike Drummondville, is home to a university (the University of Guelph) and within 20 kilometers of one of Canada's leading technologically oriented universities (the University of Waterloo). The difference shows up in the educational levels of the two workforces: 30 percent of people in Guelph between the ages of twenty and thirty-four were university graduates, compared to 14 percent in Drummondville; the Canadian average was 23 percent.[35] Not surprisingly, a nascent high-tech sector has emerged in Guelph, mainly around pharmaceuticals and biotechnologies. Guelph, in other words, has attributes that allow it to envisage future growth based on attributes other then *only* lower land and labor costs—although these remain important. Drummondville, on the other hand, has few attributes on which to base future growth other than lower land and labors costs, the latter the legacy of its past as a textile, clothing, and shoe-making town. Drummondville's future growth hangs on its ability to provide an adequately skilled workforce—but not necessarily highly educated—at a cost below that of similar locations in Canada. Average earnings in Drummondville are 25 percent lower than in Guelph.

GROWING SMALL CITIES (FAR FROM THE CENTER)

Let me now move to Moncton (population 113,000), located some 1,000 kilometers east of Montreal in the province of New Brunswick. Although the province's population has stagnated—and even declined—in recent years, Moncton has continued to grow. Moncton's success is founded on a combination of location and fortuitous accidents.[36] Moncton is located at the point—an isthmus—where the three Canadian Maritime Provinces (New Brunswick, Nova Scotia, and Prince Edwards Island) meet. As such, Moncton is strategically located to act as a service hub for the entire region. Moncton lies on the trade (railroad) corridor linking the port city of Halifax with rest of Canada. In the heyday of railroads, Moncton was the region's railway hub; the railways were long the city's major employer, including repair shops, which employed close to four thousand workers as late as the 1960s. Moncton *was*, in essence, a company town. The railways declined; the last major repair activities were shut down in 1985, provoking a major crisis. Moncton's resurgence is proof that a negative industrial legacy can be overcome. But, just as location was a primary factor in the creation of its old industrial base, so location has allowed it to renew its economic base. Over the last two decades, Moncton has emerged as a distribution, wholesaling, storage, and trucking center for the entire region. Other ancillary services, notably courier services, have also emerged as major employers. Moncton has developed into a local airline hub, with direct flights to Montreal and Toronto.[37] By the same token, consumer-oriented food and beverage manufacturing—meat processing, bakeries, dairies, bottling, etc.—has remained a source of employment. In all such cases, be it services or manufacturing, distance from the central Canadian market is an advantage, not a handicap.

Several unique features have also contributed to Moncton's success. The Maritime Provinces of Canada are home to a small but vibrant French-speaking population, the Acadians.[38] About 300,000 in number, they are largely concentrated in the province of New Brunswick, where they make up a third of the population. New Brunswick is the only Canadian province that is officially bilingual, offering French and English language services at all levels of government.[39] The greater Moncton area, where native French-speakers account for a third of the population, has emerged as the mini cultural and service metropolis for the Acadian community. This has brought a number of institutions to the city: French-language public broadcasting (radio and TV); the local headquarters of Acadian credit unions and mutual insurances companies; and, last but not least, a French-language university, the only one

in the Maritime Provinces.[40] This has given rise to a local elite of professionals, managers, and artists, further bolstered by a combination of political and
other "accidental" factors. Although not the capital of any, Moncton's location at the confluence of the three Maritime Provinces, plus the presence of
a bilingual workforce, made it the natural location for federal government
agencies and departments wishing to serve the entire region. It's also a prime
location for the offices of regional organizations and initiatives, of which the
Atlantic Lottery—managed by four provinces[41]—is a prime example. The
latter produced a small ripple effect, spawning local software firms directed at
the gaming industry, what might even be called a mini high-tech cluster.

Moncton's success story—like the Burlington and Oulu stories—demonstrates that peripheral cities can grow. But these stories also carry a warning.
All these places (urban areas) have populations above 100,000. Size matters,
especially in the periphery. The examples of rapidly growing smaller towns
in peripheral locations—unless fueled by a particularly rich resource discovery (usually oil or natural gas these days)—are much rarer. More important
still, the Moncton story highlights—yet again—the unique character of each
success story. It is difficult to draw general lessons from the Moncton story,
if only that it is indeed an exception in a part of North America where slow
growth—indeed, decline—is the rule.

Zero-sum Growth

The consequences of aging populations do not end with the rise of gray
migrants. The graying of industrialized populations is, in effect, changing the
rules of the game. Regional population decline will become more common.
The competition for people—young and educated populations, especially—
will become increasingly fierce.

Most industrialized nations have completed their demographic transition, and all will do so in the near future. National population growth will be
close to zero in many nations and declining in some. The populations of Italy
and most eastern European nations have already begun to decline. Negative
population growth will soon be a fact in Italy, Germany, Spain, and Japan.[42]
Zero or near-zero population growth is forecast for Belgium and Switzerland over the next few decades; Sweden and the Netherlands are nearing that
point. The United Kingdom and France are somewhat luckier, but national
populations will nonetheless only grow slowly in coming decades. The major
exception in Europe is the Republic of Ireland, with vigorous growth forecast
for at least the next two decades, a reflection of its still relatively young population. In New World nations (U.S., Canada, Australia, etc.) populations will

continue to grow, due in part to immigration.[43] But even in these nations, population growth will be slower than in the past.

The end of the demographic transition alters the manner in which migration affects regional growth. In the past, out-migration did not *necessarily* mean population decline since there were often sufficient new births to compensate for the loss. Migration simply meant that some regions would grow more slowly than others. That, until recently, has been the story of most lagging regions. Out-migration from the Canadian Maritime Provinces to Ontario or from Scotland to the south of England did not necessarily mean that the population of the Maritime Provinces or of Scotland would decline. This is no longer true. In a world where national populations have stabilized, places find themselves facing a zero-sum game. Out-migrants will no longer be replaced by local births. If other regions of the nation continue to attract migrants, the unavoidable outcome is that lagging regions will stop growing or decline. For nations that have passed the break-even point in the demographic transition, irreversible population decline in some places is an inevitable conclusion.

Stated more bluntly, the flip side of the first rule of regional growth in post-transition societies is that places that do not have the initial good fortune of being big or being next to a big place and do not have countervailing hedonic advantages risk seeing their populations irreversibly decline. The range of places threatened with decline will essentially depend on how close the nation is to zero population growth and the extent to which all regional growth indicators point in the same direction, favoring only one part of the nation, what I have called unidirectional growth.

Some Places Will Decline

In a zero-sum (demographic) game, decline is the corollary of growth. If some places draw in migrants other places are necessarily losing them. North America as a whole has not yet arrived at the stage of zero population growth—unlike many European nations—most notably in the United States, whose continued population growth makes it somewhat of an exception among developed nations. In the U.S., local population decline is primarily a manifestation of the forces of urban concentration and shifting regional fortunes.

THE HOLLOWING OUT OF NORTH AMERICA

Declining places in North America are not distributed at random. Declining areas are concentrated in identifiable parts of the continent—the (negative) counterparts of growth corridors. The greatest expanse of population decline is a funnel-shaped corridor with its base at the Texas-Mexico border east of El Paso and then spreading out as it moves north, covering most of the Great Plains states, culminating in the Canadian Prairie provinces of Manitoba and Saskatchewan. This is North America's dry interior, the empty quarter we met in chapter 3. Here, geography is truly taking its revenge. The message geography is sending is unambiguous: 'there are too many of you, please leave.' Technology also plays a part. Ever fewer farmers, ranchers, and local intermediaries are required to produce the same quantities—of wheat, cattle, etc . . .—and bring them to market. Whether technology, human carelessness or the environment is to blame is immaterial; it does seem, with hindsight, that large parts of the North American interior were too densely settled and exploited.

Communities located in this part of North America face an uphill battle—especially the smallest—if they are to grow in the future. They face two obvious handicaps. They are not, in most cases, cost effective locations for manufacturing activities sensitive to transport costs. For services, the regional population base is generally too sparse and too dispersed to sustain the development of competitive concentrations of advanced tradable services. Even the few large urban areas have, on the whole, found it difficult to keep up with rest. Winnipeg, the largest Canadian metropolis in this part of the continent has grown more slowly than any other major Canadian urban area. In the United States, metropolitan Kansas City and Omaha, located on the edges of this continental empty quarter, have also grown less than the national average in recent years. However, the effects of the gradual hollowing out of the continental interior are most severely felt in the least accessible, the driest, and the most climatically challenged places. Of the thirty counties in the continental United States that suffered the greatest population losses—in percentage numbers—all but three are located in the empty quarter, with the highest concentrations in western Texas and in North Dakota.[44]

This hollowing-out of the continent is in the process of altering the traditional perception of have and have-not regions in the United States. The South has always been thought of as the poorest part of America. This is no longer so, as we saw in chapter 1. Although many parts of the rural South remain miserably poor, the poorest places in the U.S. are increasingly found in the Dakotas, Montana, and Nebraska. Seventeen of the twenty poorest counties in the U.S. are located on the eastern flank of the Rockies or on the western Great Plains.[45]

THE COLD DECLINING NORTH AND EAST

Another large expanse of population decline—almost as vast as the empty quarter—stretches east across northern Ontario, takes in most of northern and eastern Quebec, and eventually engulfs the four Canadian Atlantic provinces and chunks of northern New Hampshire and Maine. Like the empty quarter, large sections of this part of North America are not terribly conducive to human habitation—certainly not dense occupation—and were chiefly settled (by Europeans and their descendants) to exploit natural resource: minerals, timber, hydroelectric power, and fish. The exceptionally rich fish stocks off the banks of Newfoundland attracted European fishermen even before the arrival of Columbus. This extreme north-eastern section of North America was never densely settled. East of Boston and Quebec City, no urban area reaches the half million mark. Halifax, with a population of about 350,000, is by far the largest urban area in this vast stretch of territory, more than three times the size of Britain. No city in northern Ontario and northern Quebec has a population above 150,000; all urban areas in this part of Canada (with populations above 50,000) have seen their populations decline since the 1990s.

This part of North America—lacking a major metropolis—thus starts out with a severe handicap in a knowledge economy that puts an ever greater premium on size. But, this is not the only handicap. The limits of resource exploitation have either been reached or exceeded in many cases. The profitable limit for cutting trees—given the constraints of climate and of geography—was reached some time ago. In the Province of Quebec, the limit has been exceeded, where a government report recently recommended a 20 percent reduction in the harvesting of trees. This has since been followed by numerous closings of saw mills and pulp and paper plants. The limits on the harvesting of ground fish, notably codfish—long the mainstay of Atlantic Canadian economy—was reached in the late 1980s, when the Canadian government declared a moratorium on cod fishing, which remains in force to this day. As in the empty quarter, geography is sending a clear message; the overexploitation of resources—be it the land or the sea—comes at a price. Many fishing villages have since closed. Harbors and fish-processing plants have fallen into disuse. The limits on the further exploration of hydroelectric power—requiring the building of new dams and the flooding of land areas—is also being reached, under the triple pressure of increasing distance (as the rivers to be dammed lie ever farther north), increasingly severe environmental regulations, and the growing compensations (royalties) demanded by native peoples on whose lands the areas to be flooded often lie.

The negative impact on local employment is further compounded by technology. New technologies and management techniques mean that ever fewer workers are required to harvest the same number of trees or fish—if there are any. Smelters, paper plants, sawmills, mines, and fish-processing plants are increasingly efficient, requiring ever fewer workers. The end result of the combined effect of greater efficiency and the limits of nature is—predictably—falling employment. Employment in these regions can only grow if substitutes are found for the jobs lost in the resource sector. The arrival of IT has not made things any easier. Management, research, and engineering functions, which previously required a local presence, can now be transferred to the big city. It is now theoretically—and often practically—possible to directly manage dams and power grids at a distance. The increasing requirement for brainpower—even in the resource sector—is pushing ever more jobs away from the periphery and towards the center. A large resource development, say a new mine, may well create more engineering and managerial jobs in the big city than jobs at the mine.

In the end, however, the principal handicap of North America's extreme Northeast is its peripheral location and absence of major cities, combined with a climate and geography that, with some minor exceptions, does not make it terribly attractive to green or gray migrants. Unlike the American South, it cannot count on the hedonic imperative to eventually come to the rescue of its declining resource-based economy. The principal hope is a new (sustained) resource boom. Oil and natural gas have been discovered—and are starting to be exploited—off the shores of Nova Scotia and Newfoundland. It is still too early to say whether this will provide a foundation for future growth. This, however, is little consolation for the northern regions of the provinces of Ontario and Quebec, where population decline appears irreversible.[46]

Other concentrations of declining places can be identified in almost every part of the continent; in the rural Deep South, a third swath of declining places stretches north from Kentucky and West Virginia, through Pennsylvania, culminating in Upstate New York on the shores of Lake Ontario and the Canadian border. This part of the U.S., specifically the southern portion, is known as Appalachia—identified with coal mining and a unique folk culture.[47] It has long been an area of chronic poverty, recalling the mining valleys of south Wales with its separate folkways and black hills, scarred by decades of accumulated debris. The great metal-bashing towns of America—Pittsburgh, Youngstown, Scranton, etc.—are located either in Appalachia or close by. Of the eighteen U.S. metropolitan areas with a population over 100,000 that saw their populations decline since 1990, all but three are located in this area.[48]

A lesson to be drawn from this admittedly somewhat gloomy journey into the sources of decline is—to paraphrase my earlier statement on growth—that different places can decline for different reasons. A particularly intriguing case is western New York State where, with some rare exceptions, most places have been underperforming for decades with stagnating or declining populations. Western New York is, it would appear, a case where high costs annul the advantages of size and location.[49] The region is not poorly located and home to several good-sized cities (Buffalo, Rochester, Syracuse, etc.) and a major Ivy League university (Cornell), which we met earlier. We might well ask why the dispersal of manufacturing out of the coastal megalopolis did not favor this part of the state rather than moving south. Western New York has a well-connected cobweb of different-sized cities, more than a match for the urban networks of North Carolina and other southern states. The answer lies in costs. Compared to other states, New York has a generally progressive political tradition with a history of generous social programs and pro-labor legislation, which is laudable from a social perspective, but translates into higher taxes and higher labor costs for firms. Crudely put, mid-sized cities in western New York are directly in competition with similar-sized cities in the South. On costs, the southern cities win, overriding the location advantages that the western New York–based cities might have.

EUROPE'S GRUYÈRE

Declining areas in Europe require less comment, since the reader will undoubtedly already have identified the principal victims. The continued concentration of growth in and near Europe's Blue Banana, in national capitals, and in hedonically favored places means that the probabilities of (future) decline *within* European nations are largely determined by relative distances from the Banana and from national capitals. The most obvious examples are the northern reaches of Britain and of the Nordic countries and the eastern extremes of nations such as Poland, Hungary, and Slovakia.

Leaving aside such obvious cases on the European periphery, population decline has not produced the same vast empty spaces as in North America, in part because of western Europe's irregular geography, but also because of the multiplicity of political and cultural boundaries. The pattern in continental western Europe is closer to that of dispersed clumps of declining communities, which is why I have conjured up the image of a Swiss cheese—a

Gruyère—with its numerous holes. The largest "holes" are to be found in the geographical center of France and—unsurprisingly—in what was once the German Democratic Republic (GDR). In France, as noted earlier, the traditional notion of what is a center and what is a periphery has literally been turned on its head, the *geographic* center emerging as the new periphery. The most challenged communities are those that are neither close to the Blue Banana or Paris nor included in France's hedonic growth crescent.

Many currently declining communities in western Europe are the offspring of negative clusters—old heavy industry and mining—which have been abundantly discussed. For such communities located in the heart of Europe—Lorraine, Saarland, Wallonia, etc.—I have argued that their decline is probably transitory. Once the effects of the negative industrial legacy wear off, the positive effects of location will, hopefully, again come to the fore. On the other hand, communities that are handicapped by both an eccentric location and a negative industrial legacy face much more of an uphill battle. Fortunately, there are not many examples in Europe. In Britain, the Tyneside area comes closest. In Spain, Asturias—the traditional heart of the Spanish coal and steel industries—is an example of a region that must deal with both the legacy of a negative industrial cluster and of a peripheral location in Europe. Its population has declined. By comparison, the declining population of Extremadura, in the extreme southwest of Spain, is essentially explained by size and location. Extremadura is a largely rural region, lacking a major metropolis, far from major markets. Little wonder that its population continues to migrate towards the large urban centers of Spain.

I shall not dwell further on the subject of community decline, not a terribly happy subject. No community envisages its decline with equanimity. But population decline does not automatically spell a decline in welfare or in living standards. Small populations and high living standards are by no means incompatible. We must never forget that national economic growth requires that populations continually move between industries, communities, and regions.

Some Places Will Continue to Grow (or Decline) for Unique Reasons

Before moving to the closing chapter, I cannot resist the temptation to tell a few last stories, if only to underline the truth that rule 4—exceptions abound—will not go away, repeatedly confounding those, like myself, in search of neat general theories. I have chosen the three cases below because they illustrate, yet again, the impact of outside events and of political choices. I shall begin with a story from my own country.

WHY TORONTO OVERTOOK MONTREAL AS CANADA'S FIRST CITY

Canada is the scene of a rare turnaround in regional fortunes: the sudden reversal in position of the nation's two largest cities, Montreal and Toronto.[50] This is highly unusual in economic geography. For most of Canada's history, Montreal was Canada's premier city, its commercial, corporate, and financial capital. It is no exaggeration to say that Montreal was Canada's New York, only on a smaller scale. Like New York, it was the nation's primary port for trade with Europe and principal point of entry for European immigrants. Like New York, Montreal developed a strong merchant culture with a distinct cosmopolitan outlook. Toronto, located some 600 kilometers to the southwest on Lake Ontario, had long been Montreal's rival, something close to the late nineteenth-century rivalry between Chicago and New York. But the relationship between the two remained very stable for more than century, with Toronto always a close second behind Montreal. Then, suddenly in the late 1960s, Montreal's growth decelerated. Toronto eventually overtook Montreal to become Canada's largest city. Toronto is today Canada's undisputed financial and corporate capital and likely to remain so. None of the first three rules of regional growth suffice to explain this outcome, the result of political and social change.

Montreal's business elite, which assured the city's national dominance before the 1960s, was overwhelmingly of Anglo-Scots origin, with Jews the principal exception. The great corporations that towered over the Canadian economy—the Canadian Pacific, the Bank of Montreal, the Royal Bank of Canada—were headquartered in Montreal, their boards of directors and management almost exclusively Anglo-Scots.[51] The language of business and social advancement was English. Yet French Canadians made up two thirds of the population, and 80 percent of the population of the province of Quebec, in which Montreal is located. Following the British conquest of Canada in 1759, an unfortunate social divide developed between English and French Canadians in Quebec, with the former on top and the latter at the bottom. French became the language of the poor and the uneducated. Perhaps the most brutal—and symbolically powerful—expression of those times was "speak white," attributed, rightly or wrongly, to obnoxious Anglos. This situation was potentially socially explosive. It could not last, and brought forth a counterreaction. Montreal went through a—fortunately brief and minor—period of terrorism during the 1960s with the FLQ (Front de Libération du Québec) placing bombs in mailboxes in predominantly English-speaking neighborhoods and blowing up statues of Queen Victoria and other symbols of British domination. The FLQ came to an unlamented end in 1970 after the bungled kidnapping of the British consul in Montreal and execution of a Quebec government minister.[52]

I do not wish to go into a detailed history of the rise of Quebec nationalism in the 1960s. It is a complex story whose unbiased telling is probably impossible, all the more so in this case since I lived through the events. Let me thus skip the details and go to the heart of the matter. Beginning in the 1960s, successive Quebec governments introduced various measures to redress the social imbalance between Francophones and Anglophones and to rehabilitate the French language. The French educational system was modernized; technical colleges, research institutes (my own included), and universities were built. French business was encouraged. The culmination was bill 101, adopted in 1977 by the Quebec legislature, which declared French the sole official language of the province, requiring all public signs to be in French and—the most controversial aspect of the law—requiring all newly arrived immigrant parents to henceforth send their children to French public schools. Before, all residents could freely choose between English and French schools; most immigrants chose English schools, threatening the long-term demographic balance between the two groups. The law is still in force—and likely to remain so—although some clauses have been softened after challenges in the courts.[53]

Viewed from a Québécois perspective, these reforms have been immensely successful. The social gap between Anglophones and Francophones was closed. A vibrant Francophone business elite emerged, giving rise to home-grown multinational corporations—Bombardier, Cascades, Quebecor—that did not exist a generation ago. French is today the dominant language of the province. English no longer poses a real threat, although the attraction of English remains (more the result today of the international preeminence of English than of internal conditions in Quebec). Young immigrants are integrating into French-Québécois society as naturally—and with the same attendant problems—as they would into American or English Canadian society. French Quebec today is full of citizens with unpronounceable names and brown skins. French Quebec, in sum, is today a modern, self-confident society. This is no mean achievement for a people who a bare generation ago saw themselves as second-class citizens in their own land.

That success came with a price: the fall of Montreal from its position at the top of the Canadian urban hierarchy. Montreal could not be both the second largest French-speaking metropolis in the world—as it sometimes proudly bills itself[54]—and the financial and corporate capital of a majority English-speaking nation, not to mention an overwhelmingly English-speaking continent. Outside Quebec, with the exception of small French-speaking populations in neighboring provinces, the rest of Canada speaks English. Language and shared culture, as noted earlier, play a crucial role in business transactions. It is simply easier—less costly in time, psychological stress, and effort—to do business with people who, literally and figuratively, speak the same language. Given the choice, individuals will naturally prefer to live and work in environments where they feel at home. Seen in this light, the flight of head offices from Montreal to Toronto during the 1970s and 1980s was entirely predictable. It also made perfect business sense for firms wishing to function primarily in English. The *relative* ease of finding a competent English-speaking secretary, lawyer, sales representative, or publicity agent is greater in Toronto than in Montreal. Unless the firm wishes to specifically service a French-speaking market, there is no compelling reason to locate in Montreal.

An additional factor propelled the move of head offices from Montreal to Toronto: the risk of separation. Since the 1970s, the separation of Quebec from the rest of Canada has been a recurring threat, waxing and waning, depending on the public mood. The victory in the provincial election of 1976 of the separatist Parti Québécois was followed by a massive out-migration of Anglophones, many undoubtedly the sons and daughters of Montreal's old moneyed elite, taking their assets, their networks, and their talents with them. Montreal's loss became Toronto's gain.[55] The probability of secession seems low at the time of writing, but the risk remains. The separatists came close to winning a referendum on Quebec independence in 1995. Besides the purely emotional reasons that drove Anglophones and others attached to their Canadian identity to move their business outside the province, business reasons should not be excluded. If a firm has most of its assets (plants, offices, outlets, etc.) or customers outside the province, it makes good sense to move its primary office outside Quebec, forestalling any financial risks or barriers to trade that an eventual separation might entail.

In the end, it is difficult to determine which was more important—the risk of separation or language legislation—for the move of head offices, financial institutions, and other business service firms from Montreal to Toronto. In the end, it does not matter. The point I wish to make is that social upheavals can upset the "natural" order of things. There was no "natural" economic or geographic reason why Montreal could not have remained the nation's financial and corporate capital, just as New York has remained the financial and corporate capital of the United States, despite the westward slide of the U.S. economy.

The Quebec story is also an illustration that cultural differences are not wholly a bad thing. Cultural differences are a barrier to trade and migration, but they also provide protection. The rehabilitation of French in Quebec caused Montreal to lose service markets outside Quebec, but in return provided Montreal with a captive market—albeit a smaller one—around a common language. As the entertainment and cultural capital of French Canada— a community of some 7 million—Montreal will always have a vibrant arts, media, and intellectual community. The attachment to place has also meant that homegrown companies are less likely to move elsewhere. New growing corporations, offspring of a rising Québécois business elite, have kept their head offices in Montreal, compensating in part for those that moved to Toronto. Attachment to place can also be a good thing.

A BRIEF TRIP TO VEGAS

Some places defy the most basic rules of economic geography. One could hardly imagine a more inauspicious location for anything than Las Vegas: a bone-dry, unbearably hot desert town in the middle of nowhere. Yet Las Vegas is one the fastest-growing metropolitan areas in the United States— it recently passed the 1 million mark—with a regional economy founded almost entirely on tourism, although a very special kind of tourism (defense establishments also play a role, but their relative weight in the local economy has declined). Las Vegas is arguably the ultimate case of hedonic growth. The demand for the pleasures that Las Vegas provides its visitors is such that it has given birth to an international airport which has become a minor hub in its own right. Las Vegas today is a fully integrated local economy founded on a constant flow of visitors from afar, although "afar" is not that far, as we shall see shortly.

Las Vegas's growth depends, in the first instance, on technology: air transport, air conditioning, and water works. The latter two, which provide the water and the electricity on which the city so dearly depends, were made possible by Hoover Dam (and its Lake Mead). This explains the conditions that have allowed Las Vegas to develop, but not its success as a mass tourist destination. For that, we need to turn to other considerations. Local policy choices are at the root of Las Vegas's success, since it is ultimately founded on territorial differences in legislation. Only in this case the difference is not the outcome of internal cultural divisions, but rather a conscious attempt by a local jurisdiction—the State of Nevada in this case—to create an advantage by legislative fiat. Such advantages can be fragile because they depend on the good—or bad—behavior of neighboring jurisdictions (nations, states, municipalities, etc.), in this instance, their policies towards socially controversial pursuits such as sex and gambling. The state of Nevada is unique in the

United States in its tolerant attitude towards gambling, prostitution (within limits), and other matters such as marriage and divorce, alcohol, adult entertainment, opening hours, etc. Las Vegas is sometimes referred to as Sin City, which nicely sums up its niche within the U.S. economy.

No neighboring state (or any other state in the union for that matter) provides a correspondingly friendly legal environment for the provision of "sinful" services, which gives Las Vegas an obvious edge. However, Las Vegas's success is not totally unrelated to geography. Market proximity also matters for sinful services. Las Vegas is near the California border, about as close to Los Angeles as one can get without actually being in California: a roughly three-and-a-half-hour drive or a forty-minute flight. The importance of market proximity is also reflected in Nevada's other sin city, Reno, which also lies close to the state border with California on the highway to the San Francisco Bay Area. It is impossible to say whether Las Vegas would have been as successful in the absence of the nearby rich Southern California market, but it seems unlikely. An additional geographic attribute gives Las Vegas a unique advantage for socially controversial services. Nevada is a largely arid, empty, state with nothing much around it in terms of population settlements. Nevada's sinful practices cannot tarnish neighboring communities because there basically are none. The drive between Los Angeles and Las Vegas crosses the Mojave Desert. If one is to build an island of sin — suitably quarantined — but still accessible to major markets, Las Vegas, Nevada, provides an ideal location. The slogan, "What happens in Vegas stays in Vegas," is appropriate in more ways than one.[56]

The fact that the rest of America has remained closed to such activities gives Las Vegas its particular edge. The other major attempt to create a similar advantage—Atlantic City in New Jersey—has been less successful, in part because sinful services could not be as easily quarantined, with the result that Atlantic City could not as easily offer the full range of sinful services. New Jersey is a densely populated state in the middle of the East Coast megalopolis. Atlantic City is a municipality and not a state, a much more constrained environment, both territorially and legally. The relationship between local authorities and—to put it bluntly—organized crime has always been more problematic. Las Vegas, in essence, enjoys a near monopoly for the services it provides in the world's biggest market. A comparison with European cities is instructive. In Europe, no one city has a monopoly on prostitution, for example. Thus, no monopoly rent is available for the taking. If one is in the business of providing a socially questionable service, it certainly helps to be in a puritanical environment where one is the only one authorized to provide the service.

Las Vegas is another example of the *relative* nature of all advantages, whether acquired or created. Earlier promoters of Las Vegas wanted the city to specialize in family-oriented entertainment activities, perhaps something on the model of Orlando (Disney World). But this did not work, precisely because Las Vegas had no particular advantage over other regions for the provision of this service. Equivalent services—Disneyland in Anaheim, for example—were available at other locations, much closer to the market and in more pleasant surroundings. Las Vegas was fortunate in developing its specific niche. But it could not have done so without the help of the good behavior of its neighbors.

WHY MIAMI BECAME THE FINANCIAL CAPITAL OF LATIN AMERICA

In other cases, it is the folly or mismanagement of neighbors that gives the place an edge. Examples are legion, especially within federations where regions (states, provinces, etc.) have broad powers. Bad tax or labor policies will drive business towards neighboring regions, just as good policies will draw them in. But such policy differences, again, are not written in stone and can be reversed.

What I have in mind are places whose economic good fortunes are the result—at least in part—of the misfortunes of others. To illustrate this, I propose a trip to Latin America. Latin America is a big place with some twenty countries united by a common language—Spanish—leaving aside Portuguese-speaking Brazil. Normally, one would have expected a major financial center to emerge, which would have become the banking and insurance capital of Latin America, along the model of London, New York, or Hong Kong. Latin America (outside Brazil) has it least two great cities—Buenos Aires and Mexico City—that appear to have the necessary size and sophistication to become great financial capitals. Yet neither has emerged as a world-class financial center or plays the role of financial capital to the continent. Why not?

We do not need to look very far for an answer: financial instability. Both Mexico and Argentina, like many Latin American nations, have unfortunate histories of inflation, collapsing currencies, and chaotic banking systems. Currencies have changed; banks nationalized and then re-privatized; regulations are unpredictable and prone to political interference. The primary ingredient of a successful financial center is confidence: confidence in the banks, confidence in the regulators, confidence in the legal system, confidence in the currency. One does not—if one has the choice—put one's life savings in a place where the currency might abruptly lose its value, where capricious regulations can prevent one from retrieving one's money, or where bankers can mismanage one's money without legal recourse. Although Mexico's banking system is becoming more solid and its currency increasingly stable—unfortunately the same cannot yet be said of Argentina—it still has a way to go before acquiring a reputation for financial responsibility comparable to that of most industrialized nations. In finance and banking, reputations are built over many decades, even centuries. In the absence of a reliable domestic financial center, Latin American savers and investors must look elsewhere, at least those—generally the rich—who have the option of doing so.[57]

Little wonder that a financial center sprung up outside of Latin America to cater to the needs of Latin Americans. Miami has effectively emerged as the financial capital of Latin America, certainly for the nations of the Caribbean and northern South America. Miami is to all intents and purposes a bilingual city, where business can be conducted in English or Spanish. Both geographically and linguistically, no city in the United States is closer to Latin America or as well poised to serve Latin American markets (and to profit from its misfortunes). Miami has also developed into the air transport hub for the region—which reinforces its position as a financial center—and become a major entertainment center for Spanish-speaking Latin America. Many Spanish-language variety and news shows for television audiences in Latin America are produced in Miami. All this activity takes place in Miami rather than in Latin America proper because the United States offers a more congenial, stable, and ordered environment in which to do business. Miami is one of the fastest-growing metropolitan areas in the U.S. Much of it is driven by hedonic choices, but much of it is also driven by Miami's role as a safe haven for Latin American business.

The safe haven principle has been a decisive factor in the growth of the Swiss economy, not only the national economy, but also the economy of its different regions. Were it not for the tumultuous history of Europe—not least, Switzerland's neighbors—Zurich would not be the international banking center it is today, nor would Geneva have become the international city it is for finance and a broad range of institutions and organizations. Bank secrecy laws are not the only explication—although they certainly helped. The prosperity of Zurich, Geneva, Lausanne, and Lugano owes much to the folly of Switzerland's neighbors. Where else in western Europe before the Second World War could one hold assets—illiquid and liquid—in the secure knowledge that they would not be expropriated, bombed out, or otherwise devalued? Not many places. In addition, Switzerland's location in the heart of Europe, overlapping three language zones—German, French, and Italian—

meant that every Swiss canton was a potential natural safe haven for its linguistic proximate neighbor. But, as the Miami example demonstrates, the safe
haven advantage only works as long as one's neighbors continue to mismanage their economies or generally misbehave, causing capital (and also people)
to seek refuge elsewhere. It is an advantage that Swiss regions are in the process of losing—fortunately, one can only say—as western Europe becomes an
increasingly stable and prosperous place.

I was not entirely honest in presenting the cases above as examples of
the fourth rule of regional growth. They are not entirely accidental, once we
think back to what we have learned. Las Vegas, we saw, would not be Vegas
without neighboring California, an illustration of the impact of location. Nor
would corporate Latino Miami be what it is today without its strategic location, only a few hours' flight away from the major centers of northern Latin
America. Toronto's overtaking Montreal makes sense once we think back
to the role of hinterlands in shaping urban fortunes. Cities, as service centers, adjust to the size of their markets. Toronto bypassed Montreal because
it acquired a larger market area—English Canada; while Montreal's natural
market area shrunk to that of the province of Quebec. This is not fundamentally different from Vienna adjusting to the smaller size of Austria. Chicago's
resurgence, by the same token, is in part explained by its continued role as
the central place for the Midwest. All stories, in the end, are a mix of unique
events and general laws.

7

What Have We Learned?

[A]s always in human experience since the invention of the telephone, the dissemination of electronic media may paradoxically even increase the need and the incentive for face-to-face contact. . . . And so, surely, this time around: the likelihood is that places with a unique buzz, a unique fizz, a special kind of energy will prove more magnetic than ever.

(SIR) PETER HALL (1999)

All throughout this book I have been fighting an uphill battle, searching for a general explanation of why some places are wealthier than others. It has been a recurrent contest between general laws and particular circumstances, with the latter victorious more often than not. If there is anything we have learned it is that actual growth and decline is highly idiosyncratic.[1] Distance and small size may be the chief constraints to growth for one place; while for another it may be its negative industrial legacy. This is frustrating for academics like me. Grand theories will constantly be overturned by troublesome exceptions. As the story of Oulu in northern Finland testified, even very peripheral places—which theory would condemn to decline—have succeeded. And, as the stories of Manchester and of Detroit demonstrate, even great cities—once models of modernity—can falter.

Some Places Will Always Be Wealthier Than Others

We have also learned that beneath the apparent serendipity there are unavoidable forces at work, which drive economic activity and people towards particular places. The lessons for developing and emerging economies are unambiguous. Economic growth will inevitably produce urbanization and urban concentration. Attempting to halt either is futile. Regional differences in wealth will emerge, most notably during the early years of development. A nation in which all places grow equally is impossible. Balanced regional growth is an oxymoron.

DISTANCE IS NOT DEAD

For rich nations, the message is no less unambiguous. Place will continue to matter. Today and in the future, some places will gain more than others from ongoing changes in technology, tastes, and demography. The need for information-rich, innovative firms to be in or near a large city will not disappear and will most probably increase in the future. Travel is not and most likely never will be costless. As long as people need to meet, the places where they can most profitably do so will continue to command a premium. As the opportunity cost of time increases with higher incomes, so will the true cost of travel.

A world in which place no longer matters is a fantasy. Were that unlikely event ever to occur, we would recognize the signs immediately. Place will have ceased to matter the day a square foot of land in, say, downtown Bismarck, North Dakota, costs the same as square foot of land in Midtown Manhattan. I leave it to the reader to evaluate the likelihood of that ever happening. The difference in price between comparable real estate in two places is a signal from the market (from thousands of investors, buyers, and entrepreneurs) that some places have a greater economic value than others—that some have a greater potential of generating (or capturing) wealth than others. Why such differences exist should now be clear.

We are now able to explain—with a fair level of assurance—why the market values land less *in places like* Bismarck and why incomes will be correspondingly lower. The basic rules of size and location explain much. Explaining why Bismarck *specifically* is more difficult. Once we attempt to explain the wealth of specific places, communities, or regions, particular circumstances inevitably creep into the picture, which in some cases can annul the forces of size and location, although seldom entirely. Explaining—or rather predicting—in what direction a place will evolve in the future is even more difficult. Future technological change is by its very nature unpredictable. Who in 1900 would have predicted the rise of Miami—then an inhospitable tropical village of 1,700 souls? For that to happen, the airplane, new medicines, and air conditioning had first to be invented.

We are able to assign probabilities. In cases where the rules of regional growth *and* particular circumstances point towards the same places, the probability of a given outcome will be heightened. The very high levels of income in Greater London—compared to the rest of Britain—are not an accident. The more regionally dispersed distribution of wealth in the U.S. is no accident either. Both have been powerfully molded by geography. In Britain, size and location, but also the hedonic imperative and the legacy of negative industrial clusters in some places, have all combined to favor the south of England. In the U.S., history and geography have combined to produce a very different picture, although the same basic forces are at play. The dispersal to the South of manufacturing out of the industrial Midwest and Northeast occurred for reasons that have as much to do with history and institutions as with pure economics.

The contrast between the U.S. and Britain is useful in that it informs us that there is no reason why all developing nations should evolve in the same manner. In some, economic growth will cause regional development differences to harden. I have pointed to the danger signals for west African nations. Where regional economic disparities are superimposed on ethnic or religious differences, the divides may become insurmountable. India, by contrast, has given birth to a surprisingly balanced economic geography, with multiple centers, not unlike the U.S. One of the reasons India has held together despite major regional differences in language and in culture may well be that there is no systematic, lopsided gap between places that have grown and those that have lagged behind.

WILL REGIONAL WEALTH DIFFERENCES DECLINE IN CHINA?

This brings me to the probable evolution of regional growth in China, no small question. Since my knowledge of China is limited, my analysis will be broad brush. China, we have seen, presents an extreme case of lopsided development with acute regional disparities in wealth. Despite this, an optimistic view of future development is not unwarranted.

Should we expect the divide between growing coastal regions and the less dynamic interior to harden over time, producing another Italy or Brazil, with one side of the nation in the modern economy and the other side systematically lagging behind, creating a parallel social divide? A first reason why this may not happen is the geographic diversity and expanse of the Chinese interior, which unlike the Italian Mezzogiorno is not a clearly defined region with a distinct institutional and cultural heritage. There is no natural or historic frontier separating the coastal provinces from the Chinese interior. The difference between growing and lagging regions is more like a continuum than an abrupt divide, especially when we consider the role played by the Yangtze and Yellow Rivers as trade routes and inland waterways. The interior is home to cities—Wuhan, Chongqing, Xi'an (Sian), etc.—which, in terms of sheer size,[2] would figure among the great cities of Europe and North America. Chongqing is already one of China's largest car manufacturing centers.

The chief reason for my optimism lies in the lessons to be drawn from the history of regional development in the United States, where we saw a precipitous decline in regional income disparities after World War I. I attributed the fall in disparities to high labor mobility—notably migration out of the South—but also to the movement of manufacturing out of the Northeast and the Great Lakes states towards the traditionally poor South. There is a priori no reason why the same thing should not eventually happen in China. China is still in the early stages of its economic take-off—although moving at breakneck speed—with still low labor costs by world standards, even in growing coastal regions. But, over time, if growth continues, costs in coastal regions—especially in and around the great urban conurbations of Beijing-Tianjin, Shanghai, and Hong Kong–Guangzhou—will come to equal those of the world's other great industrialized cities. If and when that happens—perhaps sooner than one might think[3]—the crowding out of manufacturing to lower-cost places will gather speed, with a growing transfer of mid-tech manufacturing to more inland locations.

Whether this actually happens depends in part on two preconditions.[4] The first, obvious, condition is the presence of adequate transportation infrastructures: modern highway, rail, and waterway facilities linking inland cities with the coast. Major investments have been made or are under way in transportation infrastructures. The second, less obvious, condition is the presence of efficient, fluid labor markets and accompanying institutional environments that allow more distant locations to keep costs competitive. As we saw in the U.S, the chief reason manufacturing moved south was that labor costs *were* lower there, made possible not only by the South's particular history, but also by the highly decentralized nature of the U.S. political system, which leaves local and state authorities considerable leeway in matters of labor market regulation.[5] Why would a firm (selling to world markets) choose to set up shop in inland locations in China if it does not find a compensating advantage to offset the additional costs of greater distance?

This is what I called the third rule of regional growth—*costs matter*—which pertains specifically to peripheral places.[6] The trend towards fiscal decentralization in China, plus the selling off of unprofitable state-owned enterprises, often located in inland provinces, suggests that wages in the interior will—at least in the foreseeable future—remain significantly lower than in coastal cities.[7] By the same token, the gradual dismantling of internal protectionist policies (provinces were encouraged to be self-sufficient) should also drive down wages in inland regions as less competitive firms shut down.[8] On other hand, all such moves towards greater liberalization—including the complete abandonment of the *hukou* (residence registration) system—can mean that regional income disparities will actually widen, that is, before they eventually start to fall as manufacturing moves inland. Whether this is politically and socially acceptable is another matter. More flexible regulations and more fluid labor markets necessarily mean disruptions: layoffs, plant closures, and out-migration. The speed and direction of future reforms remain political decisions. However, the move towards more open markets and a less omnipresent state seems irreversible. In sum, assuming both improved transport infrastructures and reasonably flexible labor markets, we should expect to see a gradual shift inland of mid-tech manufacturing and a corresponding decline over time in regional income disparities.

Let me, however, temper my optimism. Although a movement inland over time of manufacturing can be expected, the movement will not, even under the best of circumstances, reach all places. Much of China's far west— the vast expanses beyond, approximately, the cities of Xi'an and Chongqing— will remain inaccessible. The geography of China can be described—if I may be allowed some geographic license—as resembling that of the United States, but without the West Coast. China's largely dry western and northwestern interior has all the markings of what I have called a "periphery" throughout this book. Unlike North America's interior, it cannot look in two directions, towards two oceans. In this respect, there is little prospect that China will be able to escape the challenges inherent in center-periphery relationships. Most places in China's periphery will, in all likelihood, continue to lag behind the rest of the nation, sending their sons and daughters to the great urban conurbations of the east.[9] And, if I may push the analogy with the United States one step further, China's vast inland periphery recalls North America's vast dry interior—the empty quarter—where in many places, we saw, populations have begun to decline. As China completes its demographic and urban transition, we may equally expect populations to start to decline in many places in the Chinese periphery.

Cities Will Continue to Grow

Why people and firms will continue to flock to big cities should no longer be a mystery to the reader. This does, however, leave one question unanswered. Is there an upper limit to the size that cities can attain or will attain in the future? It is a perfectly legitimate question. After all, we have learned that there are also costs associated with city size: higher land costs, traffic congestion, pollution, etc. At some point, logically, the additional costs brought on by size will outweigh the economic gains. This seems almost self-evident. Stated differently: is there an optimal city size, to use the vocabulary of urban planners,[10] beyond which further growth will create more problems than benefits? The answer is no; there is no clear upper limit to the size that future cities might attain.

The reason for my answer is, yet again, technological change. An upper limit exists in every epoch. Prior to the mid-nineteenth century, the technology and know-how needed to manage a city of more than 3 million people—the size of London, the world's largest city at the time—was simply not available. For much of human history, 1 million was the approximate upper limit of what could be efficiently managed. Before the arrival of modern science and sanitation, cities were veritable hotbeds for communicable diseases, more unhealthy on average than the countryside. Health is no longer the primary obstacle to city size. The Greater Tokyo urban region, the world's largest—with some 30 million people—is also one of the healthiest, with infant mortality and air pollution indicators below those of most cities.[11] Indeed, large cities in the industrialized world today often have cleaner air than mid-sized cities precisely because manufacturing has fled to smaller cities. The recurring smog of Greater Los Angeles is not so much a result of its size—although that does not help—as of poor transport planning, the almost exclusive reliance on the automobile, and its particular geography where mountains trap air blowing in from the Pacific, producing atmospheric inversions. Leaving aside land and labor costs, a systematic link between quality of life indicators and urban size is difficult to demonstrate.[12]

Taking Greater Tokyo as our benchmark, the 30-million ceiling still leaves much room for growth among the industrialized world's other big cities. Greater New York, the next largest, could still grow by some 10 million and both Los Angeles and London still have room to double their populations before attaining the current size of Greater Tokyo. Whether this will ever happen is another matter. However, what the comparison demonstrates is that the current upper limit—if indeed a limit exists—is considerably higher than the population of the vast majority of the big world's cities. Does this mean that 30 million (more or less) is the maximum size that an urban metropolis can attain? Probably not. The chief obstacle to further city expansion is transportation. Most people in the industrialized world do not wish to travel more than forty-five minutes (in each direction) between their residence and place of work. Add in business's reliance on face-to-face contacts, and it is easy to see why travel time remains the chief constraint on urban expansion. Current transport technologies based on the internal combustion engine put a limit on what is possible, especially in American cities. If travel time between business meetings is defined by the speed of automobile travel, then road and traffic conditions will largely determine the maximum distance at which two firms will consent to locate from each other. Introducing rapid transit or better traffic management can alter the equation, allowing the city to encompass a wider commuting shed. The higher density of many third world cities is in part fueled by poor traffic conditions.

In short, the maximum possible size to which cities can grow depends on the current state of technology. If new, more efficient transport technologies are invented and locally adopted, the upper limits of urban size will change. New technologies for monitoring traffic—what transportation planners call *demand management*[13]—may one day eliminate congestion, while new, smart, non-polluting vehicles may one day eliminate the negative environmental effects of the automobile. Trying to determine the upper limits of city size is, in other words, very much like trying to hit a moving target. In an era of rapid technological change, the goal posts are constantly being moved, which is why the subject of optimal city size has largely gone out of style among city planners. There really is no way of knowing for sure what the size of the world's largest city will be in fifty years or so. Technology permitting, there is no reason why the population of greater Shanghai—about 20 million at the time of writing—will not one day reach 40 or 50 million. This is probably not something the inhabitants of Shanghai look forward to. I am not suggesting it will happen. However, the rapid growth of China's metropolis is a reminder, yet again, of the strength of the forces driving urban concentration.

The Diversification of the Sources of Regional Growth

The knowledge economy and the IT revolution are, we saw, continuing to fuel the growth of large cities. Knowledge and idea-rich activities in the arts, sciences, management, finance, and manufacturing require urban settings to thrive for reasons that should now be obvious. In addition, IT facilitates the centralization of production in a single place, making it possible to deliver the final product—be it a TV show, computer program, scan, scientific article, or musical piece—at almost no cost to every part of the nation. In a truly flat world with no communications costs, location becomes a winner-take-all game. One place—one big city—could theoretically serve the entire planet, certainly an entire nation.

But does this mean that the production of *all* goods and services will necessarily concentrate in the same big city? The answer, again, is no. Falling transport and communications costs do indeed facilitate the centralization of production (for a particular good or service), but—by stimulating trade and competition—they also facilitate specialization. The reason, simply, is that no two places are the same. This is no less true for big cities. Knowledge-rich cities can take different paths. There is ample room for specialization, especially in larger nations such as the U.S. All places will not necessarily compete for the same human resources. Young ambitious kids with star fever will move to L.A., while those who see their future in finance will head for New York. The maxim, "Different places grow for different reasons," applies perfectly to major U.S. cities, even more so in the IT-led knowledge economy.

Let me compare to two East Coast metropolitan areas, New York and Boston, each indisputably a magnet for talent and brains. Among those in the most highly concentrated occupations in New York are fashion designers, personal financial advisors, musicians, singers, artists, and media (film, TV, etc.) producers and directors.[14] By comparison, people in the most highly concentrated occupations in Boston include medical scientists and biotechnical engineers, graduate teaching assistants, computer and information scientists, and computer hardware engineers. Visibly, the creative scene is very different in each city. Each has specialized in a different range of niches within the broader knowledge economy. The combination of America's high labor mobility and IT has produced cities that are distinct knowledge and creative centers, sometimes serving the entire nation and beyond. The obvious corollary of this evolution is that each city will have a distinct mix of knowledge workers, and those who choose to work and live in each city will not necessarily have the same tastes and preferences. This is in part a self-selection process. Knowledge workers who like what Boston has to offer will choose Boston (if they can); those who prefer the delights of New York will go there. This is yet another irony of the modern IT economy. A technology that manifestly fosters the homogenization of tastes also contributes to the development of distinctive urban labor markets and distinctive urban cultures.

It seems almost self-evident in today's knowledge economy that having a high proportion of college graduates is good for growth (I use the words *college* and *university* interchangeably, since what are called *college graduates* in the U.S. are often called *university graduates* in other countries).[15] The relationship between a high proportion of university graduates and growth is generally positive for larger urban places.[16] But is it necessarily positive for all places, irrespective of location and—especially—irrespective of size? It is doubtful that the presence of a high proportion of university graduates was a factor in the choice of Greensburg by Honda. Indeed, in the case of Greensburg, it could be argued that it was the absence of a university—and thus also of a large pool of college graduates—that in part attracted Honda. A university plus a large proportion of graduates would have driven up wages and, perhaps, also real estate values. Smaller towns, as a rule, have lower proportions of college graduates than bigger cities. For some this may be a handicap; but for others this can be blessing if—an *if* that applies to many small places— their best hope for growth is mid-tech manufacturing or other industries that do not necessarily require a highly educated workforce.

How education affects growth is conditioned by the size and location of the community, and by its economic base. Smaller places will often specialize in activities not spontaneously associated with the knowledge economy. Even in fairly large cities, growth need not always be driven by knowledge-intensive sectors. Among the fastest-growing urban areas in the U.S. with populations over half a million are Las Vegas, which we met earlier, but also Bakersfield, Fresno, and Stockton in California's central valley. All have very low proportions of college graduates, well below the national average. The three California cities are food-processing and distribution centers for what is one of the richest agricultural areas in the world, exporting its produce far and wide. These are not industries that require highly educated labor, but which are no less essential in a growing economy. Larger urban areas such as Miami and Phoenix also have below-average proportions of adults with college degrees. Neither has developed into a major high-tech magnet—at least not yet—but that has not prevented each from growing. A highly educated local population, although obviously a good thing, is not a *necessary* condition for growth. It all depends on the type of community and consequently where its best chance for future growth lies. The rise of residential economies—propelled by the hedonic imperative and the graying of rich nations—will become an increasingly powerful driver of growth, notably in the U.S. and in France.

Growth, in short, will continue to occur in some places for reasons that have little to do with the number of PhDs and Starbucks cafés in the community. The perception that *only* highly educated, high-tech, and hip places have a future in the knowledge economy is unfortunate. All places will not become centers of higher learning, centers of excellence, or centers of cutting-edge research and innovation. Most small and mid-sized towns—and many larger cities as well—will continue to grow thanks to activities that do not require a high density of university graduates. That indeed is one of the reasons why mid-sized cities and towns exist in the first place.

Returning to education, it is essential not to confuse the good of the community with that of the individual. Education—including postsecondary education—is almost always a good investment for an individual. It goes without saying that local governments should encourage the educations of their citizens. However, higher education can increase the number of young (educated) adults leaving the community for greener pastures, that is, if the community lacks the necessary attributes for attracting industries that employ graduates, the classic dilemma facing many small peripheral communities.[17] The dilemma takes on special meaning if postprimary education is in whole or in part locally funded, a dilemma that may become more acute in the knowledge economy. The young will understandably demand ever more education, which—if not locally provided—gives the young added impetus to leave and, all too often, not return. On the other hand, if local government invests heavily in postsecondary education, it may simply be producing future out-migrants, in essence subsidizing the growth of other places, where their young have moved.[18]

The IT revolution is widening the range of choices for another reason. Services that were not traded before are now traded over long distances. Not all new tradable services require a highly educated labor force. Thus, some small and mid-sized towns, formerly too peripheral to draw any benefits from the dispersal of manufacturing, will hopefully be able to specialize in standardized services that travel well and for which labor costs are a prime consideration. Typical examples are call centers, data processing, and telemarketing. The place must, of course, have a cost advantage. If not, the firm will go to a lower-cost location with comparable attributes (language skills, education, etc.), since distance is no longer the primary cost factor. This, needless to say, goes a long way in explaining why the outsourcing of services can reach beyond national borders, with India a notable example in recent times, now a major exporter of services to the U.S. and other nations. In the end, all this is simply a restatement that places are increasingly in competition with each other for an ever-expanding range of goods and services.

The Never-ending Search for the Right Strategy

Perhaps the most important lesson to be drawn from this book is that the reasons for which a particular place prospers (or does not) will seldom be exactly that same as that for another. The search for a single explanation is understandable, but also futile. By the same token, the search for a magic formula that will deliver growth or arrest decline is no less understandable, but equally futile. The search for *the* right policy lever is ultimately as fruitless as the search for a pill to cure all human ailments.

As in medicine, gurus have come and gone. In my time—I have been in this field for some time—I have seen policy fashions come and go. When I was studying regional economics in the 1960s, growth poles were the all the rage, which have fallen out of fashion since.[19] One reason growth poles did not work was that its proponents at the time confused outcomes with causes. We saw that urban concentration is a necessary outcome of economic growth, but that it is not necessarily a cause. Artificially stimulating urban concentrations via public intervention will have little effect unless *other* conditions are also present. The growth potential of places is not *solely* a matter of size and the quantity of public infrastructures. It would be nice if things were so simple. Indeed, as I am fond of saying in my classes in regional economics, if the answers were simple, then poor, declining, or otherwise disadvantaged communities would not exist; the remedy to heal the economic divide between the south and the north of England would have been found; Rust Belt cities would all be booming; and the small towns of the Great Plains would cease losing population.

Growth-pole policies also failed because they pushed on one button only, *size*, neglecting the second rule of regional growth, *location*. One might argue that they also forgot *costs*, the third rule, since public investments were often in heavy industry with all the potential negative after-effects we now know. Changing the relative size *and* location of a place within a nation is no mean endeavor. It is difficult to imagine a significant change in relative locations without a radical transformation of national transport networks. For investments to truly alter the position of a designated growth pole—a medium-sized city, for instance—would almost always require investments over many decades on a scale beyond the means and the political will of most governments, certainly in democratic societies. Simple politics makes it almost impossible to systematically invest in one place to the detriment of all others. If several medium-sized cities are designated as growth poles (which is about what happened in France in the 1970s), then in the end none will be—that is, no designated city will be systematically favored over another. Public infrastructure investments tend to follow demand and voters. Few things are more embarrassing to politicians than white elephants: a half-empty industrial park, an abandoned airport, or underused highway.

In short, *size* and *location*—the outcome of decades, even centuries, of development—are not easily amenable to public policy. Equally, public policy cannot rewrite the past and undo the legacy of negative industrial clusters, nor can it alter the hedonic blessings (or lack thereof) that Mother Nature has bestowed on places. Such facts on the ground put severe limits on what public policy can achieve. But the third rule—*costs matter*—is perhaps the cruelest cut of all. Most places, unless highly autonomous jurisdictions like American states, have only limited leeway to alter their relative cost structures. The porous nature of regional economies sets natural constraints on the degree to which local tax or fiscal measures can deviate from that of neighboring jurisdictions, without provoking unwanted out- or inflows of people and capital.[20]

Local development strategies must be tailored to local circumstances. For an industrial city or a resource-dependant community with a severe case of the Intrusive Rentier Syndrome, improved labor relations and worker retraining might be appropriate priorities. For a large metropolis and service center, the upgrading of its institutions of higher learning might well be the appropriate priority, or perhaps the expansion of its airport. Strategies that foster growth in big cities will not necessarily be appropriate for small cities. Local economic development is messy by its very nature, which is perhaps self-evident, but is nonetheless a useful reminder that fashionable strategies, which push on only one button, are seldom efficient.

The long history of local economic development strategies contains a powerful message: nothing really changes if all places adopt the same strategy. If all big cities, for instance, invest heavily in higher education, the *relative* position of each city will remain unchanged; those on top will still be on top and those on the bottom still on the bottom, which is another reason why national economic geographies are so infuriatingly stable. If every place invests in high-tech industrial parks, then again *relative* positions will remain unchanged. And in any spending contest the rich (or big) will always be able to outspend the poor (or small). Chicago will always be able to put more money into its symphony orchestra than Peoria.

The power of local policies to change the *relative* standing of the community within the nation is necessarily even more limited than that of higher orders of government. Actions at the local level demand even more imagination. The best strategy may sometimes be to bet against the market, so to speak.[21] If the current policy fashion for big cities is, for example, investing in local cultural institutions—very much in vogue at the time of writing—then perhaps the appropriate strategy is to focus on something totally different (while not necessarily neglecting culture). The first question to ask is, what *unique* advantage does the community have over others? On what attributes can the community truly compete?

My primary purpose in writing this book is not to propose policy recipes, but to explain. As in medicine, the essential first step to a cure is an accurate diagnosis. And as in medicine, a proper diagnosis requires combining an understanding of general laws with an understanding of the patient's particular circumstances, which fairly well sums up what I have been trying to do throughout this book.

The New Importance of Place: People

Perhaps the reader still has lingering doubts about the real importance of place in modern economies. Granted, geography was important in the past in determining where people settled and which cities rose to greatness. But surely today with the Internet and airplanes, great cities no longer need to be ports, to take but one example. Great cities can rise up almost anywhere. That is true in large part. The precise location where great cities will rise up is less constrained by physical geography than in the past. Great centers have sprung up in what would have formerly been thought unlikely places. The growing cities of the American Sun Belt—Los Angeles, Miami, Phoenix, and others—owe much to technology and improvements in sanitation and health care, as do growing cities in tropical or otherwise difficult climates—the Singapores, Mumbais, and Riyadhs of this world. The constraints of physical geography on human behavior are indeed less restrictive today.

This is good news. Past handicaps have become assets. In the rich, graying societies of North America, Europe, and east Asia, the most visible manifestation is the spectacular growth in green and gray migrants in search of places—to visit or settle—inaccessible or uninhabitable not so long ago. The new geography of development has opened up opportunities over an ever wider range of places, perhaps to places on Mars tomorrow. Geography no longer is destiny—physical geography, that is. But the decreasing importance of physical constraints does not mean that the importance of *place* has diminished. Quite the opposite is true.

The new importance of place has less to do with physical geography—although it still matters greatly—than with people and with access to people, ideas, and markets. Meeting, working, and conferring with others demand time and effort. A distinguishing feature of modern knowledge intensive economies is the shift towards products—goods and services—whose production requires that people come together, often at irregular intervals, to exchange ideas, discuss, negotiate, learn, and create. Travel and trade have become irrevocably intertwined. Where before, the dominant consideration was access to the land or to a natural resource, the principal consideration today is access to the right people at the right time—customers or creators—in increasingly distance places. Despite the Internet—indeed in part because of it—never has business travel been so widespread. The Internet and similar information technologies have accelerated the need to meet and to travel.[22] To paraphrase Robert E. Lucas: why are all these businesspeople flying around—with increasing frequency—if it is not to meet other businesspeople? And the reason they *need* to meet—the answer is almost too obvious—is that people live and work in different places.

The new economic reality of place is first and foremost a geography of people, people as creators and as consumers. Place will cease to matter the day all people live in exactly the same place, which for equally obvious reasons is not about to happen. Each place, city, town, or village is, by its very nature, a unique mix of people. No two places will, or can, have the same inhabitants with exactly the same talents, abilities, and skills. No two places will, or can, provide the same access, either on the spot or because of proximity to other places, to the same network of customers, contacts, and faces. No one place—even the New Yorks and Londons of this world—will ever house all the talents and all the know-how needed to produce every good and every service. Production in modern economies is increasingly differentiated and non-standardized, meaning an ever-growing demand for contacts with people in different places. *The* expert on a particular subject may well live in Boston, Delhi, Cannes, or Cape Town. Distance will continue to matter so long as travel—face-to-face contact—requires time and effort, and so long as time is not free. In the end, the principal culprit in the story is time. The truly rare resource is time, not money. Distance will only cease to matter the day people no longer need to meet and goods no longer need to be shipped to customers.

The forces that drive people towards big cities also produce countervailing pressures. This is one of the fundamental laws of economic geography. Even in the absence of differences in physical geography, places of varying sizes will emerge with different economic profiles. Not all industries need—or want—to be in the same place. For some, small size and distance from major metropolitan areas will be an asset. True, globalization fuels the growth of high-profile jobs in global cities, which tend to steal the limelight,[23] but other forces are also at work. There are good economic reasons why different-sized cities emerge at different locations and why they will continue to exist. This, again, is good news, notably for smaller communities, not necessarily destined to be at the cutting edge of the knowledge economy. During each epoch, certain activities will be centralizing, while others will be moving in the opposite direction. The balance between the two is not preordained. Future landscapes founded on people attributes rather than on physical attributes have the potential—at least, such is my hope—of producing less unequal geographies. In today's rich nations, extreme regional income inequalities are the exception, not the rule.

As the share of trade in the world economy grows, so will, inevitably, the importance of place. When markets were essentially local, firms had little choice but to locate near customers. But, in a world where more and more goods and services are traded over longer distances, picking *the* right place— *the* place that maximizes access to people and to markets[24]—is an increasingly frequent choice. Place is becoming more important, simply because firms are increasingly able to choose where to locate, certainly within nations, the predictable outcome of rising scale economies combined with falling transport and communications costs. Location becomes paramount in a world where a single firm can supply the entire nation (or world) from a single plant or office. Once all barriers to commerce are lifted, all that remain are physical distance and the attributes of place. Some places will always be closer than others. Some will always be bigger than others, and no two places will ever have precisely the same mix of people.

The more the world shrinks, the more *place* matters. In a completely flat world with no barriers to trade or interaction, what matters is access to the right places with the right people. New technologies, some not yet invented, will make it ever cheaper to move people and goods. The cost of moving information is already close to zero. But, at the same time, the need to interact with others will grow. This is one of the ironies of recent times, which makes the study of regional economies so fascinating and ensures that geography will not wither away.

Data Sources: Tables, Figures, and Maps

Tables

Table 1.1. OECD Territorial database (http://www.oecd.org/gov/territorialindicators), Eurostat, and the following national statistical agencies for non OECD nations:

- Instituto Brasileiro de Geografia e Estatística (http://www.ibge.gov.br/home), Diretoria de Pesquisas, Departamento de Contas Nacionais (Brazil)
- Ministry of Statistics and Programme Implementation, Government of India (http://www.mospi.nic.in)
- National Bureau of Statistics of China, China Statistical Yearbook, 2005 (http://www.stats.gov.cn/englis)

Table 2.1. Ciccolla (1999), PRISMA (1996), Prud'homme (1997), Weiss (2001), World Bank (1991). The author's calculations are based on national accounts and census data for the U.S., Canada, France, the UK, and China.

Table 5.1. Principal sources: Cipolla (1962), Kuznets (1966), World Bank (2002).

Figures

Figure 1.1. U.S. Census (2000). Summary File 4. For housing costs, the variable is median gross rent (per housing unit) as defined by the U.S. Bureau of the Census (http://www.census.gov).

Figures 2.3 and 2.4. 2001 Census of Canada, Statistics Canada, (special tabulations for INRS); U.S. Census (2000). Summary File 4. Bureau of the Census (http://www.census.gov).

Figure 4.1. For the U.S.: Bureau of Economic Analysis, U.S. Dept. of Commerce (http://www.bea doc.gov/bea/regional); For Canada: Statistics Canada (periodic). *Provincial Economic Accounts*, Catalogue No. 13-213. Ottawa: Statistics Canada.

Figure 5.1. Historical data on urbanization draws on various sources. The principal sources are: Breese (1966), Cipolla (1962), Kuznets (1966), United Nations (2004), World Bank (annual), paper before 1993, online since (http://devdata.worldbank.org/dataonline).

Figure 5.2. World Bank (2003) Word Bank Development Indicators: tables 1.1 and 3.10.

Figures 5.3 and 5.4. Principal sources: Breese (1966), Cipolla (1962), Kuznets (1966), World Bank (2004).

Maps

Maps 1 and 2. Eurostat (2002) (http://epp.eurostat.ec.europa.eu) and EuroGeographics (http://www.eurogeographics.org).

Map 3. Eurostat (1993, 2003) (http://epp.eurostat.ec.europa.eu) and EuroGeographics (http://www.eurogeographics.org).

Maps 4 through 7. For the U.S.: U.S. Census (2000) (http://www.census.gov). For Canada: Statistics Canada (2001) (http://www.statcan.com).

Map 8. Centro de Estudios de Finanzas Públicas de la Cámara de Diputados de México (2006) (http://www.cefp.gob.mx).

Map 9. Government of India, Ministry of Statistics and Programme Implementation (2001) (http://www.mospi.nic.in).

Map 10. National Bureau of Statistics of China, China Statistical Yearbook (2005) (http://www.stats.gov.cn/englis).

Maps 11 and 12. Eurostat (2002) (http://epp.eurostat.ec.europa.eu) and EuroGeographics (http://www.eurogeographics.org).

Notes

Preface

1. My undergraduate degree (BA) was in economics from City College, City University of New York, and my subsequent degrees (MA and PhD) in Regional Science and in City and Regional Planning, respectively, both from the University of Pennsylvania.

2. I have the additional good fortune of having a varied personal background. I was born in the Netherlands—where I spent my early childhood—of Viennese parents (German was the language of the home), grew up in New York City—where I spent my formative years—and then settled in Montreal, where I have happily lived since.

3. In 1947, Jean François Gravier, a French geographer, published *Paris et le désert français* (*Paris and the French Desert*), which nicely captured the spirit of the time, and which became an immediate bestseller.

4. GDP per person in Shanghai, the richest area, exceeded that in Guizhou, the poorest province, by a ratio of eleven to one in 2002 (Bils 2005).

5. The Regional Science Association International, with it is various national and regional affiliates, is the principal scholarly grouping where economists, geographers, and other like-minded academics and practitioners regularly come together. Annual North American and European meetings usually draw several hundred participants, which is not all that bad but still far below attendance at equivalent annual meetings of economists or geographers, which run in the thousands. Britain has also spawned the Regional Studies Association, which is more UK- and European-oriented. The two respective websites are http://www.regionalscience.org and http://www.regional-studies-assoc.ac.uk.

6. One of the reasons, undoubtedly, for the confusion –at least in the English-speaking world—is that the field is relatively young. Until the Second World War, the field, with some exceptions, was largely a German monopoly. The German generic name for the field was *Raumwirtschaft* (literally, spatial economy). It is instructive that the American economist, Walter Isard, the father of regional science, initially employed the term *space economy*, but which never caught on, for obvious reasons. Perhaps, if man one day settles Mars, it will come back into vogue.

7. Thus, I am by no means original in the emphasis I place on historical accidents as determinants of the economic geography of nations. Accidents and exceptions are recurrent themes in the writings of the Princeton University economist and Nobel Prize winner, Paul Krugman,

a leading pioneer of the new economic geography. By the same token, I am by no means alone in emphazing the role of deep-seated structural forces, a leitmotif in many of the writings of Alan Scott of the University of California at Los Angeles, a leading economic geographer. The writings of Edward Gleesaer and of Vernon Henderson, two of America's leading urban economists, have also profoundly influenced my thinking. Appropriate references to all are found in the bibliography.

Acknowledgments

1. INRS, part of the University of Quebec system, is a research institute and graduate school. The initials stand for *Institut National de la Recherche Scientifique* (National Scientific Research Institute). I am attached to INRS Urbanisation, Culture et Société in Montreal, which focuses on the social sciences. For more information see http://www.ucs.inrs.ca as well as http://laser .ucs.inrs.ca for information on the Spatial Analysis and Regional Economics Laboratory, where I do most of my work.

Chapter 1

1. The interchangeable use of product (GDP) and income per person is somewhat unorthodox, and will undoubtedly displease specialists. I do it for simplicity's sake in order not to unnecessarily disrupt the flow of ideas. GDP (gross domestic product) and income data are not strictly comparable, although the difference is seldom major, especially for nations as a whole. GDP measures the market value of goods and services produced in a given place, while income refers to the income received by the residents of that same place. For smaller entities (cities, towns, regions, etc.), the two may diverge because the place of production (say, an auto plant)—where added value is generated—may not match the place of residence of all those who derive income from the plant. Shareholders or owners may live elsewhere. GDP figures tend to exaggerate the true wealth of resource-rich regions since the royalties, taxes, and other income generated by resources (oil, for example) may in part accrue to residents of other places. Per capita GDP figures tend to accentuate disparities, especially in richer nations where incomes also include transfers (pensions, social insurance, etc.), which act to lessen income disparities between places. Data availability largely determines my choice of information. In cases where differences between income and product data matter, I will comment on it.

2. Although the relationship between in-migration and higher incomes generally holds true, it is nonetheless somewhat of an oversimplification. The relationship weakens considerably for the very largest places such as New York and London, at the top of the urban hierarchy.

3. U.S. Dept. of Commerce, Bureau of Economic Analysis, *Regional Economic Accounts* (http://www.bea.gov/regional/reis/default.cfm?catable=CA1-3&section=2).

4. National Association of Realtors Median Sales Price of Existing Single-Family Homes for Metropolitan Areas (http://www.realtor.org/research/research/metroprice).

5. To ensure data comparability across nations, the information on table 1.1 refers to per capita GDP (gross domestic product) and not to income. To minimize deviations due to particular circumstances and geographies, the following are excluded in table 1.1: Federal District (Brazil); Nunavut, NWT and Yukon (Canada); Macao and Hong Kong (China); Départements d'Outre-Mer (France); Chandigarh, Pondicherry, and Goa (India); District of Colombia and Alaska (U.S.).

6. A word of caution is in order for table 1.1. The results (ratios) are sensitive to the size of spatial units. The smaller the units—states, provinces, regions, etc.—the higher one would expect the ratios to be. Thus, in the U.S., per capita income (or product) variations between counties will be higher than between states. Recall the wide income variation between Manhattan (New York County) and Loup County, Nebraska, a ratio of more than ten to one. Caution is thus called for in comparing results between nations. The distortions are probably minor on table 1.1 because all spatial unities are fairly large. However, a direct comparison between the U.S. and Britain, for example, is not warranted because of the difference in country size.

7. China has administrative controls on internal migration—the *hukou* residence registration system—but which have not been terribly effective. The system is being dismantled but is still in place in parts of China. Much internal migration continues to occur in a legal limbo.

8. Product per person in the Greater London area has (with the exception of the surrounding southeast region) systematically remained at about twice the level of other regions in Britain. Referring to the gap between Greater London and the rest of Britain, Budd (2006, 262) writes that "once real price differences are taken into account . . . both income and productivity (per person) show no sign of narrowing." See also: UK Statistics, *Regional Trends 38* (http://www.statistics.gov.uk/STATBASE/ssdataset.asp?vlnk=7648).

9. I have consciously avoided mentioning Scotland, primarily because I am not sufficiently familiar with Scotland, but also because Scotland has its own distinctive geography with its own center-periphery relationship.

10. The great French geographer Onésime Reclus (1893, 40–41) wrote: "Liverpool, on the Mersey, almost rivals London as the world's greatest trading center; no European port imports as much cotton from America; none sends off as many European emigrants to the New World. . . . Manchester, a mere 50 kilometers away, weaves the cotton, whose finished products England sells to the world." Of Birmingham, Reclus wrote that it "has no equal in the iron industry; she produces every imaginable metallic object in impressive quantities, needles, machinery, pot ware . . ." (my translation). In order not to overburden the endnotes with references, I shall limit the reference citation to the family name and the date of publication—as in "Reclus (1893)." This is common practice in the scholarly literature.

11. The quote is in fact that of a character in one of Disraeli's novels, *Coningsby, or The New Generation*, book 1, chapter 1, third paragraph (digitized version). Harvard College Library (Philadelphia: Carey & Hart, 1844), found on Google. An e-book version can also be found at http://www.gutenberg.org/etext/7412.

12. In the early 1950s, about a half of UK merchandise exports still went to the Commonwealth (Sterling Area); the European share was about a third, the same as on the eve of the First World War (1913). (*Encyclopaedia Britannica* 1960, volume 10, 727, table LIX.) Europe's share today is around 60 percent.

13. The lagging development of the north of England remains a subject of grave concern in Britain. It is almost impossible to enumerate the government policy papers and initiatives that have sought to address the issue over the years. For a recent assessment, see Godchild and Hickman (2006).

14. For this insight I thank my colleague, Richard Shearmur, at INRS in Montreal. The idea had been taking shape in my mind for some time, but a recent study allowed me to formulate it more clearly. Looking at Canada, Shearmur, Apparicio, Lizion, and Polèse (2007) apply a statistical technique called geographically weighted regression (GWR), which allows researchers to test whether the explanatory power of a given variable changes with location. For example: do a

high proportion of university graduates have the same positive impact on growth in all places? The answer is obvious—no—but was not easy to see before. Indeed, there is no logical reason why persons with postgraduate degrees should have the same impact in a fishing community than in a high-tech center, which is precisely why graduates will earn more in the latter and, consequently, move there. For a similar study for the U.S., see Partridge et al. (2008b).

15. Among U.S. metropolitan areas east of the Mississippi, Detroit went from twelfth place in 1900 to fourth place in 1950. It has since fallen back to fifth place.

16. *Herald Tribune*, Batesville, Indiana, June 28, 2006 (http://www.batesvilleheraldtribune .com).

17. According to the U.S. Bureau of Labor Statistics, average hourly earnings in May 2007 were $15.90 in non-metropolitan Southern Indiana, which includes Greensburg. In nearby Indianapolis and Cincinnati, average hourly wages were $19.15 and $19.45, respectively. U.S. Department of Labor, Bureau of Labor Statistics, *Occupational Employment Statistics* (http://www.bls .gov/oes).

18. *Economist* (2006a, 36).

19. I'm not advocating that small towns such as Greensburg should not pay attention to urban planning and quality of life issues. These are commendable objectives in their own right. What I am saying is that they will rarely be *the* decisive factors in the town's economic future.

20. The word *cities* is used throughout this book as a generic term to refer to stand-alone urban areas of different sizes. Urban areas are defined differently by different national statistical agencies. Among the most commonly used criteria are population size and density and commuting flows. For larger urban areas, drawing the appropriate boundary is the main problem. In the United States, metropolitan statistical areas (MSAs) are principally defined on the basis of commuting sheds. Thus, the New York consolidated metropolitan statistical area (CMSA), with a population of about 20 million, refers to New York's labor market, which covers a wide area. The term *city* does not—unless stated otherwise—refer to political or administrative entities. When I refer to New York, I mean the metropolitan area and *not* the City of New York, with about 8 million inhabitants, which covers a much smaller area. To avoid confusion, where the word *city* does, exceptionally, refer to a political unit, I will use a capital *C*, as in *City of Paris*.

21. *Habitations à loyer modique*, literally, low-cost housing.

22. Hall (2000).

23. Hall (2000). The first part of the quote is part of Hall's opening statement (639); the second part is the closing sentence of Hall's article (649).

24. Indeed, if we are to follow Peter Hall's advice, then pleasant, safe, and secure cities are the polar opposites of creative cities.

25. Kraska and Kaup (2005). The region beyond Munich identified by Kraska and Kaup covers all of Bavaria south of Nuremburg and parts of the *Land* of Baden-Württemberg.

26. Florida (2002).

27. For electricity to be transported to the other side of the Gulf of St. Lawrence would require a major engineering feat, either lines bridging the gulf or tunneled under it.

28. Local development planners take great pride in the area's specialization in aluminum. The development of a cluster—*La Vallée de l'Aluminium* (Aluminum Valley)—is a core element of the region's development strategy.

29. We first proposed this in Polèse and Shearmur (2002). The idea, to be honest, is not all that original. The Intrusive Rentier is basically a regional version of what economists call the Dutch Disease. In the early 1970s, I believe, the discovery of petrol and natural gas in the North

Sea off the Dutch coast caused the Dutch currency—the guilder—to suddenly appreciate, in turn threatening the international competitiveness of its manufacturing sector. The term has since been applied to any situation where high demand for local resources "artificially" increases production costs in other sectors of the local economy.

30. In 2005, Chicoutimi's sister city, Jonquière, had the dubious distinction of being the only place in North America—so it seems—where union organizers succeeded in unionizing a Wal-Mart Superstore. I believe that Wal-Mart has since closed the store.

31. Why lunch box? Because the father would leave in the morning for the factory with his lunch box packed with food—by his wife, of course.

32. For that opportunity, I am indebted to the British Council, which generously funded my trip to the United Kingdom. Thanks to the British Council, I was able to go on what is best called a fact-finding tour on local economic development, involving meetings with academics and practitioners, which took me to London, Birmingham, Manchester, Liverpool, Newcastle, and Glasgow.

33. The reader may wish to consult a map of Belgium to see exactly where Charleroi and Mons are located. The province of Hainault is in the east of Wallonia, hugging the French border.

34. *Jim Crow* is commonly used shorthand for the infamous Black Laws promulgated by Southern states after Reconstruction (1865-1877)—the short period of relative freedom and Northern occupation—following the Civil War. The Black Laws, which entrenched segregation, relegated African Americans to what can only be called the status of an underclass. Segregation was finally declared illegal by the U.S Supreme Court in the early 1950s.

35. Economic *rents* are not only created by nature or location. Rents can also be generated by legislation, for example, special protection accorded particular producers. Thus, slavery, which allowed producers to employ labor at costs below that of a free market, generated a rent for slave owners.

36. Social conflict—sometimes violent—between landowners and peasants has remained a feature of daily life in many parts of northeastern Brazil.

37. Minnesota's unique political heritage is also reflected in the existence of the Farmer Labor Party, merged with the Democratic Party in 1944, to create the Democratic-Farmer-Labor Party, which long dominated state politics. This is probably the closest any U.S. state has come to a social democratic heritage, America's mini-Scandinavia, as it were. Unlike much of Europe, early socialist parties in North America often had rural roots. This is also reflected in the rural roots of Canada's socialist party, The New Democratic Party, whose origins lie in neighboring Saskatchewan and Manitoba, where it is often the ruling party.

38. The Renaissance Center in Downtown Detroit is among the most well-known initiatives. However, when I visited Detroit, which admittedly was some time ago, the Renaissance Center—a large modern office complex—basically stood alone in the middle of a desperately desolate central neighborhood.

39. Many (white) slave owners were refugees, so to speak, who fled Saint Domingue, as it was then called, in the late 1790s and early 1800s after the successful slave revolt—the only such case in the Americas—and subsequent war against Napoleon's armies, which freed Haiti from French rule. Haiti's history since is not a happy one. It is a sad irony that the nation which was the first to free itself from slavery has found it most difficult to free itself of the social and psychological wounds left by slavery. Perhaps no better proof exists of the indelible mark left by that repugnant system.

40. The population of metropolitan Atlanta was about 4.1 million compared to 1.3 million for New Orleans (2000 census figures). The terrible tragedy of Hurricane Katrina in 2005 has since reduced New Orleans's population further. Clearly, New Orleans has not been a lucky place in recent times.

41. Appelbome (1996, 10).

Chapter 2

1. The concept goes back to the earliest writings on industrial location (Isard 1956; Hoover 1948; Weber 1909), and is now a standard element in urban and regional economics. It is at the center of much recent research and writings in the New Economic Geography. Parr (2002) provides a good discussion of the uses and limits of the concept.

2. The list of empirical studies in academic journals on agglomeration and on industrial location is almost endless. Edward Glaeser and Vernon Henderson are among the most prolific authors. Gilles Duranton and Diego Puga have also published numerous empirical studies. References are provided in the bibliography.

3. Years differ on table 2.1. However, the relationships portrayed are unlikely to fluctuate significantly over short periods of time.

4. The high ratio for Shanghai is also in part a reflection of bottled-up rural migration, resulting from the *hukou* (residence registration) system, which discourages internal migration.

5. Manchester was discussed in chapter 1. For Montreal, see chapter 6.

6. Trade and specialization have, all throughout history, been a source of wealth creation, well before the Industrial Revolution. The economic foundation for this is the law of comparative advantage, which—simply put—states that we all gain if each of us works at what he or she does best (specializes, in essence) and that the fruits of our specialized labor are traded.

7. To identify these non-monetary costs, economists have coined the terms *opportunity cost* (for the value of time lost) and *transaction costs* (for the psychological costs involved in negotiating contracts and other business).

8. Held et al. (1999, 170).

9. The term *Bollywood* is a play on *Hollywood*, the *H* being replaced by *B* for Bombay, now called Mumbai.

10. Cairncross (2001).

11. Marshall (1890, 225). Quoted in Fujita and Thisse (2002, 7).

12. Michael Porter (1998; 2000) is undoubtedly the best-known advocate of local economic development strategies founded on the cluster concept.

13. Much of the recent literature on the impact of agglomeration economies focuses on the role of information and knowledge. Economists have coined the concept of *knowledge spillovers* to identify the positive externalities associated with the geographic concentration of related firms.

14. Gaspar and Glaeser (1998).

15. Lichtenberg (1960).

16. Since the 2008 subprime crisis, I am less convinced of the veracity of these two statements. Perhaps bankers should have traveled more. Had more actually met the families whose mortgages they were financing and then packaging in impenetrable financial instruments, perhaps the crisis would not have occurred or at least have been less severe.

17. The possibility of others poaching the firm's most valuable workers is a constant pre-

occupation among firms in high-tech clusters (such as Silicon Valley). A customary, but not always efficient, way of reducing such risks is to write specific conditions into hiring contracts, forbidding workers from going to work for competitors (located within x kilometers of the firm) for x months or years after his or her departure from the firm. Such clauses are notoriously difficult to enforce.

18. In the language of economists, services purchased by firms are intermediary inputs (into the production process). They are also sometimes referred to as *producer services*.

19. Of the top ten agencies with a combined income of $28 billion in 2002, about half was generated by firms located in New York (http://www.adage.com).

20. Economist (2005, 6).

21. One of the most popular books on the subject is *Edge Cities: Life on the New Frontier* (Garreau 1992). Garreau argues that traditional central business districts in the heart of the city are increasingly outmoded, to be replaced by shining new edge cities. Although suburban businesses have emerged in many places, I am far from convinced that the old CBD is on its way out.

22. Given this demonstration, the reader may well ask why the American film industry is not concentrated in New York. The answer is weather. The almost constant sun and warm weather of Southern California significantly reduces the risks (for outside filming) of days lost due to bad weather. In nations where climatic differences are not a factor, the film industry will indeed be concentrated in the largest city.

23. This terminology is rooted in Central Place Theory, whose origins are attributed to the German geographer Walter Christaller. His pioneering work, *Die Zentralen Orte in Süddeutschland* (1935), constituted the first attempt to explain the spatial distribution of market centers in a systematic manner. Central Place Theory laid the foundation for explaining urban hierarchies.

24. Gerald Carlino, an economist at the Federal Reserve Bank of Philadelphia, has strongly argued this point. In the jargon of economists, agglomeration is not only a production good (sought by firms) but also a consumption good (sought by consumers). Several studies have shown that *real* wages—once higher local living costs have been factored out—are sometimes lower in larger than in smaller cities. In other words, workers are willing to pay a premium (i.e., accept lower *real* wages) in order to live in larger cities. See Carlino (2005) and Tabuchi and Yoshida (2000). Glaeser and Gottlieb (2006, 1297) have taken this one step further, arguing that "[t]he success and failure of big cities depends in large part on the urban edge in consumption, not production."

25. Admittedly, the pull of the center—of great cities—also draws on less noble human traits: vanity, the desire to show off, self-importance. Tom Wolfe's 1987 novel *The Bonfire of Vanities* is, in this respect, an excellent fable of New York.

26. I say "essentially" because it is always possible to expand the perimeter of what constitutes central London. But there are limits to this expansion, precisely because firms and people seek to be near each other. A location farther from the center defeats the very purpose of nearness.

27. Mumbai, Vancouver, and San Francisco, where the central business district is located on a peninsula, are other examples of the impact of geography on supply. Supply can also be constrained by legislation, for example, by limits on the maximum height of construction or by zoning ordinances. Such legislative constraints on supply are more common in Europe than in North America, in large part because of heritage and architecture considerations.

28. In this paragraph, I am referring to average land prices in communities and cities. I am not dealing with neighborhood choice and housing markets, which are quite different issues.

29. Local ordinances limiting the maximum height of buildings are the most frequent countervailing force. As noted earlier, such measures are more common in Europe, but also found in some U.S. cities, most notably in Washington, D.C., to ensure that public structures such as the Washington and Lincoln monuments are not dwarfed by high-rise buildings.

30. A PhD student at INRS in Montreal, Sylie Arbour, carried out a regression analysis for all North American metropolitan areas with populations over 500,000 in 2000 (ninety urban areas in all) with wages in knowledge-rich occupations as the dependent variable. Wages, as expected, showed a positive relationship with urban size. However, when housing prices were introduced, *real* wage differences largely disappeared, suggesting that the productivity premium associated with size is largely captured by firms and not by workers. This is consistent with my earlier comments on the consumption value of big cities. In other words, workers are willing to forego the (real) wage gains associated with higher productivity in return for the benefits of living in a big city. Ms Arbour's PhD dissertation was not yet completed at the time of writing.

31. This is why economists will generally advocate road pricing—at least, where it is technically feasible—as the most efficient means of combating traffic congestion.

32. I choose this figure (a fourfold population increase) because this is approximately what occurred in Europe between 1800 and 2000; this, despite two world wars and massive out-migration to the New World. Thus, a fourfold population increase is very conservative. Over the same period, North America's population increased tenfold.

33. This is a simple mathematical result. If population increases fourfold (say, from 100 to 400) and the urban percentage goes from 10 percent of 100 (thus 10) to 90 percent of 400 (thus 360), the end result is a 36-fold increase in the total urban population.

34. Figure 2.2, although a stylized picture, is a fairly accurate representation of what has occurred in industrialized nations over the last one hundred years or so. The exact shares may vary from one nation to another, but the general trend is that pictured.

35. An abundant literature has accumulated on the stability of national urban hierarchies. Henderson et al. (2001, 98) observe for the U.S. that the 1900 and 1990 relative city size distributions overlap almost perfectly. For Germany, see Brakman et al. (2004); for Japan, see Davis and Weinstein (2002); for France, see Eaton and Eckstein (1997) and Guérin-Pace (1995); for India, see Sharma (2003).

36. This point is persuasively argued by Davis and Weinstein (2002), in which they show that the relative distribution of the population over Japanese prefectures has barely changed over a thousand years.

37. In the economic geography literature, the terms *producer services* and *high-order services* are often used interchangeably. Both refer to services that concentrate at the top of the urban hierarchy.

38. This is part of the vocabulary of central place theory, referred to earlier, one of the foundations of economic geography.

39. Glaeser (1998) argues that the opportunity cost of time—to use the vocabulary of economists—has increased in modern societies, therefore raising the economic cost of travel.

40. Most trade was limited to primary products (spices, wheat, furs, precious metals, vegetable oils, dried fish, etc.) and early manufactured goods (cloth, clothing, iron and copperware, etc.).

41. Using economic reasoning, crowding out is admirably explained by Henderson (1997). For a London example, see Graham and Spence (1997).

42. The idea of comparing transport costs for inputs and for outputs as a framework for

analyzing industry location was first introduced by Alfred Weber (1909). Weber's ideas were later refined and further developed by the American economists Edgar Hoover (1948) and Walter Isard (1956), all pioneers of modern industrial location theory.

43. The opposite cases are called market-oriented industries. A market-oriented product—recall the example of industrial bakeries—is one for which the costs of getting the final product to the customer, including the cost of time, outweigh the costs of bringing the primary ingredients—flour, sugar, yeast, etc.—to the plant.

44. The same reasoning applies to smelting activities (iron ore, copper, zinc, etc.), where the produced ingot uses only part of the raw resource and thus weighs less. Smelting activities are, as a rule, located near mines.

45. The nomenclature is that of NAICS—the North American Industrial Classification System—introduced in both countries in 1997. This industry class includes management, accounting, and engineering consultancies, as well as services related to marketing, research, design, advertising, and computer programming. It is by far the fastest growing component of modern economies, with an approximately tenfold growth in employment in the United States and Canada between 1970 and 2000.

46. For larger urban areas (populations above 100,000), these are Metropolitan (or Consolidated) Statistical Areas in the U.S. and Census Metropolitan Areas in Canada. I thank Laurent Terral, postdoctoral scholar at INRS from 2003 to 2005, for his help with these tabulations.

47. Employment in other modern services—financial, management, and information services exhibits similar symmetrical distributions in the United States and Canada

48. There are very few exceptions to the rule that a nation's financial center is also its largest city. Frankfurt, Germany's financial center and the seat of the European Central Bank, is such an exception. This can in part be attributed to Germany's comparatively short existence as a unified state—founded in 1870—and to its turbulent history since. Had things evolved differently, Berlin might well have replaced Frankfurt in the course of time.

49. The move to manufacturing technologies requiring more space (horizontal rather than vertical plants) has accelerated the process, plus the need for space for trucks to load and to park.

50. This conclusion—stated here in admittedly simple language—is consistent with an equilibrium view of how economies work; an important foundation of theoretical spatial economics. In most theoretical economic models, the system tends toward equilibrium—that is, until the next shock arrives.

51. The idea of organizing data in this way—by city size and by distance—was first developed in 1988 in an article with my colleague William J. Coffey at the University of Montreal, to whom I am intellectually indebted; see Coffey and Polèse (1988). Much of my work since on industry location has its roots in my earlier work with William J. Coffey.

52. For a detailed study of the location behavior of various industries, using Canadian data, see Polèse and Shearmur (2006).

53. *The Economist* (2006, 72–73) cites a typical example. Novartis, a major pharmaceutical company, announced the establishment of a $100 million research facility in Shanghai. The company declared—notes *The Economist*—that its choice "was not motivated by a desire to cut costs." By locating in Shanghai—the article further notes—perhaps China's most expensive city, Novartis turned down inland areas where prices were lower and government inducements abounded.

54. The postulate of a featureless plain with a central point toward which economic activity

converges is the starting point for many theoretical models in economic geography. Some two hundred years ago, the German economist Heinrich von Thünen (1826), one of the great pioneers of regional economics, began his theoretical exercise with the same postulates, laying the groundwork for all those to follow.

55. For the U.S., Partridge and Rickman (2008) show that poverty rates increase with rural distances from successively larger metropolitan areas, while Hanson (2005) demonstrates the positive relationship between average wages and market access. For Canada, Shearmur et al. (2007) find a strong positive relationship, growing over time, between local employment growth and continental market access.

56. Minneapolis–St.Paul was discussed in chapter 1.

Chapter 3

1. Paul Bairoch, a leading economic historian, argues that income differences between regions or nations before the Industrial Revolution were seldom more than 30 percent (Bairoch 1992, 14). Braudel (1979, 36) also argues that development differences were less acute before the onset of the Industrial Revolution. This does not mean an absence of wealth differences in riches, notably between the great trading cities in each epoch (Venice, Bruges, Amsterdam, etc.) and other areas. However, the disparities, which were harsh, concerned small numbers, since the great mass of humanity was still outside the market, living in poverty.

2. Columbus, we know, thought he had landed in India, which is why its inhabitants were initially called Indians. Near my home city of Montreal is a community called Lachine (China, in French), so called because of a similar misunderstanding by early French explorers. The first explorations were also driven by the partial closure of the traditional trade route to Asia after the fall of Constantinople (today's Istanbul) to the Ottoman Turks in 1453.

3. The idea that the first events—which determined where future big cities would spring forth—are "accidents" is today widely accepted by economic geographers. I am not original in the choice of the term "accident," which I use with some poetic license. I use the term as a convenient shorthand for events—be they political, technological, or social—which are not predetermined. Political boundaries, for instance, are not predetermined, nor are technological innovations. An accident can also come in the shape of a particular individual who altered the course of history. The list of possible accidents is interminable.

4. Ireland is the exception. Ireland's history is special and its story is by no means always a happy one. But it is a story with an unexpected happy ending for a part of the island. Since the 1990s, the Republic of Ireland has achieved a level of economic prosperity comparable to, and even surpassing, the most advanced nations of Europe. This is a remarkable historical turnaround.

5. Cole and Deane (1965, 33) are very clear on this point: "At the beginning of the twentieth century, there were five or six countries which could be said to have undergone an industrial revolution. They were the United Kingdom, the United States, Germany, France, Belgium, and possibly Holland."

6. Although the Blue Banana already figured in Brunet's earlier work, it only became popular following a report submitted to the French regional planning board in 1989. The concept has since gained wide acceptance. Some versions of the Blue Banana exclude northern Italy, while others include it.

7. Map 2 highlights variations *within* nations, which is different from standard maps pub-

lished by the European Union, where the reference point is the EU average, not the average for each nation. Map 2 refers to per capita GDP, not income. Recall my earlier comments on the difference between the two. GDP data can create distortions for regions where high locally generated resource rents do not necessarily accrue to local populations as income. This explains the high per capita GDP in eastern Scotland, a measure of the value of North Sea oil production, but not necessarily of local incomes.

8. Besides the Dutch cities of Amsterdam, Rotterdam, and The Hague, the Randstaad (literally, rim-city) also includes Utrecht, Haarlem, and Leiden, as well as a number of smaller cities, with an estimated total population about 7 million. The Rhine-Ruhr conurbation covers the great German steel and coal towns (Essen, Dortmund, etc.) of the Ruhr Valley as well as, according to some definitions, Cologne and Düsseldorf, located on the Rhine. Using the broadest definition, the area has some 11 million inhabitants. The Rhine-Main conurbation is centered on the cities of Frankfurt, Mainz, and Manheim, with a population of approximately 5 million.

9. The three exceptions are the Bulgarian-Rumanian boundary along the Danube, Rumania's eastern boundary along the River Pruth, and Germany's southeastern boundary (west of the Neisse River) with today's Czech Republic and Austria. However, the last two cases are not really exceptions. Rumania's eastern border changed several times since 1900. The current one (although the same as in 1900) now separates it from a different country (Moldova and Ukraine, rather than Russia). As for Germany's southeastern boundary, it was erased after Hitler's annexation of Austria, the Sudetenland, and the Czech Lands (1938, 1939) and then reinstated in 1945 after the fall of the Third Reich. A de facto international boundary existed from 1947 to 1990 between the Federal Republic of Germany (West Germany) and the now defunct German Democratic Republic (East Germany).

10. The other two cases are Switzerland (Berne) and Scotland (Edinburgh), recognizing Scotland as a historically (if not politically) distinct nation. It is certainly not an accident that the first is a highly decentralized federation.

11. Mak (2007, 53), more poetic, asks, "Vienna: how could this symbol of the illustrious empire suddenly have become a monstrous fish floundering on a dry seabed?" His metaphor is entirely apt. Great cities, in order to breathe, need to draw oxygen from a wide field. Vienna remains a glorious city, but is no longer the center of intellectual ferment it was prior to World War I.

12. Hanell and Neubauer (2006).

13. The precise quote from Hanell and Neubauer (2006, 14) is as follows, with reference to populations with a university education and for professions requiring a university education: "The regional distribution of these human resources . . . displays the very familiar pattern of the Blue Banana, supplemented by national capitals and larger metropolitan areas. In virtually all European countries, capital and other metropolitan areas account for the lion's share of this human capital."

14. Brülhart (1998), looking at manufacturing in the European Union from 1961 to 1990, found that employment in industries sensitive to labor costs was shifting to the EU periphery. In a more recent study, covering 1975 to 2000, Brülhart (2006, 227), observes that "Accession to the EU has favored countries' peripheral regions in terms of manufacturing employment and their central regions in terms of service employment."

15. Drenthe's GDP per capita is below the (Dutch) national average, as is that of the Slovak region of eastern Slovakia compared to the Slovak average.

16. Portugal and Greece do not fit into this scheme because it is difficult to establish a priori

which regions are less—or more—accessible to the European heartland. In both cases, the picture is closer to a pure national center-periphery model, centered on the national capital, respectively Lisbon and Athens.

17. Together with Jean Paelinck, I first expounded the idea of a general law of this nature in an article in 1999 (Paelinck and Polèse 1999).

18. Note that Burgenland was not part of pre–World War I Austria. After the war, it was transferred from Hungary to the new Austrian Republic because it was largely German-speaking.

19. The Spanish did arrive first in Florida. But Florida (ceded to the United States in 1821) did not develop into a major area of human settlement until the twentieth century.

20. Gottman (1961).

21. The Saint Lawrence Seaway, opened in 1959, had little effect on Montreal's position as a break-bulk point for ocean-going ships arriving from the Atlantic. Incoming or outgoing cargo still needs to be transferred from one transport mode to another. Most shipping on the Seaway is carried by *lakers*, specifically designed for that purpose.

22. The Hudson River Valley was already a well-established trade route and, incidentally, the traditional route of invasion (in both directions) for British, French, colonial, and American armies at varies moments in history.

23. Rappaport and Sachs (2003, 5) make a similar point, observing that "counties within 80km of an ocean or Great Lakes coast accounted for 13 percent of the continental U.S. land area but 51 percent of population and 57 percent of civilian income in 2000." Both shares have been rising.

24. According to recent estimates, Greater London's population was in the order of 11 million, about half that of metropolitan New York (CSMA).

25. Until the First World War, people moved fairly freely across the border, which was largely artificial in most places. Often the same groups and families would settle on both sides of the U.S.-Canada border. But times have changed.

26. Garreau (1981). The area to which I refer does, however, not entirely match that referred to by Garreau, which includes larger parts of the West.

27. Bonnifield (1978). The classic novel of that period remains *The Grapes of Wrath* by John Steinbeck.

28. These central valleys are the northern parallel in the Western Hemisphere of Chile's Central Valley, tucked between the Andes and the coastal ranges of the South Pacific.

29. In a now classic (but difficult to obtain) study some forty years ago of the location of U.S.-owned manufacturing plants in Canada, Michael Ray, a Canadian geographer, found a strong relationship between the location of plants and the location of their U.S. head offices. Chicago-based companies were, for example, more likely to have plants in (nearby) southern Ontario than Boston-based companies, proportionately more likely to invest in Quebec or the Maritime Provinces of Canada.

30. Some Loyalists also settled in Prince Edward Island and in Nova Scotia—both largely English-speaking provinces—which refused to join the American rebellion.

31. *Real* per capita income refers to income adjusted for cost of living differences. For the most recent figures, the reader should consult *The World Bank Development Indicators*, published annually (http://devdata.worldbank.org/dataonline).

32. Depending on sources, the population of Tenochtitlan has been variously estimated at

anywhere between 100,000 and 200,000 at the time of its fall to the Spanish in 1521, larger than most contemporary European cities.

33. The Spanish had the charming habit of first destroying the ancient Indian cities and their temples and then proceeding to build their churches on top of them as visible signs of their conquest and power.

34. A colleague of mine who knows Mexico well (and who shall remain unnamed) once remarked—with a touch of sarcasm, I admit—that the Spaniards and the Aztecs were made for each other, which perhaps explains in part why the conquered Aztecs and associated Indian peoples so rapidly adopted the Catholic religion and its institutions. The society that eventually grew out of this encounter of two cultures—the foundation of modern Mexico—constitutes arguably the most impressive example in the Americas of the fusing of European and Indian cultures.

35. But here again, one should beware of geographic determinism. The Mayan civilization in what is now Southern Mexico and Northern Central America arose in a largely tropical clime. The rise and the fall of the Mayan civilization remain a mystery to this day.

36. It is useful to recall that pre-European civilizations in the Americas lacked horses and did not use the wheel, which further increased transport costs and reduced the incentive to trade.

37. The only part of Mexico that arguably falls within one of North America's two economic centers is Tijuana on the U.S. border, de facto an urbanized southern extension of the San Diego metropolitan area. But this is, precisely, a recent development.

38. Data is for 1990–2000, All references to Mexican urban areas are for metropolitan areas as defined in the *Sistema Urbano Nacional*, based on census data published by INEGI (*Instituto Nacional de Estadística, Geografía e Informática*), the Mexican National Statistical Agency. My thanks to Isabel Angoa and Salvador Pérez-Mendoza of the Economics Department of the *Universidad Autónoma de Puebla* for their help in obtaining and in structuring the data.

39. The Zapatista uprising in 1994 in Chiapas and a particularly tumultuous political crisis—involving riots and some deaths —occurred in the state of Oaxaca in 2006. At the time of writing, the Zapatistas—with the much-mediatised, ski-masked, *Subcomandante* Marcos as their leader—continued to occupy a slice of territory in the Chiapas jungle close to the Guatemalan border. Both states have an unhappy history of political mismanagement and corruption, high even by Mexican standards.

40. Rodríguez-Pose and Sánchez-Reaza (2005, 254–55) are unequivocal in their assessment of the impact of NAFTA on regional disparities in Mexico, concluding, "States farthest away from the United States have lost out in relative terms," and observing "a widening of the gap between a relatively rich north . . . and an increasingly poor south." See also Esquivel et al. (2003).

41. These are my own projections and, of course, pure speculation. However, the numbers are not farfetched. Vienna's population at the outbreak of World War I (1910 census) was already 2.1 million, up from about 1.4 million twenty years earlier. Berlin's population was already well above 4 million in the 1920s, up from some 1.6 million in 1890. The figures are drawn from diverse sources. One can also speculate how the port city of Trieste would have evolved had the territorial and economic integrity of the Danube Basin—the core of the Habsburg monarchy— been preserved, which was its natural hinterland.

42. This brings to mind the following story (not to be taken seriously): following World War I, newly independent Poland and Soviet Russia disagreed on where the international

boundary should be drawn. A commission, headed by Lord Curzon, was set up to enquire what the local population thought. Interviewers were sent into the field. A Ukrainian farmer, asked whether he preferred his village to be incorporated into Poland or into Russia (as a Ukrainian, he was expected to be noncommittal), spontaneously answered, "Definitely Poland." When the interviewer asked why, the farmer's response was, "Because I can't stand those Russian winters."

Chapter 4

1. The word *disparity* has a negative connotation, suggesting that something is wrong and needs to be corrected (via government action). Terms such as *regional inequality* and *unbalanced growth* send a similar signal. Language is a powerful marker of political opinion. Such terms are generally avoided by persons (scholars included) leaning towards the right end of the political spectrum. My choice of the word *disparity* should not be construed as a political statement. I simply find it the handiest word around, which instantly evokes the subject being discussed.

2. Coe et al. (2007) do a good job of presenting what might be called the alternative—Marxist-based—perspective.

3. An important recent work on the subject is Barro and Sala-i-Martin (1995) in which they show that the historical trend is towards income convergence (reduced disparities) in developed nations, examining long-term trends in the twentieth century for North American, European, and Japanese regions. The trends for developing nations (Brazil, Mexico, and China, notably) are less clear-cut. Recent evidence for Europe suggests a widening of regional disparities for some nations since the 1980s, as well as a loosening of the link between growth and income convergence: Geppert and Stephan (2008); Petrakos et al. (2005); Puga (2002); Rodríguez-Pose and Gill (2004).

4. A minor cottage industry of studies on the subject has sprung up in recent years, especially in Europe. In the scholarly literature, the term most often employed to identify the object of study is *convergence*: such studies seek to measure whether regional (income) convergence has occurred or not for the time periods studied. How to precisely measure convergence remains an object of debate among scholars.

5. I have chosen to present an easy-to-understand measure of regional disparity; the ratio of per capita income in the two richest states (provinces) to that in the two poorest. Other more complex measures exist, but which basically show the same trends over time.

6. For a more technical presentation of the economics of regional equality, see Puga (1999).

7. Barro and Sala-i-Martin (1995). The results are for GDP per capita, using standard deviations as measures of regional disparity. Standard deviations fell between 1950 and 1980 in all of the five largest nations: France; Germany (West); UK; Italy; and Spain.

8. The apparent sudden surge in regional disparity in Canada following World War II should not be misinterpreted. This is solely attributable to the entry into the Canadian Federation of Newfoundland in 1949, since then (and still) Canada's poorest province.

9. Among industrialized nations, the United States has by far the most unequal distribution of income. The share of national income in the U.S. going to the poorest 10 percent of the population is about one-third of that in Japan, the industrialized nation with the most equal distribution of income. Data are published annually in *The World Bank Development Indicators*.

10. In most industrialized nations today, with the U.S. again an exception, the existence of income maintenance programs (unemployment insurance, social welfare payments, family allowances, etc.) means that, except in extreme cases, total income loss is rare.

11. Rodríguez-Pose and Gill (2004) observe an increase in regional disparities in the EU between 1990 and 2000, as measured by the variance of the log of regional GDP per capita. Geppert and Stephan (2008) also observe a widening of disparities in Europe.

12. This is understandable. Regional policy is a major component of the EU budget. The amounts involved are far from insignificant. Spending on regional policy over the 2001–2006 fiscal exercise was in the order of 200 billion euros. Most of this went for infrastructure investments in designated areas.

13. Duranton and Monastiriotis (2003) observe that earnings in Greater London were 121 percent of the national average in 1982, but 137 percent in 1997.

14. Shearmur and Polèse (2005). We examined the evolution of income and earning differences in Canada between 1971 and 2001 for 382 territorial units.

15. Seen in this light, the EU criterion for identifying regions eligible for aid—per capita GDP 25 percent below the EU average—seems quite appropriate. It is unfortunate, however, that the EU uses GDP rather than income figures. As noted in note 1 (chapter 1), using GDP can create distortions, especially in resource-rich regions.

16. Myrdal (1957).

17. I shall not attempt to explain the reasons behind the word *endogenous*, since the explanation is rather technical and does not really add anything to the understanding of their argument. The relevant references are Lucas (1988, 1990) and Romer (1989, 1994, 1996).

18. Lucas and Romer, although among the most well-known, are not the only authors. For a very readable presentation of the arguments of new growth theory, see Easterly (2002). The idea of increasing returns—at the heart of the matter—also has its roots in the writings of Krugman (1991, 1995).

19. If I may be forgiven for boasting, albeit somewhat belatedly, I proposed a similar framework in my PhD thesis almost forty years ago (Polèse 1972). My explanation was not as elegant as that of Lucas and Romer, but I similarly attempted to demonstrate how in-migrants—via their possible positive impact on local productivity—indirectly increased local demand for labor, annulling their downwards supply effect on wages. I should perhaps have given greater exposure to my intellectual exercise. At the time, I didn't think it all that important.

20. The dependency rate refers to the ratio of non-working-age persons (the very young and the old) to those of working age.

21. This is one of the classical dilemmas in local economic development. Education is often seen (not incorrectly) as a means of promoting the development of depressed communities. However, investments in education may be counterproductive (for the community, but not for the individual) if they simply increase out-migration. A minister of education of the province of Nova Scotia (Canada) once commented to me in frustration: "Half of my money serves to subsidize Ontario, paying for kids who will pack up and move to Toronto." But then, should Nova Scotia cease to educate its sons and daughters? A true dilemma, to which I return in chapter 7.

22. Argentina also exhibits extreme regional disparities. The ratio (GDP per capita) between the richest and the poorest province was eleven to one (Cao and Vaca 2006). Development in Argentina has always been very polarized in and around Buenos Aires and the La Plata River Basin.

23. Williamson (1965).

24. For my analysis of South Korea, I owe a considerable intellectual debt to two former students, Minhee Park and Chang-Hoon Yoo (the latter now a university professor in Seoul) and my old friend Joseph Chung, one of Canada's first urban economists and a former associate of

the Korea Research Institute for Human Settlement, who was kind enough to first invite me to South Korea.

25. All data is from *The Korean Statistical Yearbook* (annual publication), cited in Yoo (2001).

26. Between 1965 and 1995, the coefficient of variation for regional GDP per capita—a measure of disparity—fell from 0.31 to 0.16, and then to 0.15 for the year 2002 (Chang et al. 2004). My thanks to Minhee Park for the translated tables.

27. All this will necessarily change the day Korea reunites, as it one day must. Seoul is located on the Northern edge of the republic, but smack in the middle of an eventually united Korea. The centralizing forces favoring Seoul would be compounded in a united Korea, leaving aside the frightening prospect of truly massive out-migration from the much (much) poorer north. Northeastern Korea might well be transformed into a true marginalized periphery, unless eastern Manchuria (neighboring China) and Vladivostok (neighboring Russia) turn into economic powerhouses, which seems unlikely at the time of writing.

28. As noted earlier, the two "disparities" should not be confused. They sometimes are in South Korea. I have heard South Koreans lament the high level of regional disparity in their country, when in fact they were really referring to the high concentration of economic activity in Seoul. The term *disparity* is best reserved for differences in per capita income or other measures of welfare.

29. The regional units (provinces/states) are of comparable size in both nations. Thus the observed difference in regional disparity, as measured, cannot be attributed to differences in region size.

30. Studies of migration, especially in developing nations, find that migrants often migrate in stages from one generation to another. The first move will be to a nearby town or city.

31. I shall not pursue this question any further since my knowledge of India's economic geography and history is limited.

32. If Bihar and the National Capital Territory (the two extremes) are excluded, all "rich state/poor state" ratios (for GDP per capita) fall below 2.8, which is low by developing nation standards.

33. For my analysis of China, I should like to thank my colleague Nong Zhu at INRS in Montreal. I am especially indebted to him for providing me with detailed regional data for China. Nong Zhu has written on internal migration and regional development in China (Luo and Zhu 2006; Zhu and Luo 2006).

34. The spread of economic reform—notably via the establishment of special economic zones—undoubtedly further contributed to the widening of the gap between coastal and interior provinces. The first five zones, created in the early 1980s, were located in coastal provinces. Only in the 1990s was the so-called Open Door Policy applied to the whole country (Bils 2005). Ying (2006) also argues this point persuasively.

35. Bils (2005, 15, table 5). The data are for the year 2002.

36. Bils (2005, 16, table 6).

37. For Canada, the sharp decline in disparity noted on table 1.1 is attributable to the quirks of the GDP measure. The high disparity in 1980 is inflated by the economic boom at the time of the oil-rich province of Alberta.

38. However, if skilled labor is scarce (and valued), interpersonal wage disparities between skilled and unskilled workers might be very high. As noted earlier, there is no *necessary* correlation between the level of interpersonal and interregional income disparities.

39. U.S. Department of Commerce, Bureau of Economic Analysis, *Regional Economic Accounts* (http://www.bea.gov/regional/reis/default.cfm?catable=CA1–3&section=2). The other exception is the Washington, D.C., area, for reasons that are not difficult to guess.

40. The Irish government has established the Western Development Commission—a special function agency—to deal with the economic problems of the western counties, but which excludes the *Gaelteacht*, the Irish-speaking region in the extreme southwest.

41. The ratio of per capita GDP in the Bratislava region to that in eastern Slovakia was three to one in 2005, very high by developed nation standards. The following lines from the *Slovak Spectator* (March 7, 2005) are worth quoting: "Although purchasing power per capita is growing in Slovakia, regional disparities are getting larger. . . . Slovakia's richest region is Bratislava. . . . Purchasing power is lowest in . . . southern central Slovakia and the remote districts in the East" (http://www.itapa.sk.index.php?ID=427).

42. Birth rates in Ireland have since fallen, and are now close to the western European norm. However, the recent history of high birth rates has left Ireland with a younger population compared to most European nations, which is part of its good fortune. The luck of the Irish, as the saying goes.

43. I say viewed from afar, because I do not know Slovakia well. I did visit Slovakia during the Communist era when Czechoslovakia was still one nation. At the time, I had a contact in Slovakia's central planning office, a former classmate at the University of Pennsylvania. He took me to the outlying regions of eastern Slovakia. To be perfectly honest, all I remember is drinking far too much plum brandy, courtesy of overly gracious managers of the collective farms we visited.

44. I do not include Birmingham because—as noted earlier—I see it increasingly as an extension on of the south English economy.

45. The nations, moving from west to east, are Mauritania, Senegal, Gambia, Guinea-Bissau, Guinea, Sierra Leone, Liberia, Ivory Coast, Ghana, Togo, Benin, and Nigeria.

46. Source: http://www.world-gazetteer.com.

47. The port of Beira, farther north, is the natural outlet for Zimbabwe (former Rhodesia). But with the almost total collapse of the Zimbabwe economy—at the time of writing—even that small counterweight to the irreversible pull of Maputo and the South African economy has disappeared.

48. In this scenario, southeastern Austria, on the southern side of the Alps—specifically the *Länder* of Styria and Carinthia—could be considered peripheral. Their GDP per capita is below the national average.

49. Recall also my earlier comments on the probable under-exploited potential of the former German provinces of Silesia and Pomerania.

50. The German Democratic Republic, also called East Germany, existed from 1947 until the fall of the Berlin wall in 1990. After 1990, the East German *Länder* were reunited with the rest of Germany as part of the German Federal Republic.

51. Reclus (1893) does not even mention Johannesburg in his chapter on what was then the Boer Republic of Transvaal. Only the two small nascent urban centers of Pretoria (the capital) and Potchefstroom are mentioned.

52. The Bantustans of the old white-dominated apartheid regime, which collapsed in the early 1990s, were literally black reserves—largely rural—to which much of the black African population was forcibly tied by a complex regime of internal passports and other restrictive measures.

53. The exact proportion for each trading partner continues to evolve. China is in the process of replacing Canada as the U.S's principal trading partner. The point, however, remains valid: U.S. international trade is not unidirectional.

54. I am not the first person to point out the existence of such growth corridors in the United States, which generally follow the contours of the interstate highway system. See, for example, Lang and Dhavale (2005).

55. I am not the first to suggest this. Short (2007, 15) also argues in favor of an extended megalopolis, but he stops at Charlotte, North Carolina, while I go further south.

56. By "South" at the time, I mean those who could vote—the white population, in other words. Remember also my earlier comments on Jim Crow and the Black Laws.

57. Neither Spain nor Portugal was formally part of the Western Alliance (NATO) until much later. In the years following the Second World War, both were viewed with some suspicion because of their non-democratic regimes and pro-Axis proclivities during the war. Both only became truly democratic states during the 1970s. In addition, Spain—and Portugal even more so—were technologically far less advanced than France at the time.

58. In case Belgian readers should think me overly critical of Belgium, I can assure them that I have nothing against Belgium. Quite the contrary. I spent several very enjoyable months of a postdoctoral year in the university town of Leuven (Louvain), drinking far too much Belgian beer, which, be it said, is among the best in the world. And nothing beats Belgian french fries and chocolate, not necessarily to be consumed together.

59. Taking the ratio of richest to poorest region (per capita GDP), Felsenstein and Portnov (2005), looking at 23 European nations, found that Belgium had the third highest ratio, exceeded only by Slovakia and Britain.

60. Actually, the working-class patois of Brussels is a wonderful mix of both languages. I remember once sitting next to a couple, trying to figure whether they were speaking Dutch or French. They were speaking the local patois.

61. The reader may well ask: what about the EU, which provides for labor mobility within European space? That is true. But language remains a powerful barrier.

62. Were it not for Brussels, Belgium would most probably have split into two separate nations long ago.

Chapter 5

1. South Korea completed the transition in a mere generation, undoubtedly the fastest on record, going from 80 percent rural in 1955 to 80 percent urban in 1990.

2. Understanding the origins of modern economic growth is, arguably, the most important question in economics. Besides David Landes's *The Wealth and Poverty of Nations* (1998), I recommend the now classic *Towards a Theory of Economic Growth* (Kuznets 1968), as well as two more recent books: *The Elusive Quest for Growth* (Easterly 2002) and *Economic Growth* (Barro and Sala-i-Martin 1995). The latter is rather technical.

3. Numerous studies have, time and again, confirmed the positive (statistical) relationship between national per capita income and urbanization levels: Fay and Opal (2000); Jones and Koné (1996); Lemelin and Polèse (1995); Tolley and Thomas (1987).

4. Kuznets (1968, 6).

5. World Bank (2001). The difference between Dutch and Indian per capita incomes falls to roughly ten to one if incomes are adjusted for cost of living differences.

6. Bairoch (1992, 1997); Landes (1998); Maddison (1995, 2001).

7. DeLong (1998).

8. On the social consequences of modernization, Karl Polanyi's 1944 classic, *The Great Transformation*, remains an essential reference.

9. World Bank (2004, table 1.1).

10. Baudhuin (1996); World Bank (1998, 2002), Economist (1990).

11. *World Development Report: World Development Indicators* (World Bank 1998, table 4.10).

12. I use the term *agriculture-based* in its broadest meaning to include all products derived from industries producing foodstuffs: farming, fishing, hunting, ranching, etc.

13. Economist (2001, 26).

14. *World Development Report: World Development Indicators* (World Bank 2002; 2003, table 3.3).

15. It is no accident that Easterly (2002) entitles his book *The Elusive Quest for Growth*.

16. Most industrialized nations suffer from agricultural overproduction, signifying that the share of labor in agriculture has not fallen far enough, in part the result of generous farm price support programs, especially in the European Union, contested by developing nations who see such programs as a form of protectionism, not without reason.

17. The positive statistical relationship between GDP per capita and urbanization levels is very strong. For the data on figure 5.2, some 82 percent of the variation in urbanization levels between nations is statistically explained by differences in per capita product.

18. World Bank (2003, table 2.5). According to China's national statistical agency, the ratio of urban to rural income was close to three to one in 2002.

19. The distinction between static (allocational) and dynamic effects may seem somewhat esoteric to non-economists. Much of economic analysis and theory is essentially static. Methods of production (technology) are generally assumed to be constant. When economists refer to a more efficient allocation of resources—labor, in this instance—this is under given technological conditions. Long-term economic growth, by contrast, necessarily implies technological change, which is the principal source of productivity growth and rising per capita incomes. See the pioneering work by Denison (1967, 1985) and, more recently, Barro and Sala-i-Martin (1995).

20. I have developed this argument in greater detail in Polèse (2005). Henderson (2003a, 50) makes a similar point: "The paper finds little support for the idea that urbanization per se drives growth. Urbanization is a 'by-product' of the move out of agriculture and the effective development of a modern manufacturing sector, as economic growth proceeds, rather than a growth stimulus per se."

21. Polèse (2005).

22. Taking the U.S. as our benchmark (U.S. = 100), per capita GDP adjusted for cost of living differences was, respectively, 35 for Argentina, 27 for Chile, and 26 for Uruguay (World Bank 2003, table 1.1).

23. Fay and Opal (2000) make a strong case for the argument that urbanization has progressed in Sub-Saharan Africa in the absence of economic growth. However, they note that the rapid progression of urbanization in Africa since 1980 is not exceptional when seen in the light of Africa's under-urbanization before 1980 and the very high urban-rural income disparities existing at the time. Wages in industry and services in the 1970s were on average about nine times higher than in agriculture.

24. Private transfers—notably money sent home by relatives working in richer nations—will also serve to bolster incomes and local consumption.

25. It is worth quoting Gugler (1988, 82–83) at length on this point: "A substantial body of research on rural-urban migration has accumulated over the last two decades, and the evidence is overwhelming: most people move for economic reasons . . . studies throughout the Third World report time and again that the great majority of migrants consider that they have improved their condition and that they are satisfied with their move." Although Gugler's work is now somewhat dated, his conclusions remain valid. Reader (2004, 163) observes: "The quality of life for the majority of people (in today's African cities) is desperately low, with squatter or slum housing being the norm. . . . So why do people migrate to cities in such numbers? The answer, contrary to the idealized Western view of the countryside as a haven to which city-dwellers yearn to escape, is that prospects are even worse in the rural areas. The cities may be poor, but the countryside is poorer still."

26. Taking modern sanitary infrastructures (drainage, sewage facilities, etc.) as a benchmark, 61 percent of urban dwellers in India had access to such facilities in the year 2000, compared to 15 percent for the rural population (World Bank 2003).

27. The author well remembers talking to a city official in Cape Town during the dying days of apartheid, who frankly admitted that the city had all but lost control over the inward movement of rural black migrants.

28. The negative consequences of the lack of tenure security are not difficult to guess. The absence of clear property rights makes it impossible for a mortgage market to develop and for residents to use their house or land as collateral. This in turn makes business start-ups or other productive investments all the more costly to undertake, in essence making it more difficult for the urban poor to grow out of poverty. Hernando De Soto (2000), a Peruvian economist, argues this point persuasively.

29. European farmers, especially the French, have been richly subsidized since the beginnings of the Common Market. The common agricultural policy (CAP) accounts for some 40 percent of the European Union budget. This has not prevented the share of the French labor force in agriculture from declining to about 2 percent of the national total today.

30. Engel's law is no less valid at the level of the planet. As the planet grows richer (well, at least some parts), demand for food products will account for an ever-decreasing share of global demand. The world as a whole currently suffers from agricultural overproduction, localized famines notwithstanding, which are largely caused by distribution failures and administrative breakdowns, often as a result of war and civil strife.

31. My comments on rural development are in part founded on my experience in Mexico, where I was affiliated for several years with an NGO (non-governmental organization) providing teaching and training for rural populations, located in the Sierra Norte de Puebla, one of the most marginalized areas of Mexico.

32. Language training is often part of education. In the Sierra Norte de Puebla (Mexico), emigration to the city was proportionately less prevalent in communities where the indigenous language was still predominant (Náhuatl in this case, the language of the Aztecs).

33. Reader (2004, 72).

34. Data before 1947 refer to unified British India, which includes today's Bangladesh and Pakistan.

35. World Bank (2002, table 2.20).

36. Kuznets (1966) and World Bank (2002).

37. Kessides (2005, 60).

38. Mills and Hamilton's *Urban Economics* (5th ed., 1994) and O'Sullivan's *Urban Economics*

(4th ed., 2000) are among the leading textbooks currently on the market. My comment should not be interpreted as criticism. These are quality university textbooks. Institutions are simply not a major issue in urban and regional economics.

39. Public goods, in the language of economists, refer to goods and services that will not be provided by the private sector, in part because all users cannot be billed for the service. Sidewalks, streets, and public safety are typical examples.

40. Historical experience also suggests that changes in land use (land markets), which necessarily accompany urbanization, operate more smoothly under conditions where the rural economy is largely made up of small farmers rather than large landowners. Institutions and laws are in part the historical legacy of geography and climate, a point persuasively argued by Diamond (1997).

41. The clash of cultures can create confusing situations, exacerbating the insecurity of marginal urban dwellers. I remember, in French-speaking west Africa, an urban planner pointing out areas that were subject, simultaneously, to communal tribal law, Islamic law, and French civil law. Little wonder that land tenure is uncertain and ownership difficult to ascertain. Such problems are not exclusive to the developing world. In Canada, land claim disputes involving native populations, whose traditions are often communal, continue to make the headlines.

42. Easterly (2002) remains an excellent reference on this point.

43. Jacobs (1969, 1984). My arguments are developed in more detail in Polèse (2005, 2006).

44. *The Wealth of Nations* (Smith, first published in 1776).

45. Landes (1998)

46. On the cultural foundations of economic growth, Max Weber's classic, *The Protestant Ethic and the Spirit of Capitalism* (first published in German in 1905), remains a landmark. The influence of Protestantism—specifically Calvinism and its offshoots—on the early economic development of western Europe is difficult to deny. It was certainly *not* an accident that the outlying European nations which caught up most rapidly in the first half of the twentieth century were all Protestant: Scandinavian nations plus Iceland and Finland. Contrast this with the evolution of Catholic Spain and Portugal at the same time. The Protestant-Catholic divide has far less economic significance today.

47. Diamond (1997).

48. W. Easterly and R. Levine (2002) in *Tropics, Germs, and Crops* make very much the same point.

49. In recent years, the very largest U.S. metropolitan areas—those with populations over 5 million—have on average grown more slowly than metropolitan areas in the 500,000 to 5 million range, suggesting that agglomeration economies are approaching their upper limits under current technological conditions.

50. At the time, the two cities played similar roles in their respective national economies: the chief points of entry for European immigrants and the chief ports for (prairies, pampas) grain exports to the rest of the world.

Chapter 6

1. Florida (2002).

2. Cheshire and Magrini (2006); Rappaport and Sachs (2003); Rappaport (2004).

3. Quoting Glaeser (2005, 137): "No variable can explain state and city growth over the past 80 years as reliably as temperature." Glaeser also points out the role of technology in the rise of

Sun Belt cities. He also notes, as I do, that the positive relationship between human capital (the presence of an educated labor force) does not necessarily hold for places that have been blessed by Mother Nature.

4. An old Latin proverb, certainly familiar to many readers, literally: "About tastes and colors one should never argue."

5. Some groups—notably in the arts and in knowledge-intensive professions—are apparently prepared to pay a premium to live in large cities. Recall my earlier observation for North American cities that *real* wages—adjusted for cost of living differences—often decline with city size.

6. A particularly revealing example is a report (Lilly 2002) commissioned by the Trade Development Alliance of Greater Seattle, a city which certainly need not be envious of Barcelona's economic success. The report waxes absolutely poetic over Barcelona's city planning and economic development strategy.

7. Much of the evidence is indirect, based on studies that examine the relationship between the presence of human capital (as measured, generally, by the share of the population with advanced degrees) and subsequent growth. Most of the studies are for the United States. Probably no scholar has studied the relationship more than Edward Glaeser at Harvard University. See, for example, Glaeser and Saiz (2003) and Berry and Glaeser (2005). In the 2003 paper, the authors found that metropolitan areas where more than 25 percent of adults had a BA degree or over grew by 45 percent between 1980 and 2000, compared to 13 percent for metro areas where degree holders accounted for less than 10 percent of the adult population.

8. Webometrics, an Internet scientometrics tool, ranks Berkeley, MIT, Harvard, and Stanford as, respectively, the four best universities in the U.S. (and in the world) in that order (http://www.webometrics.info/index.html). The first and fourth are located in the San Francisco Area and the other two in the Boston Area. A second source places these four universities among the world's five best, together with Cambridge University in England (*Academic Ranking of World Universities 2006*, Institute of Higher Education, Shanghai Jiao Tong University [http://ed.sjtu.edu.cn/rank/2006/ARWU2006_Top100.htm]).

9. Pierre Lafitte, a professor at the time at the University of Nice, first launched the idea in an article in the daily *Le Monde* in August 1960 under the title "Un Quartier latin aux champs" (A Latin Quarter in the countryside). In a an interview recounting the beginnings of Sophia Antipolis, Lafitte goes on to state: "For all of us, coal and heavy industry [were] associated with the nineteenth century, with the smoke and fog of Pittsburgh, Pennsylvania; Birmingham, England; Lorraine, France; Ruhr, Germany. This was western Europe, geologists' Hercynian domain, with outcrops of carboniferous strata. Quality of the environment, attractive sites, joy of living [were] associated in our minds with the Mediterranean shores. . . . Geologists tell us this is an effect of Alpine orogeny, an effect also present in California, that other region so attractive to innovators. This is the first factor that made us choose the French Riviera for our International Science Park, Sophia Antipolis, the City of Wisdom north of Antibes, the former Antipolis across from Nice. We were guided by a second major reason: the proximity [fifteen minutes by car] from an international airport directly linked to the main cities of Europe and the world." Excerpt from *Corps Écrit* 29 (March 1989) at: http://www.sophia-antipolis.org/index1.htm.

10. In North Carolina, the idea of creating a research park was also initiated by a university professor: Howard Odum of the University of North Carolina at Chapel Hill (in the 1950s). Interestingly, neither Pierre Lafitte nor Howard Odum were in disciplines that have anything to do with business or technology. Pierre Lafitte was a professor literature and Howard Odum a

professor of sociology. It's comforting to discover that even professors in the social sciences can sometimes do useful things.

11. Webometrics ranks Cornell as the tenth best university in the world, ahead of any European university: http://www.webometrics.info/index.html. The Institute of Higher Education (Shanghai) has Cornell in twelfth place after nine U.S. universities and two European universities (Cambridge and Oxford): http://ed.sjtu.edu.cn/rank/2006/ARWU2006_Top100.htm.

12. The population of Vermont barely grew between 1870 and 1950, from 330,000 to 377,000. It has since grown to 623,000 (2005). Source: U.S. Bureau of the Census. According to 2000 census figures, 86.4 percent of the Vermont population over twenty-five years of age holds at least a BA degree, which is above the national average of 80.4 percent.

13. Source: http://www.city-data.com/us-cities/The-Northeast/Burlington-History.html.

14. Five years after locating its plant in Burlington, IBM chose to locate another major plant in France in the area that was to become Sophia Antipolis, which suggests that the managers at IBM at the time were indeed looking for places able to attract and hold a particular type of workforce.

15. Shearmur (2007).

16. Davezeis (2008).

17. Boca Raton, Florida, is one of the most expensive and upscale beach communities in the U.S.

18. There's an old joke about France, often told by the French themselves. One day when God was creating the world, He decided to outdo himself. He created France. He gave it everything: majestic mountains, rolling lush hills, fertile plains, a temperate climate, beautiful beaches and shorelines, the best wine-growing soils in the world, truly everything. Contemplating His handiwork, God became concerned. What have I done?! Such perfection will create jealousy and wars. I must do something to redress the imbalance. So God created the French.

19. It is no accident that Nice's seafront is called "La promenade des Anglais" (English promenade).

20. Italy and Spain have attracted Brits, but I would argue that cultural links are not as strong as with France.

21. One of the distinguishing features of France's geography is that few places close to Paris have much to offer, which further increases the relative attractiveness of France's periphery.

22. The same point is made by Chishire and Magrini (2006) and Portnov and Schwartz (2008).

23. Cuadrado-Roura (2001) identifies a list of growth attributes based on an exhaustive study of European regions. His list is not very different from what I propose here.

24. Personal income per capita was $43,714 in Chicago (MSA) and $61,337 in San Francisco (MSA) in 2007 (http://www.bea.gov/newsreleases/regional/mpi/2008/xls/mpi0808.xls).

25. Territorial units—counties in the U.S. and census divisions in Canada—are generally larger in the West and the North since they are often sparsely populated or were settled more recently. This can create an illusion of population growth, especially in the Southwest (Arizona, Nevada, Colorado, and New Mexico), where populations are indeed growing rapidly, but in much more concentrated settlements than map 7 leads one to believe.

26. On map 3, variations are with reference to *national* (not European) averages, highlighting growth (or declines) due to internal shifts, chiefly attributable to internal migration.

27. Some examples: Brusco (1982), Cooke and Morgan (1991), Goodman et al. (1989), and Leonardi and Nanetti (1987).

28. Dunford and Greco (2006) persuasively argue this point, noting that the predominance in Italy of family-owned companies with strong kinship ties and small size acts as constraints on investments in R&D and marketing.

29. The slower growth of Swiss regions is surprising. One would expect much of Switzerland to fall in this growth corridor. The fact that it does not suggests that Switzerland is paying a price for staying outside of the European Union.

30. Hanell and Neubauer (2006) observe a strong concentration of knowledge-intensive employment in the southern tier of Germany, which includes not only Bavaria, but also the *Land* of Baden-Württemberg and the Rhine-Main conurbation.

31. Brunet (2002), the father of the Blue Banana, identifies a Mediterranean arc in recent thematic maps.

32. The position of Boston as a magnet for young professionals needs no further explanation. Hamburg is no less of a magnet in the German and European context. As the chief western port of entry to the East, the fall of the Berlin Wall has further strengthened its position. Hamburg has one the highest GDPs per capita in Europe, in the same league as Brussels and London.

33. The word *cities*, as used in this book, it useful to recall, refers to urban areas and not to municipalities. The populations given are from the 2001 Canadian census for, respectively, the Census Metropolitan Area (CMA) of Guelph and the CA (Census Agglomeration) of Drummondville.

34. Average earnings (2001) in Guelph were 88 percent of those of Toronto; earnings in Drummondville were 80 percent of those of Montreal. Statistics Canada, *Community Profiles, 2001* (Ottawa: Statistics Canada, 2001). Catalogue No. 93f005XIE (http://www12.statcan.ca/english/profil01/CP01/Index.cfm?Lang=E).

35. Ibid.

36. My thanks to Pierre-Marcel Desjardins, professor of economics at the University of Moncton, for his helpful insights on the evolution of the Moncton economy.

37. The link between courier services (with major players such as Purolator, DHL, and Federal Express) and airports is not difficult to guess.

38. The Acadians (*Acadiens* in French), the original (European) settlers of what is now Nova Scotia, were expelled by the British in the eighteenth century after France lost l'Acadie. Many migrated to Louisiana, then still French territory. The word *Cajun* is a corruption of *Acadien*. Not all were expelled and some returned. Today's Acadians are the descendants of those that remained or returned.

39. The Canadian *federal* administration is officially bilingual; but provincial administrations are not obliged to be bilingual, although they can (and often do) provide services in the minority language where justified by numbers.

40. A small French-language university—Université Sainte-Anne—also exists in Nova Scotia, but this is really a liberal arts college.

41. The three Maritime Provinces plus the province of Newfoundland and Labrador.

42. United Nations, *World Population Prospects* (annual, 2004 revision).

43. The United States is somewhat of an exception. Fertility rates have remained systematically higher than in most of the industrialized world and have recently rebounded, though still low by historical standards. Since the early 2000s, fertility rates were close to replacement level: 2.1 children per mother.

44. The author's calculations are based on U.S. census data for 1990 and 2000. Of the 30 counties showing the greatest population declines, twelve were in North Dakota and eight in

Texas. The three counties outside the empty quarter were in Nevada (two) and West Virginia (one). The United States has 3,140 counties in all.

45. Economist (2005b). Of the ten poorest counties, eight were located in Montana, one in Nebraska, and one in North Dakota.

46. Because of the concentration of Aboriginal and Inuit (Eskimo) populations with higher birth rates, the northernmost regions will grow in population, though not necessarily prosper economically.

47. The traditional definition of Appalachia includes only the southern portion of western New York State. In its broadest definition, Appalachia stretches south into Alabama and Mississippi. Parts of southern Ohio can also be considered as belonging to Appalachia.

48. The author's calculations are based on U.S. census data for 1990 and 2000. The ten metropolitan areas (MSAs) in this part of the country that exhibited the most pronounced population declines were: Steubenville (Ohio), Utica (New York), Binghamton (New York), Wheeling (West Virginia), Johnstown (Pennsylvania), Scranton-Wilkes-Barre (Pennsylvania), Buffalo (New York), Jamestown (New York), Pittsburgh (Pennsylvania), and Syracuse (New York). Of the three MSAs lying in other parts of the U.S. and also exhibiting population declines, two are in the Deep South and one (Decatur, Illinois) neighbors the empty quarter.

49. I owe this insight to Mark D. Partridge, professor in the Department of Agricultural, Environmental, and Development Economics, Ohio State University, Columbus.

50. For a more detailed analysis of the Montreal-Toronto reversal, see Polèse and Shearmur (2004c).

51. Jews were excluded from the boards of directors of these old-money corporations. Fortunately, times have changed.

52. This sad episode is generally referred as the October Crisis, because of the month in which it occurred. This was no minor event in Canada's history. In reaction to the perceived threat posed by the FLQ—at the time of the kidnapping, nobody knew the true size of the FLQ—the then–prime minister, Pierre Elliot Trudeau, declared the war measures act, which brought the army to the streets of Montreal and led to the summary arrest of hundreds of individuals. The downfall of the FLQ, however, had little to do with the government's actions. The FLQ forfeited all public support—it was quite popular among young politicized Francophones at the time—when one if its cells killed Pierre Laporte, a government minster. Blowing up statues was fine, but actually executing someone in cold blood—one of your own, on top of it— went beyond what even the most militant Québécois could accept.

53. English is permitted on public signs, but French must be predominant. On the whole, the Supreme Court of Canada has upheld the spirit of Bill 101, recognizing that French is a minority language in North America in need of protection. Quebec's language legislation is much less stringent than that in Flanders. Quebec maintains a complete English-language public school system. Public services, both provincial and federal, are generally available in French and in English.

54. It does so less these days because a number of French-speaking African cities—Kinshasa, certainly—may have overtaken it.

55. Many members of Toronto's business elite are former Montrealers. The most notorious example—I use the word deliberately—is the ex-newspaper magnate Conrad Black, born and bred in Montreal, currently doing time in a U.S. prison for misuse of corporate funds.

56. Las Vegas's isolation contributes to economic growth in other ways. Money spent in the town will tend to stay in town, spent on local construction companies, repair shops, and other

services. Much money will flow out, but more—proportionally—will be spent locally because of the absence of nearby competing service centers.

57. The poor are the principal victims—as so often—of a bad banking system. They have little choice but to use local institutions, if indeed they use them at all. The unreliability of the local banking system discourages savings and productive investment, a major problem in many developing nations. In the Mexican village in the Sierra Norte de Puebla, where I worked, most people did not have a proper bank account and distrusted banks for understandable reasons. The distrust is mutual. Banks do not like to lend to poor peasants.

Chapter 7

1. The partly idiosyncratic nature of regional growth is reflected in the limited success of scholars to "explain" variations in growth (of employment, income, or product) via the use of statistical models. Even the most successful models seldom explain more than 50 percent of the observed variations over time (an R^2 of 0.50 in regression models). This necessarily means that much remains unexplained, a reflection of accidents, exceptions, and particular circumstances—rule 4, in sum.

2. Wuhan, Chongqing, and Xi'an had, respectively, metropolitan populations of 7 million, 6.4 million, and 4 million in 2005.

3. Another factor keeping down costs in China at the time of writing was the low value of the Chinese currency, the yuan, which many analysts feel has been kept artificially undervalued by the policies of the Bank of China. A rise in the value of the yuan would immediately raise costs.

4. Bils (2005) finds that some dispersal of manufacturing inland is already occurring, notably towards the province of Anhui to the west of Shanghai. She notes no similar inland dispersal out of the Hong Kong–Guangzhou conurbation.

5. Italy provides a counterexample. In a recent survey of Italy, *The Economist* (2005a, 14) notes: "A big reason why unemployment is so high [in the south] is that wages tend to be set nationally, when they really ought to be lower in the south."

6. The cost advantage must be *real*, taking into account labor force skills, local infrastructures, the quality of public services, and other determinants of labor force productivity. If lower wages are simply the reflection of lower productivity—lower skills, especially—then there are no real savings for the firm.

7. The flip side of greater fiscal decentralization, which generally means reduced national government transfers to poor provinces, is greater regional income inequality. Here we meet another of the central dilemmas of regional development policy. Transfers surely promote greater income equality, but if overly generous (difficult to define) they can artificially raise local costs and wage expectations, making it more difficult to attract industries to peripheral regions. Defining the right mix between social justice (transfers from rich to poor) and greater labor market flexibility is a question to which there is no—and probably never will be—a simple answer.

8. On the impact of internal trade barriers in China, see Poncet (2005).

9. Sinkiang and Tibet, the two most westerly regions, have distinct cultures. Since I am not sufficiently familiar with this part of the world, I will refrain from further comment.

10. The debate surrounding the idea of optimal city size goes back many decades. See, for example, *The Economics of Urban Size* (Richardson 1975).

11. United Nations (1990).

12. Contrary to popular perception, there is, for example, no link between crime and city size. In the U.S., the four metropolitan areas with the highest homicide rates were (respectively) New Orleans, Birmingham, Mobile, and Los Angeles, while the four safest were Honolulu, Portland (Oregon), Albany, and Boston (FBI 2003).

13. Demand management refers to measures that seek to regulate the level of traffic. As electronic monitoring devices become more sophisticated, road pricing is becoming increasingly feasible, but is generally not politically popular.

14. Currid (2006) calculates location quotients (which measure relative specialization) for selected occupations for twelve Metropolitan Statistical Areas (MSAs) in the United States for the year 2004, using Occupational Employment Statistics (OES) survey data, taken form the Bureau of Labor Statistics.

15. In both cases, I employ the term to refer to persons who hold a bachelors degree (BA, BS, etc.) or higher, usually obtained at about twenty-one years of age.

16. Even this statement needs to be tempered. The strength of the relationship can differ, depending on how urban centers are defined and on city size.

17. The real choices facing governments are generally more complex: Should more public money be spent on vocational training or on general education? On graduate or on undergraduate education? What proportion of the costs should be born by students? Etc.

18. The situation will be different for communities in nations where all education is centrally funded (or by states or provinces in federations). Actions by community leaders will focus on lobbying the central government. Every community will—understandably so—lobby to attract (or keep) educational institutions. Every major town will want its university.

19. For a useful review of the rise and fall of growth poles, see Parr (1999, 1999a).

20. A danger of fiscal competition between neighbouring places is what is sometimes called the race towards the bottom, where each place attempts to systematically underbid its neighbor (offering ever more generous breaks to incoming firms), with the local taxpayer in the end picking up the bill.

21. On the other hand, once a policy fad takes off, communities may have no choice but to join in if they want stay in the race. If all competitors are investing in education, museums, technology parks, or whatever, then not copying them may also imply a cost. However, as noted, if all follow, relative positions will remain unchanged.

22. Recall my earlier comments on the complementary relationship between IT and face-to-face meetings. Communication by e-mail or via mobile text messages, for example, rarely occurs in isolation, without having been preceded or followed up by meetings.

23. Saskia Sassen, a sociologist at the University of Chicago, is one of the principal pioneers of the study of global cities. See Sassen (1991).

24. Several studies confirm the *growing* importance of access to markets or to large urban centers. For Canada, Apparicio et al. (2007) and Shearmur et al. (2007) studied the relationship between continental market access and local employment growth over a thirty-year period. For the U.S., Partridge et al. (2008) looked at the relationship between local population growth and distance from large centers over a fifty-year period (1950–2000). In both cases, the strength of the relationship increased over time.

Bibliography

Apparicio, P., G. Dussault, M. Polèse, and R. Shearmur. 2007 *Transport Infrastructure and Local Economic Development. A Study of the Relationship between Continental Accessibility and Employment Growth in Canadian Communities*. Montreal: INRS Urbanisation, Culture et Société (http://www.inrs.ucs.c).

Appelbome, Peter. 1996. *Dixie Rising*. New York: Times Books.

Bairoch, Paul. 1992. *Le Tiers-monde dans l'impasse. Le démarrage économique du XVIIIe au XXe siècle*. Paris: Gallimard.

Barro, R. J. and X. Sala-i-Martin. 1995. *Economic Growth*. New York: McGraw Hill.

Baudhuin, Fernand. 1966. *Principes d'économie contemporaine*, tome 4—la consommation. Verviers, Belgium: Marabout.

Berry, C. and E. Glaeser. 2005. "The Divergence of Human Capital Levels across Cities," Discussion Papers No. 2091, Harvard Institute of Economic Research (http://post.economics.harvard .edu/hier/paper_list.html).

Bils, Barbara. 2005. *What determines regional inequality in China? A survey of the literature and official data*. Bank of Finland: Institute of Economics in Transition. BOFIT Online No. 4 (http://www.bot.h/bofit).

Black, D. and V. Henderson. 1999. "Spatial Evolution of Population and Industry in the United States." *American Economic Review* 89 (2): 321–27.

Bonnifield, Paul. 1978. *The Dust Bowl: Men, Dirt, and Depression*. Albuquerque: University of New Mexico Press.

Brakman, S., H. Garretsen, and M. Schramm. 2004. "The Strategic Bombing of German Cities during World War II and Its Impact on City Growth" *Journal of Economic Geography* 4 (2): 201–18.

Braudel, Fernand. 1979. *Civilisation matérielle, économie et capitalisme: 3—Le temps du monde*. Paris: Armand Colin.

Breese, Gerald. 1966. *Urbanization in Newly Developing Countries*. Englewood Cliffs, New Jersey: Prentice Hall.

Brülhart, M. 1998. "Trading Places: Industrial Specialization in the European Union." *Journal of Common Market Studies* 36 (3): 319–46.

Brülhart, M. 2006. "The Fading Attraction of Central Regions: an Empirical Note on Core-Periphery Gradients in Western Europe." *Spatial Economic Analysis* 1 (2): 227–35.

Brunet, R. 2002. "Les lignes de force de l'espace européen." *Mappemonde* 66 (2): 14–19.

Brusco, S. 1982. "The Emilian Model: Productive Decentralisation and Social Integration." *Cambridge Journal of Economics* 6:167–84.

Budd, Leslie. 2006. "London: From City-state to City-region?" In *The Rise of the English Regions?* ed. I. Hardill, P. Benneworth, M. Baker, and L. Budd: 245–66. London: Routledge.

Cairncross F. 2001. *The Death of Distance 2.01. How the Communications Revolution Will Change Our Lives*. New York: Norton.

Cao, H. and J. Vaca. 2006. "Desarollo regional en la Argntina: la centenaria vigenvia de un patrón de asimettría territorial" *EURE: Revista Latinoamericna de Esudions Urbanas Regionales* 32 (95): 95–111.

Carlino, Gerald. 2005. "The Economic Role of Cities in the 21st Century" *Federal Reserve Bank of Philadelphia, Business Review* (third quarter): 9–15 (http://www.philadelphia.org).

Chandler T. and G. Fox. 1974. *3000 Years of Urban Growth*. New York: Academic Press.

Chang, J. H., Y. G. Choi, and M. G. Heo. 2004. *Economic Growth and Regional Economic Disparity*. Seoul: Korea Institute for Industrial Economics and Trade (available in Korean only).

Cheshire, Paul C. and Stefano Magrini. 2006. "Population Growth in European Cities: Weather Matters—But Only Nationally" *Regional Studies* 40 (1): 23–37.

Christaller, W. 1935. *Die Zentralen Orte in Süddeutschland*. Jena, Germany: Fischer Verlag.

Ciccolla, Pablo. 1999. "Globalización y dualización en la región metropolitana de Buenos Aires. Grandes inversiones y reestructuración socioterritorial en los años noventa." *Revista Latinoamericana de Estudios Urbano Regionales* 25 (76): 5–28.

Cippola, C. 1962. *The Economic History of World Populations*. Baltimore: Penguin.

Coe, N. M., P. F. Kelly, and H. W. Yeung. 2007. *Economic Geography. A Contemporary Introduction*. Malden, MA: Blackwell.

Coffey, W. J. and M. Polèse. 1988. "Locational Shifts in Canadian Employment, 1971–1981, Decentralisation versus Decongestion." *The Canadian Geographer* 32 (3): 248–55.

Cole, W. A. and P. Deane. 1965. "Chapter 1: The Growth of National Incomes." In *The Cambridge Economic History of Europe, Volume VI—The Industrial Revolutions and After: Incomes, Population, and Technological Change* (II), ed. H. J. Habakkuk and M. Postan, 1–59. Cambridge: Cambridge University Press.

Cooke, P. and Morgan, K. 1991. "The Intelligent Region: Industrial and Institutional Innovation in Emilia-Romagna," *Regional Industrial Research Report No. 7*. Cardiff University, Wales.

Cuadrado-Roura J. R. 2001. "Regional Convergence in the European Union: From Hypothesis to Actual Trends." *Annals of Regional Science* 35:333–56.

Currid, Elizabeth. 2006. "New York as a Global Creative Hub: A Competitiev Analysis of Four Theories on World Cities." *Economic Development Quarterly* 20 (4): 330–50.

Davezies, Laurent. 2008. *La république et ses territoires; La circulation invisibles des richesses*. Paris: Seuil.

Davis, R. D. and D. E. Weinstein. 2002. "Bones, Bombs, and Break Points: The Geography of Economic Activity." *American Economic Review* 92 (5): 1269–89

De Soto, H. 2000. *The Mystery of Capital: Why Capitalism Triumphs in the West and Fails Everywhere Else*. New York: Basic Books.

DeLong, J. B. 1998. "Estimating World GDP, One Million B.C.–Present." Department of Economics, University of California, Berkeley (http://econ161.berkeley.edu/TCEH/1998_Draft/World_GDP/Estimating_World_GDP.html).

Denison, Edward. 1967. *Why Growth Rates Differ*. Washington, DC: The Brookings Institution.

Denison, Edward. 1985. *Trends in American Growth 1929–1982*. Washington, DC: The Brookings Institution.

Diamond, J. 1997. *Guns, Germs, and Steel: The Fates of Human Societies*. New York and London: W. W. Norton & Co.

Dunford, M. and L. Greco. 2006. *After the Three Italies: Wealthy, Inequality, and Industrial Change*. Oxford, UK: Blackwell Publishing.

Duranton, G. and D. Puga. 2001. "Nursery Cities: Urban Diversity, Process Innovation, and the Life Cycle of Products." *American Economic Review* 91 (5): 1454–77.

Duranton, G. and D. Puga. 2002. "Diversity and Specialization in Cities: Why, Where, and When Does It Matter?" In *Industrial Location Economics*, ed. P. McCann, 151–86. Cheltenham, UK: Edward Elgar. (Updated version of an article [same title] in *Urban Studies* 37, no. 3 [2000]: 533–55.)

Duranton, G. and V, Monastiriotis. 2002. "Mind the Gaps: The Evolution of Regional Earnings Inequalities in the UK, 1982–1997," *Journal of Regional Science* 42 (2): 219–56.

Duranton, Gilles. 2000. "Urbanization, Urban Structure, and Growth." In *Economics of Cities: Theoretical Perspectives*, ed. J.-M. Huriot and J.-F. Thisse, 290–317. Cambridge: Cambridge University Press.

Easterly, W. and R. Levine. 2002. *Tropics, Germs, and Crops: How Endowments Influence Economic Development*. National Bureau of Economic Research, Working Paper 9106 (http://www.nber.org).

Easterly, William. 2002. *The Elusive Quest for Growth*. Cambridge, MA: MIT Press

Eaton, J. and Z. Eckstein. 1997. "Cities and Growth: Theory and Evidence from France and Japan." *Regional Science and Urban Economics* 27:443–74.

Economist. 1990. *Book of Vital World Statistics*. New York: Times Books.

Economist. 2001. "The Future of Farming: The Great American Desert." *Economist*, December 15, 26.

Economist. 2005. "The Town of the Talk: A Survey of New York." *Economist*, February 19 (special section).

Economist. 2005a. "A Survey of Italy: Southern Cross." *Economist*, November 26 (special section).

Economist. 2005b. "The Poorest Part of America. Not Here, Surely?" *Economist*, December 10, 31–32.

Economist. 2006. "Novartis—A Novel Prescription—A Big Western Company Moves into China, but Not for the Usual Reasons." *Economist*, November 11, 72–73.

Economist. 2006a. "Interstate Highways: Roads to Somewhere" *Economist*, June 24, 36–37.

Encyclopaedia Britannica. 1960. "Great Britain." In *Encyclopaedia Britannica*, volume 10. London, Chicago, and Toronto: Encyclopaedia Britannica Inc., William Benton, Publisher.

Esquivel G., D. Lederman, M. Messmacher, and R. Villoro. 2003. "Why NAFTA Did Not Reach the South." In *Development Strategy for the Mexican Southern States*. Washington, DC: World Bank.

Fay, M. and C. Opal. 2000. "Urbanization without Growth: A Not So Uncommon Phenomenon." Working Paper Series (WPS) no. 2412. Washington, DC: The World Bank.

FBI. 2003. *Crime in the United States, Metropolitan Statistical Area 2003*. Federal Bureau of Investigation, Washington DC (http://www.fbi.gov/ucr/ucr.htm#cius).

Felsenstein, D. and B. A. Portnov. 2005. "Understanding Regional Inequalities in Small Countries." *Regional Studies* 39 (5): 647–58.

Florida, Richard. 2002. *The Rise of the Creative Class*. New York: Basic Books.

Florida, Richard. 2002a. "Bohemia and Economic Geography." *Journal of Economic Geography* 2 (1): 55–71.

Fujita, M. and J.-F. Thisse. 2002. *Economics of Agglomeration*. Cambridge: Cambridge University Press.

Garreau, J. 1981. *The Nine Nations of North America*. Boston: Houghton Mifflin.

Garreau, J. 1992. *Edge Cities: Life on the New Frontier*. New York: Anchor.

Gaspar, J. and E. Glaeser. 1998. "Information Technology and the Future of Cities." *Journal of Urban Economics* 43:136–56.

Geppert, K. and A. Stephan. 2008. "Regional Disparities in the European Union: Convergence and Agglomeration." *Papers in Regional Science* 87 (2): 193–217.

Glaeser, E. L. 1994. "Cities, Information, and Economic Growth." *Cityscape* 1 (1): 9–77.

Glaeser, E. L. 1998. "Are Cities Dying?" *Journal of Economic Perspectives* 12 (2): 139–60.

Glaeser, E. L. 2000. "The New Economics of Urban and Regional Growth." In *The Oxford Handbook of Economic Geography*, ed. G. Clark, M. Feldman, and M. Gertler. Oxford: Oxford University Press.

Glaeser, E. L. 2005. "Reinventing Boston 1630–2003." *Journal of Economic Geography* 5:119–53.

Glaeser, E. L. and J. Gottlieb. 2006. "Urban Resurgence and the Consumer City." *Urban Studies* 43 (8): 1275–99.

Glaeser, E. L., H. D. Kallal, J. A. Scheinkman, and A. Shleifer. 1992. "Growth in Cities." *Journal of Political Economy* 100 (6): 1126–52.

Glaeser, E. L. and A. Saiz. 2003. "The Rise of the Skilled City." *Discussion Paper No. 2025*. Harvard Institute of Economic Research (http://post.economics.harvard.edu/hier/paper_list .html).

Glaeser, E. L., J. A. Scheinkman, and A. Shleifer. 1995. "Economic Growth in a Cross-section of Cities." *Journal of Monetary Economics* 36 (1): 117–43.

Godchild B. and P. Hickman. 2006. "Towards Regional Strategy for the North of England? An Assessment of 'The Northern Way.'" *Regional Studies* 40 (1): 121–33.

Goodman, E., J. Bamford, and P. Saynor. 1989. *Small Firms and Industrial Districts in Italy*. London: Routledge.

Gordon, John S. 2004. *An Empire of Wealth. The Epic History of American Economic Power*. New York: Harper.

Gottman, Jean. 1961. *Megalopolis: The Urbanized Northeastern Seaboard of the United States*. New York: The Twentieth Century Fund.

Government of Canada. 1924. *The Canada Year Book*. Ottawa: Minister of Trade and Commerce.

Government of Japan. 2004. *Annual Report on the Japanese Economy: Economy and Public Finance 2003–2004—Prefectural Accounts*. Tokyo: Cabinet Office (http://www5.caogo.jp/zenbum).

Graham, D. and N. Spence. 1997. "Competition for Metropolitan Resources: The 'Crowding Out' of London's Manufacturing Industry." *Environment and Planning A* 29:459–84.

Gravier, J-F. 1947. *Paris et le désert français*. Paris: Le Portulan.

Guérin-Pace, F. 1995. "Rank-Size Distribution and the Process of Urban Growth." *Urban Studies* 32 (1): 551–62.

Gugler, J., ed. 1988. *The Urbanization of the Third World*. New York: Oxford University Press.

Hall, Peter. 1999. *Cities in Civilization. Culture, Innovation, and Urban Order*. London: Phoenix Giant.

Hall, Peter. 2000. "Creative Cities and Economic Development." *Urban Studies* 37 (4): 639–49.

Hanell, T. and J. Neubauer. 2006. *Geographies of Knowledge Production in Europe*. Nordregio Working Paper No. 2006:3. Nordregio, Stockholm (http://www.nordregio.org).

Hanson, Gordon. 2005. "Market Potential, Increasing Returns, and Geographic Concentration." *Journal of International Economics* 67:1–24.

Held, D., A. McGrew, D. Goldblatt, and J. Perraton. 1999. *Global Transformations: Politics, Economics, and Culture*. Palo Alto, CA: Stanford University Press.

Henderson, V., Z. Shalizi, and A. J. Venables. 2001. "Geography and Development." *Journal of Economic Geography* 1:81–205.

Henderson, V. 1988. *Urban Development: Theory, Fact, and Illusion*. New York: Oxford University Press.

Henderson, V. 1997. "Medium-sized Cities." *Regional Science and Urban Economics* 27:583–612.

Henderson, V. 2003. "Marshall's Scale Economies." *Journal of Urban Economics* 53:1 28.

Henderson, V. 2003a. "The Urbanization Process and Economic Growth: The So-What Question." *Journal of Economic Growth* 8:47–71.

Hoover, E. 1948. *The Location of Economic Activity*. New York: McGraw Hill.

Howe, F. 1915. *The Modern City and its Problems*. New York: Charles Scribner's & Sons.

Huriot, J.-M. and J.-F. Thisse, eds. 2000. *Economics of Cities: Theoretical Perspectives*. Cambridge: Cambridge University Press.

Isard, Walter. 1956. *Location and Space Economy*. Cambridge, MA: MIT Press.

Jacobs, Jane. 1969. *The Economy of Cities*. New York: Vintage.

Jacobs, Jane. 1984. *Cities and the Wealth of Nations*. New York: Vintage.

Jones, B. and S. Koné. 1996. "An Exploration of Relationships between Urbanization and Per Capita Income: United States and Countries of the World." *Papers in Regional Science* 75 (2): 135–53.

Kessides, Christine. 2005. *The Urban Transition in Sub-Saharan Africa: Implications for Economic Growth and Poverty Reduction*, African Region Working Paper Number 97. Washington, DC: The World Bank.

Kraska, S. and S. Kaup. 2005. *Metropolregionen in Deutschland*, BBR-Referat I 1. Bonn, Germany: Bundesamt für Bauwessen und Raumordnung.

Krugman, P. 1995. *Development, Geography, and Economic Theory*. Cambridge, MA: MIT Press.

Krugman, Paul. 1991. "Increasing Returns and Economic Geography." *Journal of Political Economy* 99 (3): 483–99.

Kuznets, S. 1966. *Modern Economic Growth: Rate, Structure, and Spread*. New Haven and London: Yale University Press.

Kuznets, Simon. 1968. *Towards a Theory of Economic Growth*. New York: W. W. Norton & Co.

Landes, D. 1998. *The Wealth and Poverty of Nations: Why Some Are So Rich and Some So Poor*. New York and London: W. W. Norton & Co.

Lang, R. E. and D. Dhavale. 2005. "American Megapolitan Areas" *Land Lines, Lincoln Institute of Land Policy*. (July): 1–4.

Lemelin, A. and Polèse, M. 1995. "What about the Bell-shaped Relationship between Primacy and Development?" *International Regional Science Review.* 18:313–30.

Leonardi, R. and R. Nanetti, eds. 1987. *The Region and European Integration: the Case of Emilia-Romagna.* London: Pinter.

Lichtenberg, R. 1960. *One-tenth of a Nation.* Cambridge, MA: Harvard University Press.

Lilly, Dick. 2002. *A Competitive Region in a World Economy: Report on the Greater Seattle Chamber of Commerce and Trade Development Alliance of Greater Seattle's Ninth International Study Mission, May 3–11, 2002.* Barcelona (http://www.seattle.gov/tda/missions/barcelona/barcelonareport.htm).

Lucas, Robert. 1988. "On the Mechanics of Economic Development." *Journal of Monetary Economics* 22:3–42.

Lucas, Robert. 1990. "Why Doesn't Capital Flow from Rich to Poor Countries?" *American Economic Review* 80 (2): 92–96.

Lucas, Robert. 2001. "Externalities and Cities." *Review of Economic Dynamics* 4:245–74.

Luo, X. and N. Zhu. 2006. "China's Lagging Region Development and Targeted Transportation Infrastructure Investment." In *Regional Disparities in China*, ed. S. Anwar, C. Shen, and H. Zou. Washington, DC: World Bank (in Chinese).

Maddison, Angus. 1995. *Monitoring the World Economy, 1820–1992.* Paris: OECD.

Maddison, Angus. 2001. *The World Economy: A Millennial Perspective.* Paris: OECD.

Mak, Geert. 2008. *In Europe: Travels Through the Twentieth Century.* New York: Vintage Books.

Marshall, Alfred. 1890. *Principles of Economics.* London: Macmillan.

Mills, E. S. and B. Hamilton. 1994. *Urban Economics,* 5th ed. New York: HarperCollins.

Myrdal, Gunnar. 1957. *Economic Theory and Underdeveloped Regions.* New York: Harper Torchbooks.

O'Sullivan, Arthur. 2000. *Urban Economics,* 4th ed. Boston: Irwin McGraw-Hill.

Olson, Mancur. 2000. *Power and Prosperity.* New York: Basic Books.

Paelinck, J. and M. Polèse. 1999. "Modeling the Regional Impact of Continental Economic Integration: Lessons from the European Union for NAFTA." *Regional Studies* 33 (8): 727–38.

Parr, John. 1999. "Growth-pole Strategies in Regional Economic Development Planning: A Retrospective View. Part 1. Origins and Advocacy." *Urban Studies* 36 (7): 1195–1215.

Parr, John. 1999a. "Growth-pole Strategies in Regional Economic Development Planning: A Retrospective View. Part 2. Implementation and Outcome." *Urban Studies* 36 (8): 1247–68.

Parr, John. 2002. "Agglomeration Economies: Ambiguities and Confusions." *Environment and Planning A* 34:717–31.

Partridge, M. D. and D. S. Rickman. 2008. "Distance from Urban Agglomeration Economies and Rural Poverty." *Journal of Regional Science* 48 (2): 285–310.

Partridge, M. D., D. S. Rickman, K. Ali, and M. R. Olfert. 2008a. "Lost in Space: Population Growth in the American Hinterlands and Small Cities." *Journal of Economic Geography* 8 (6): 727–57.

Partridge, M. D., D. R. Rickman, K. Ali, and M. R. Olfert. 2008b. "The Geographical Diversity of U.S. Nonmetropolitan Growth Dynamics: A Geographically Weighted Regression." *Land Economics* 84 (2): 241–66.

Petrakos, G., A. Rodríguez-Pose, and A. Rovolis. 2005. "Growth, Integration, and Regional Disparities in the European Union." *Environment and Planning A* 37 (10): 1837–55.

Polanyi, Karl. 1957. *The Great Transformation* (first paperback ed., original copyright 1944). Boston: Beacon Press.

Polèse, Mario. 1972. "Interregional Migration and Regional Economic Disparities." PhD diss. University of Pennsylvania, Philadelphia.

Polèse, Mario. 2005. "Cities and National Economic Growth: A Reappraisal." *Urban Studies* 42 (8): 1429–51.

Polèse, Mario. 2006. "On the Non-City Foundations of Economic Growth and the Unverifiability of the 'Jacobs Hypothesis': A Reply to Peter Taylor's Comment." *Urban Studies* 43 (9): 1631–37.

Polèse M. and R. Shearmur. 2002. *The Periphery in the Knowledge-Based Economy: The Spatial Dynamics of the Canadian Economy and the Future of Non-Metropolitan Regions in Quebec and the Atlantic Provinces.* Montreal: INRS-UCS (http://www.inrs-ucs.uquebec.ca).

Polèse, M. and R. Shearmur. 2004a. "Is Distance Really Dead? Comparing Industrial Location Patterns over Time in Canada." *International Regional Science Review* 27 (4): 1–27.

Polèse, M. and R. Shearmur. 2004b. *Économie urbaine et régionale.* Paris: Economica.

Polèse, M. and R. Shearmur. 2004c. "Culture, Language, and the Location of High-order Service Functions: The Case of Montreal and Toronto." *Economic Geography* 80 (4): 329–50.

Polèse, M. and Shearmur. 2006. "Growth and Location of Economic Activity: The Spatial Dynamics of Industries in Canada 1971–2001." *Growth and Change* 37 (3): 362–95.

Poncet, S. 2005. "A Fragmented China: Measure and Determinants of Chinese Domestic Market Disintegration." *Review of International Economics* 13 (3): 409–30.

Porter M. 1998. "Clusters and the New Economics of Competition." *Harvard Business Review* 76 (6): 77–90.

Porter, M. 2000. "Location, Competition, and Economic Development: Local Clusters in the Global Economy." *Economic Development Quarterly* 14 (1): 15–34.

PRISMA. 1996. *La Evolución de la Red Urbana y el Desarollo Sostenible en El Salvador.* San Salvador: Programa Salvadoreño de Investigación sobre Desarrollo y Medio Ambiente.

Prud'homme, Rémy. 1997. "Urban Transportation and Economic Development." *Région et Développement* 5:40–53.

Puga, Diego. 1999. "The Rise and Fall of Regional Inequalities." *European Economic Review* 43 (2): 303–34.

Puga, Diego. 2002. "European Regional Policies in Light of Recent Location Theories." *Journal of Economic Geography* 2:373–406.

Rappaport, J. 2004. "Moving to Nice Weather." Research Working Paper 03-07. Federal Reserve Bank of Kansas City.

Rappaport, J. and S. Sachs. 2003. "The United States as a Coastal Nation." *Journal of Economic Growth* 8:5–46.

Ray, D. M. 1967. *Regional Aspects of Foreign Ownership of Manufacturing in Canada* (mimeo). Waterloo, Ontario: University of Waterloo.

Reader, John. 2004. *Cities.* London: Vintage.

Reclus, Onésime. 1893. *La Terre à Vol d'Oiseau.* Paris: Librairie Hachette & Co.

Richardson, H. 1975. *The Economics of Urban Size.* Westmead, UK: Saxon House/Lexington Books.

Rodríguez-Pose, A. and N. Gill. 2004. "Is There a Global Link between Regional Disparities and Devolution?" *Environment and Planning A* 36, (12): 2097–2117.

Rodríguez-Pose, A. and J. Sánchez-Reaza. 2005. "Economic Polarization through Trade: Trade Liberalization and Regional Growth in Mexico." In *Spatial Inequality and Development*, ed. R. Kanbur and A. J. Venables, 237–59. Oxford: Oxford University Press.

Romer, P. 1989. *Human Capital and Growth: Theory and Evidence.* NBER working paper no. W3173. Cambridge, MA: National Bureau of Economic Research (http://www.nber.org).

Romer, Paul. 1986. "Increasing Returns and Long-Run Growth." *Journal of Political Economy* 94:1002–37.

Romer, Paul. 1994. "Origins of Endogenous Growth." *Journal of Economic Perspectives* 8 (1): 3–22.

Rosenthal, S. R. and W. C. Strange. 2001. "The Determinants of Agglomeration." *Journal of Urban Economics* 50:191–229.

Sassen, Saskia. 1991. *The Global City.* Princeton, NJ: Princeton University Press.

Scott, Alan. 2006. *Geography and Economy.* Oxford: Oxford University Press.

Sharma, Shalini. 2003. "Persistence and Stability in City Growth." *Journal of Urban Economics* 53:300–320.

Shearmur, Richard. 2007. "The New Knowledge Aristocracy: A Few Thoughts on the Creative Class, Mobility, and Urban Growth." *Work, Organization, and Labour* 1 (1): 31–47.

Shearmur, R., Ph. Apparicio, P. Lizion, and M. Polèse. 2007. "Space, Time, and Local Employment Growth: An Application of Spatial Regression Analysis." *Growth and Change* 38 (4). 691–717.

Shearmur, R., M. Polèse, and Ph. Apparicio. 2007. "The Evolving Impact of Continental Accessibility on Local Employment Growth, 1971–2001." Working Paper 2007-4, INRS Urbanisation, Culture et Société, Montreal (http://www.ucs.inrs.ca/default.asp?p=pl).

Shearmur, R. and M. Polèse. 2005. La géographie du niveau de vie au Canada, 1971–2001. INRS Urbanisation, Culture et Société, Montreal (http://www.ucs.inrs.ca/default.asp?p=rr).

Short, John R. 2007. *Liquid City: Megalopolis and the Contemporary Northeast.* Washington, DC: Resources for the Future.

Smith, Adam. 1776. *The Wealth of Nations.* New York: Modern Library (1994 ed., first published in 1776 in London).

Statistics Canada. 1979. *Historical Statistics of Canada,* 2nd ed. Ottawa: Statistics Canada.

Statistics Canada. (Periodic). Provincial Economic Accounts, Catalogue No. 13-213. Ottawa: Statistics Canada.

Steinbeck, John. 1939. *The Grapes of Wrath* (first ed.). New York: Viking Press.

Tabuchi, T. and A. Yoshida. 2000. "Separating Urban Agglomeration Economies in Consumption and Production." *Journal of Urban Economics* 48: 70–84.

Thünen, Johann-Heinrich (von). 1826. *Der isolierte Staat in Beziehung auf Landwirtschaft und Nationalökonomie.* Hamburg [publisher unknown]. Translated as *The Isolated State* (Oxford: Pergamon, 1966).

Tolley, G. S. and V. Thomas, eds. 1987. *The Economics of Urbanization and Urban Policies in Developing Nations.* Washington, DC: The World Bank.

United Nations. 1990. *Cities: Life in the World's 100 Largest Metropolitan Areas. Statistical Appendix,* ed. Sharon Camp. New York: United Nations Population Crisis Committee.

United Nations. 2004. *World Urbanization Prospects,* 2003 revision. New York: United Nations Department of Economic and Social Affairs, Population Division (http://www.un.org/esa/population/publications/wup2003/2003WUP.htm).

United Nations. (Annual). *World Population Prospects,* 2004 revision. New York: United Nations Population Division (http://esa.un.org/unpp).

Weber, Alfred. 1909. *Über den Standort der Industrie.* Tübingin, Germany [publisher unknown]. Translated by Carl J. Friedrich as *Alfred Weber's Theory of the Locationof Industries* (Chicago: University of Chicago Press, 1929).

Weber, Max. 1905. *Die protestantische Ethik und der Geist des Kapitalismus* (reedited). Tübingen, Germany: Mohr-Siebeck Verlag. Translated by Talcott Parsons as *The Protestant Ethic and the Spirit of Capitalism* (New York: Charles Scribner's Sons, 1930).

Weiss, Marc. 2001. "Productive Cities and Metropolitan Economic Strategy." Theme Paper at the International Forum on Urban Poverty (mimeo). Marrakech, Morocco.

Williamson, J. G. 1965. "Regional Inequality and the Processes of National Development: A Description of the Patterns." *Economic Development and Cultural Change* 13:3–54.

Wolfe, T. 1987. *The Bonfire of the Vanities*. New York: Bantam Books.

World Bank. 1991. *Urban Policy and Economic Development: An Agenda for the 1990s*. Washington, DC: The World Bank.

World Bank. 1994. *World Development Report: Infrastructure for Development*. Washington, DC: The World Bank.

World Bank. 1998, 1999, 2000, 2001, 2002. *World Development Report: World Development Indicators*. Washington, DC: The World Bank.

World Bank. (Annual, since 2003). WDI Online, World Bank Development Indicators (http://devdata.worldbank.org/dataonline).

Ying, Lon Gen. 2006. "An Institutional Convergence Perspective on China's Recent Growth Experience. A Research Note." *Papers in Regional Science* 85 (2): 321–30.

Yoo, Chang-Hoon. 2001. "L'évolution du système urbain d'un nouveau pays industrialisé: la Corée du sud 1955–1996." PhD diss. INRS-Urbanisation, University of Quebec, Montreal.

Zhu, N. and X. Luo. 2006. "Regional Differences in China's Urbanization and Its Determinants." In *Regional Disparities in China* (in Chinese), ed. S. Anwar, C. Shen, and H. Zou. Washington DC: World Bank.

Index